Protecting Our Children

Understanding and Preventing Abuse and Neglect in Early Childhood

Sharon Thompson Hirschy
Collin College

Elaine Wilkinson
Collin College

WADSWORTH
CENGAGE Learning™

Australia • Brazil • Japan • Korea • Mexico • Singapore • Spain • United Kingdom • United States

Protecting Our Children: Understanding and Preventing Abuse and Neglect in Early Childhood
Sharon Thompson Hirschy and Elaine Wilkinson

Executive Editor: Marcus Boggs

Acquisitions Editor: Chris Shortt

Assistant Editor: Caitlin Cox

Editorial Assistant: Linda Stewart

Associate Media Editor: Ashley Cronin

Marketing Manager: Kara Parsons

Marketing Assistant: Dimitri Hagnere

Marketing Communications Manager: Martha Pfeiffer

Content Project Manager: Samen Iqbal

Creative Director: Rob Hugel

Art Director: Maria Epes

Print Buyer: Paula Vang

Rights Acquisitions Account Manager, Text: Margaret Chamberlain-Gaston

Rights Acquisitions Account Manager, Image: Mandy Groszko

Production Service: Sara Dovre Wudali, Buuji, Inc.

Photo Researcher: Martha Hall, Pre-PressPMG

Copy Editor: Linda Ireland

Cover Designer: Bartay

Cover Image: © Michael Prince/Corbis

Compositor: NewGen

For product information and technology assistance, contact us at:
Cengage Learning Customer & Sales Support, 1-800-354-9706.
For permission to use material from this text or product, submit all requests online at **www.cengage.com/permissions.**
Further permissions questions can be e-mailed to **permissionrequest@cengage.com**

Library of Congress Control Number: 2008936785

Student Edition
ISBN-13: 978-1-4283-6124-9
ISBN-10: 1-4283-6124-3

Wadsworth
10 Davis Drive
Belmont, CA 94002-3098
USA

Cengage Learning is a leading provider of customized learning solutions with office locations around the globe, including Singapore, the United Kingdom, Australia, Mexico, Brazil, and Japan. Locate your local office at **www.cengage.com/international.**

Cengage Learning products are represented in Canada by Nelson Education, Ltd.

To learn more about Wadsworth, visit **www.cengage.com/wadsworth**
Purchase any of our products at your local college store or at our preferred online store **www.ichapters.com.**

Printed in Canada
1 2 3 4 5 6 7 13 12 11 10 09

Brief Contents

Contents

About the Authors

Sharon Thompson Hirschy has been an educator, social worker, and advocate for families and children for 35 years. She has a Bachelor's degree in Social Welfare and a Master's in Child Development and Family Relations, and is completing coursework for a doctorate in Early Childhood Education. She is a college professor teaching Child Development and Education, including Child Abuse Prevention courses. Ms. Hirschy is a former protective services caseworker. She is a certified teacher and has taught preschool, first grade, special education, English as a Second Language, and has been a teacher and administrator in child care programs.

Ms. Hirschy is a Certified Family Life Educator who has authored many parenting and child care publications, including several parenting programs. She serves on the advisory board for several national, state, and local boards related to children and families. She has been the Assistant Director for the University of North Texas Center for Parent Education and a leader in the development of parent educator standards in Texas. Recognition has included the 2000 Parent Educator of the Year by Practical Parent Education and the Brous Leadership Award for advocacy for early childhood by the Fort Worth Association for the Education of Young Children.

Elaine Wilkinson has a Bachelor's in Early Childhood, Special and Elementary Education, a Master's in Educational Leadership, and is All But Dissertation (ABD) in Child Development. She is currently the Academic Chair/Professor of Child Development/Education, and has taught as a certified teacher in preschools, special education, elementary, high school, and, currently, college classes for more than 30 years, including Child Abuse Prevention courses. She has served on the Texas State Advisory Board for curriculum development for the Texas Higher Education Coordinating Board, the North Central Texas Workforce Commission as the sole child care representative on the board, and the Parent Network Advisory Board for the Texas A&M Co-operative Extension Branch. Ms. Wilkinson was invited by the Ministers of Education as an Ambassador to Beijing, China, and Budapest, Hungary, to visit and observe Early

Childhood classrooms in both the farming and city communities in those countries. She traveled to Moscow, Russia to present at the Association of Childhood Education International. Ms. Wilkinson also serves on numerous boards advocating for the rights of young children. Among her honors are being recognized as the 2008 Trainer of the Year by Collin County Association for the Education of Young Children and the 2005 Professor of the Year in the Social Science Division at Collin College.

Preface

This book has been in our thoughts for some time. Sharon Thompson Hirschy, one of the authors, was a caseworker for several years working with all aspects of abuse and neglect, including intake, investigation, disposition, and treatment. Working with children who had been abused and neglected and their families changed Sharon's life. Returning to school to pursue an advanced degree focused on family life education and later in working as a parent educator and teaching other parent educators, the faces of those children whose lives had been so altered by maltreatment shaped the paths that were taken. Elaine Wilkinson was a teacher of at-risk students for several years, working in inner-city schools and with children who had been abused and neglected. Those faces are still there in dreams and thoughts . . . and hopes that they were able to overcome their experiences. This book is in part an effort to remember them, the lessons they taught and the pain they endured.

Both of the authors as teachers and administrators in public school and in child care came into contact with children of abuse. We found ourselves not only reporting new cases of abuse, but also trying to repair the damage caused by the maltreatment of some of the children in our care. We often found it difficult to decide whether or not to report something we thought might be abuse. It was also hard to understand and guide children who had suffered severe abuse or neglect. When we became college professors and consultants in early childhood, we found so many teachers struggling with these same issues, and little written that could help them. It is for these reasons that this book has been written.

This book has been written to assist teachers, child care and education administrators, health care providers, social service workers, and all who work with young children to recognize and understand the abuse and neglect of children. While the book is focused on educational interventions, it also provides information and ideas for professionals in child welfare and health care as well as anyone working with young children. The book contains practical ideas on working with families and children, and information that should better inform their practice. This book includes not only history and theory, but also best practices in working with young children. There are forms and resources to help those who work with and teach young children.

It is our goal to provide a research-based, practical guide to understanding and working with maltreated children. Our hope is that this book will enable you to not only identify abuse and neglect, but develop an understanding of the many facets of child maltreatment, find practical ideas to help children and their families, and ultimately reduce the incidence of child abuse and neglect nationally as well as globally.

ACKNOWLEDGMENTS

A book about abuse and neglect is a difficult one to write. We are so appreciative to the many friends and our editors who have encouraged us in this project.

We would like to acknowledge our husbands, John and Gene, and our children and parents for their patience, understanding, love, and support through this project. We are grateful for the assistance of the following who critiqued the chapters and whose suggestions were invaluable: Renee McMenamy, Lindy Dutra, Kris Hermonant, Jessica Dundon, Salama Timimi, Krystal Smith, Priscilla Arriaga, Jennifer Young, Kimberly R. Lane, Kimberly A. Jones, Natalie Morgan, Jennifer Volkers, Susan Skinner Wyatt, Gail Goldstein, Kim Brown, Pamela Davis, Jennifer Johnson, David Dean Richey, Patricia Weaver, Karen Roth, Sandra Hughes, Rose Weiss, and Janet Hale. We would like to acknowledge the many professionals at the Collin County Children's Advocacy Center for their willingness to share information and for their support.

We dedicate this work to Glenda, Darin, Elena, Linda, and all the children whose lives have been altered through abuse and neglect, and who taught us through their courage and resilience. Finally, this book is dedicated to our grandchildren, Jovi, Corbin, Emily, and Joseph, in the hope that all those who teach them and touch their lives will nurture and be vigilant in their protection.

SUPPLEMENTS

Website

The book-specific website at www.cengage.com/education/hirschy offers students a variety of study tools and useful resources, including learning objectives, tutorial quizzes, links to related sites, downloadable forms, case studies, flashcards, and more.

The instructor area of the book companion website offers access to password-protected resources such as sample syllabi, PowerPoint® slides, and an electronic version of the Instructor's Manual.

Instructor's Manual

The Instructor's Manual contains resources designed to streamline and maximize the effectiveness of your course preparation. The contents include chapter summaries and outlines, outcomes, teaching tips, activities, discussion questions, projects, workshop suggestions, a test bank, and additional resources.

CHAPTER 1

History and Theory of Child Maltreatment

WHAT YOU WILL LEARN

- The definitions and descriptions of abuse and neglect
- The history of abuse and neglect
- How theories about children and families apply to child abuse and neglect
- The laws and legal implications that impact children who have been abused and neglected

INTRODUCTION

The abuse of a child . . . heartbreaking, overwhelming, beyond understanding. According to the U.S. Department of Health and Human Services Administration for Youth and Families (U.S. Department of Health and Human Services [USDHHS], 2007a), more than 3.6 million children were investigated by Child Protective Services and 899,000 children were conclusively identified as victims of abuse and neglect during the Federal Fiscal Year (FFY) 2006. Every day in this country, every minute, a child suffers from some type of maltreatment. The residual effects of the abuse, neglect, and sexual abuse experienced by children can be seen again and again.

What is child maltreatment? Why does it occur? What are the laws? Should I report it if I think a child is being abused? What if I am wrong and accuse a parent unjustly? These are questions that teachers, nurses, and all those who work with young children like Joey ask themselves. *Child maltreatment,* another term for *child abuse and*

VIGNETTE

It was late July and four-year-old Joey walked in the classroom with long sleeves and pants. He kept his head down and moved very slowly. One of the other children grabbed his hand and pulled him over to a table. Joey cried out in pain. Mrs. Sheritt hurried over and asked where it hurt. Joey pointed to his upper arm. When his shirtsleeve was pulled up, she was horrified to see bruises all the way up his arm. She took him in the bathroom and, with the assistant director, had him take off his shirt. His arms, chest, and back were covered in large welts and dark bruises. Mrs. Sherritt asked Joey what had happened. Unable to meet her eyes, he looked at the floor and said, "I fell."

1

neglect, is a national epidemic that is often "swept under the rug" or ignored. Many refuse to act to protect young children out of fear or uncertainty. *Professionals who learn to understand and recognize what abuse is, and what can be done, make a difference in the lives of these children.*

DEFINING CHILD ABUSE AND NEGLECT

One single definition of child maltreatment or child abuse and neglect is difficult to develop. There are so many terms, for example, *injury to a child, abuse, neglect, child maltreatment,* and *battered child syndrome* (Helfer, Kempe, & Krugman, 1999). What constitutes abusive behavior can vary over time, social situations, and cultures (Goldman & Wheeler, 1986). "Different societies accept and condone different levels of violence toward its members, including children" (Maher, 1985, p. 54). There is a general consensus among researchers that five factors should be taken into consideration when defining whether maltreatment has occurred: **severity**, the nature and intensity of maltreatment; **type**, the form of maltreatment; **chronicity**, the duration and repeated instances of a child's maltreatment experience; **age of onset**, when maltreatment first began; and **frequency**, the number of reports and the duration of maltreatment (English et al., 2005; Herrenkohl, 2005).

A number of definitions are currently accepted. David Gil (1970, p. 50) defined child abuse "as an occurrence where a caretaker injures a child, not by accident, but in anger or deliberately" (Gelles, 1976). The World Health Organization provided this definition: "child abuse or maltreatment constitutes all forms of physical and/ or emotional ill-treatment, sexual abuse, neglect or negligent treatment or commercial or other exploitation, resulting in actual or potential harm to the child's health, survival, development, or dignity in the context of a relationship of responsibility, trust or power" (World Health Organization [WHO], 1999, p. 59).

The definitions found in the federal Child Abuse Prevention and Treatment Act are those most commonly used:

> The Federal Child Abuse Prevention and Treatment Act (CAPTA) . . . , as amended by the Keeping Children and Families Safe Act of 2003, defines child abuse and neglect as, at minimum: Any recent act or failure to act on the part of a parent or caretaker which results in death, serious physical or emotional harm, sexual abuse or exploitation; or An act or failure to act which presents an imminent risk of serious harm. (Child Welfare Information Gateway, 2007)

However, many states have modified this definition and have defined specific forms of abuse and neglect, yielding no universally accepted legal definitions of child maltreatment (Horton & Cruise, 2001; National Center on Child Abuse and Neglect [NCCAN], 1988).

We will use *child maltreatment* and *child abuse and neglect* interchangeably as the terms for the multiple forms of child abuse and neglect, and their characteristics, that you will read about in this text. For the purposes of this book, **child maltreatment** is defined as ***the endangerment of a child's physical or emotional health and development by actions or failure to act.***

Typically, four specific categories of child maltreatment have been used, but due to current research, we feel it appropriate to identify an additional one. Hence, we will explore the following five categories of child maltreatment: **physical abuse**, **sexual abuse**, **emotional abuse**, **neglect**, and **child exploitation**.

HISTORY OF CHILD ABUSE

— Fast Fact —
The first real definition and description of child abuse was written by a French physician, Ambroise Tardieu, in 1860 (Labbe, 2005).

When does history first record evidence of child abuse? Children's fate has often been tied to the culture, socioeconomic group, and time in which they lived. Cultures suffering economic hardships, famine, and war have had higher rates of abuse and neglect, as have those cultures that did not support stable marriages and strong family systems (Breiner, 1990). Since earliest times, some children have been love, nurtured, and educated, while others have been ignored, abandoned, killed, and abused.

Ancient Cultures

Many ancient cultures supported **infanticide**, the intentional killing of infants through violence or neglect. Children of Greece and Rome were not given names until they were several days or months old. Prior to naming they were not considered human, and parents were free to do anything with them. In Greece, it was common for infants to be left on mountainsides, in large jars, or even in the streets to die or for people to claim if they so chose (Van Hook, 1920). The Spartans required infants to be exposed to the elements after birth to determine if they were strong enough to be accepted into the culture. Infants that were weak or had defects were killed immediately. Ancient Chinese culture required infants to be left unfed in a room for three days to see if they would be able to survive (Breiner, 1990). The Twelve Tables, the foundation of Roman law, stated, "an obviously deformed child shall be quickly killed" (Cicero, 450 B.C.). Plato in the Republic advocated "putting away" deformed children. Many early societies—including ancient Greek, Roman, and Chinese cultures—sacrificed infants and young children to gods or to ward off evil magic (Breiner, 1990).

Children who survived infancy were often subjected to harsh treatment. They were the property of the parent who could kill, sell, or abandon them. Societies, such as those of ancient Rome and Greece, perpetrated many atrocities on children. Young boys were sexually used and abused, often by their teachers. Starvation of young children was prevalent. Children were often used in Roman "games" where they were tortured, mutilated, and assaulted as Roman citizens watched and cheered. Roman and Greek cultures appear to have valued children initially, but as these civilizations deteriorated, abuse became more prevalent.

History indicates that as a society became less family oriented and corruption increased, so too did abuse, neglect, and the murder of children (Breiner, 1990). Not all children in early cultures were treated harshly. Many records indicate there was an abundance of nurturing and caring for children in ancient Rome and Greece. Also, during the same time period, other cultures demonstrated less harsh treatment of young children. Ancient Egyptians, Hebrews, and Chinese for the most part exhibited a nurturing attitude toward children. Many of the dynasties of ancient Egypt considered children sinless, and fathers were especially affectionate and nurturing (Breiner, 1990). Infants were nursed and carried until they were three years old. However, when time, war, and famine broke down the government and family structure in Egypt, child abuse became more common. The Hebrews did not allow infanticide. Harsh treatment of children went against their law. Education was important. But even these cultures saw children as the property of parents, and government was often limited in its ability to force parents to treat children appropriately.

— **Fast Fact** —
Cultures such as China, Egypt, and Israel that supported and encouraged strong family units appear to have had fewer incidents of harsh treatment of children.

Middle Ages to Nineteenth Century

Conditions for children (and their families) were harsh during the Middle Ages and the Renaissance. Most children did not survive due to poor sanitation, lack of adequate food, no medical care, and abuse. Parents often valued children only as products to be sold or to be used as workers as soon as they could walk. Children were to be seen and not heard and were typically apprenticed or sent away at very young ages to schools or work situations, and often subjected to harsh treatment. Babies with mothers who were unable to nurse usually died. Bottles were made of cloth or wood, which absorbed bacteria and led to many early deaths (Fuchs, 1982). Mothers who could afford it often placed their babies with **wet nurses**, women who had given birth during the previous year and still had breast milk. Such children were often sent to live with the wet nurses in rural areas, where minimal care was given and neglect common. Infanticide and child abandonment were still common during medieval times, and child abuse and neglect were not recognized as crimes, although society began at this time to be harsher with those who committed blatant infanticide.

Literature of this time period often bore descriptions of children's abuse. The many tales collected by the Brothers Grimm (Degh, 1979) describe children abandoned by parents, neglected, eaten by witches, having their hands cut off by their fathers, locked up, starved, and generally mistreated. Children's nursery rhymes also portrayed children who were denied food, beaten, and neglected.

Lack of appropriate care led to so many deaths that in the early 1700s **Dr. William Cadogan** stated half the children born died under the age of five years. He berated wealthier families who sent their children out to wet nurses to be suckled, as the process provided them with inappropriate care and nurturing (Cadogan, 1749).

Many religions, particularly in the United States during the 1700s, were harsh in their perception of children and contributed to abusive situations. Puritans and Calvinists taught that children were born sinful and discipline should be severely applied. John Robinson, the pastor of the original Pilgrims, stated, "Surely there is in all children . . . a stubbornness and stoutness of mind arising from natural pride, which must, in the first place be broken and beaten down . . . for the beating and keeping down of this stubbornness parents must provide . . ." (Ashton, 1851, p. 246). The prevailing attitude of the Puritans was that the "devil must be beaten out of children."

Child maltreatment often resulted from ignorance or well-meaning attempts to increase a child's health. **Rousseau** (2005 [1762]) in *Emile* stated,

Children's nursery rhymes often described harsh treatment and care for the young:
There was an old woman who lived in a shoe.
She had so many children; she didn't know what to do.
She gave them some broth without any bread,
Then whipped them all soundly and put them to bed.

"Experience shows that children delicately raised are more likely to die. . . . Accustom them therefore to the hardships they will have to face; train them to endure extremes of temperature, climate, and condition, hunger, thirst, and weariness" (p. 66). Many interpreted this to mean that children should routinely be left hungry, and put out with little clothing in extreme cold.

Toward the end of the eighteenth century there was some movement toward recognition of children's need to be nurtured and more emphasis on gentler treatment of children. **Johann Pestalozzi,** an educational reformer, spoke out vigorously against the practice of infanticide and promoted the education and provision of social services for the poor and unwed mothers. He also took abandoned children from the streets of Switzerland and brought them to a farm where he began an educational experiment that provided a basis for later educational reformation (Lascarides & Hinitz, 2000).

Nineteenth Century to Present

The high incidence of child deaths internationally began to be recognized as a serious problem in the late 1700s and early 1800s. Dr. A. I. Coffin (1878) wrote, "It appears from the annual registry of the dead, that almost one half of the children born in Great Britain die under twelve years of age." Medical doctors began to recognize child abuse as a syndrome. The first publication that systematically examined children who were maltreated was presented in 1860 by **Ambroise Tardieu** (Labbe, 2005) using case studies to identify child abuse and to call for doctors to begin to recognize child maltreatment as a serious problem. He said, "I wish to speak of those deeds, described as acts of cruelty and ill treatment, of which young children fall victim from their parents, their schoolmasters, and all who exert over these children some degree of authority" (p. 326). Even with so encompassing a report on abuse, doctors still refused to recognize maltreatment of children as a concern. Dr. Samuel West in 1888 wrote a paper identifying swellings found on children, including newborn infants in the same families, that sound very much like abuse. Dr. West did not even mention abuse as a possibility, but instead concluded that rickets (even though the symptoms were not the same) was the cause (Knight, 1985).

The nineteenth century brought a new attitude in England, Europe, and the United States toward children. It marked the beginning of events that culminated in legal and social protection for children. Children began to be viewed as needing to be protected. Within a 20-year period, France had a threefold increase in the number of prosecutions for child maltreatment, not due to increased incidence, but rather due to changes in law to recognize abuse and neglect of children. The primary focus on protecting children in the 1700s and 1800s was for the poor, abandoned, or unsupervised child. The rate of infant abandonment in Paris was 4,000–5,000 babies a year (Fuchs, 1982). However, by 1811, all the major French cities had **foundling** (orphan) homes that provided care for abandoned infants. Most of these homes had a turnstile system on which an infant could be placed, a bell rung, and the turnstile would rotate the child into the foundling home. Robert Owen, a British industrialist in the early 1800s, found that children as young as five were working 12-hour days in his father-in-law's factory. He inherited the factory and required that children be at least 10 years old to work there, and he also provided a nursery school for younger children (Lascarides & Hinitz, 2000).

Parents and society focused more on education and moral development of children. The prevailing attitude was that abuse and neglect were concerns only in relation to the poor. The best way to avoid delinquency and future problems when abused or neglected children became adults was to rescue them and protect them. The effort was not just to protect children, but also to protect society. Child abuse and neglect were reasons that children become thieves, beggars, and murderers. Child maltreatment was defined primarily in the early nineteenth century as not teaching or supervising children properly.

Nineteeth-Century Prevention Programs. Prevention programs of various types developed internationally. The purpose was to provide protection to children not by changing the family, but by educating or separating the child from the family. In England and the United States, almshouses (free institutions) took in poor, insane, and abandoned children. **Maria Montessori,** a medical doctor in Italy, was approached by a group who asked her to establish a nursery program for children of the slums who were left alone all day while their parents worked. She developed curricula and materials for them, which led to the founding of the Montessori method of early childhood education (Lascarides & Hinitz, 2000). Many of the nursery school programs founded in the United States and Great Britain in the 1800s and 1900s were also efforts to provide care for children left unsupervised or neglected. Private charities and benefactors during this time began to establish orphan asylums and special programs and facilities for children who were abandoned, abused, or neglected.

The United States had **Children's Aid Societies** that were established and supported by private and public funds to protect urban children considered neglected. They also wanted to protect children they felt were exposed to people and situations that would encourage delinquency by removing them to juvenile institutions or to homes in rural areas. Although ideally this would protect children, it did not always do so; sometimes it put children in greater danger than before.

Charles Loring Brace, a minister, in 1850 saw great poverty and abandonment of children in New York City and the urban areas of the North.

National Archives

Carlisle school, a Native American boarding school, 1878.

The prevailing values and attitudes of the times were that if these children were raised in rural areas with farm families they would be healthier and better contributors to society. He orchestrated the placement of over 150,000 children over 70 years into rural families, a movement known as the **Orphan Train**. These children were placed with families chosen by the local ministers or by town committees to learn the virtues of hard work and Christian life, but often they became a cheap labor source for farm families, and many were treated harshly. This method of dealing with abuse and neglect was recognized and accepted internationally during this time as an appropriate course of action (Children's Aid Society, 2007).

One of the most shameful periods of history in the United States occurred during the 1800s and early 1900s. It involved the separation of Native American children from their families because the government felt the

Mary Ellen Wilson

families were neglecting their children by teaching them their native culture. The children were placed in boarding schools where the purpose was to "kill the Indian and save the man" by assimilating them into European American culture and destroying any ties to Indian culture (Pratt, 1892). Children were removed from their homes, by force if necessary, and sent to boarding schools where they were forced to speak only English, were given new names, and were not allowed to practice their culture with the justification that their home situations were neglectful and inappropriate (Mannes, 1995).

Mary Ellen Wilson. The case that is seen as the defining moment when physical abuse of children in the United States was finally recognized as a significant problem and addressed legally was the case of **Mary Ellen Wilson** in the 1870s in New York (American Humane Society, 2007). Mary Ellen was a little girl whose father had died, and whose mother had abandoned her. She was living with a woman whose former husband (then deceased) had claimed to be her father. The child was 10 but looked to be about five. She was kept locked in the house, never taken out, and put in a closet when the woman left. She did the chores in the house and had multiple bruises, cuts, and scars. **Etta Angell Wheeler,** a church social worker, was visiting another woman at the tenement apartments where Mary Ellen lived when the woman told her of hearing Mary Ellen crying and screaming. Mrs. Wheeler went to the apartment, saw Mary Ellen, and began a crusade to help her. She was told that the current laws would not allow anyone to remove Mary Ellen, and so she contacted Henry Bergh, the founder of the Society for the Prevention of Cruelty to Animals, for help. He advised her to secure evidence of Mary Ellen's ill treatment and offered to help. Mrs. Wheeler gathered letters from others in the tenement to attest to Mary Ellen's treatment, and with that evidence Mr. Bergh was able to get a court order for her removal. Mary Connolly, the woman with whom Mary Ellen lived, was found guilty of assault. Mr. Bergh contacted the news media as this case unfolded, and the subsequent publicity set the stage for new laws and the formation of the **Society for the Prevention of Cruelty to Children**. As a result of this case, new organizations, public and private, as well as new legislation for the protection of children were created.

Child Maltreatment in the Modern World. The United States during the early 1900s held several White House Conferences on the Care of Dependent Children. These conferences, particularly the one in 1930, recognized the role of government in the protection of children and that abuse and neglect of children developed from multiple causes that might require treatment or intervention with families and children. Juvenile court systems and child protective agencies were founded. Neglected children were the primary focus of these groups. The prevailing attitude was still that parents knew what was best and that physical abuse was a rare occurrence in families.

In the 1960s, a new perspective on child abuse and neglect came about when, as a result of new x-ray and imaging technology, doctors were able to examine children closely for injuries that were not apparent through a routine physical examination. **Dr. Henry C. Kempe** in 1961 coined the phrase **battered child syndrome** after seeing so many unexplained internal injuries that were identified as "accidents" by parents. Dr. Kempe went on to identify criteria for the identification of abuse. His work brought about a transformation in attitudes and understanding of abuse and neglect that resulted in sweeping changes in laws and practice for the protection of children from abuse and neglect. Dr. Kempe's recognition of various forms of maltreatment became the basis for many current laws and interventions internationally (Kempe et al., 1962; Leventhal, 2003).

Was there more abuse and neglect of children in the past than now? Some historians say yes (deMause, 1998). Other historians point out that the culture and times were different and that it is unfair to judge past treatment of children by the cultural norms and values that we have today (Knight, 1985). Some declare that history has misinterpreted the past and that the treatment of children was far more loving and caring than previously stated (Pollock, 1984). A culture in which most children died of natural causes, and where there was little food and great need for everyone to participate in activities to provide food and shelter, would need children in the labor force much younger and would view children in a different way. A culture in which most children had enough food, lived to adulthood, and had parents who could provide food, shelter, and care, as well as playtime, for them would recognize more rights for children and appropriate care.

As we think about child abuse, it is important to recognize that circumstances and culture often create different views of children and child maltreatment. Some in the world today would consider leaving a child of nine alone to be neglect, while others would see a child of nine as an adult. Many would consider the ear piercing of a female child or the circumcision of a male infant to be cruel, but both are common occurrences in many modern societies. The past seems to be a series of horrific events for children, but it must be seen in the context of culture. Cultural understanding of child maltreatment is better understood by examining the laws and legal descriptions used to define and protect against abuse and neglect. The following section examines the development of child abuse and neglect laws in the United States (see also Figure 1.1).

LAWS AND LEGAL IMPLICATIONS

The relationship between federal and state legislation in regard to abuse and neglect has been at times difficult. Some states provide very detailed legal definitions of abuse and are more punitive in regard to all abuse and neglect. Other states have more general definitions and are less punitive. These definitions of child maltreatment are the basis from which cases are reviewed, adjudicated, and prosecuted, and therefore are critical.

Federal, State, and Local Laws

Laws traditionally were enacted to protect adults. Parents owned their children, and by law that meant that anything they chose to do to them was okay. But toward the end of the nineteenth century and into the twentieth, this attitude changed, and legislation in both state and federal government began to reflect concern for children and rejection of child maltreatment.

During the early 1900s, laws began to address labor issues with children and to limit the use of child labor. Laws were also enacted to establish children's

— **Fast Fact** —
"While laws and social actions aimed at reducing and preventing the incidence of child maltreatment have improved significantly over the last seventy years, the incidence of child maltreatment in the United States is still staggeringly high" (Paulsen, 2003, p. 63).

1729	America's first orphanage opened in New Orleans, to care for children whose parents died as the result of Indian massacres and a smallpox epidemic.
1819	The Factory Act limited the working day for children in cotton mills to 12 hours. Children under the age of nine were not to be employed, but this was not enforced.
1836	Massachusetts passed the nation's first child labor law, which required that children under 15 who worked also receive at least three months of schooling a year.
1842	Massachusetts began limiting children's workdays to 10 hours; soon other states did the same. The Mine's Act limited children under 10 and women from working underground. Boys under 15 were not allowed to work machinery.
1850	The Factory Act established the standard working day.
1853	The New York Children's Aid Society began the "orphan train" movement, a controversial plan that shipped homeless city children to farms out West. It is considered to some to be a forerunner to the foster care system.
1881	The first national convention of the newly formed American Federation of Labor passed a resolution calling on states to ban children under 14 from all gainful employment.
1889	Children who suffered violence at home could get help from the National Society for the Prevention of Cruelty to Children (NSPCC).
1898	Columbia University offered the first class on social work. Police could arrest anyone found ill-treating a child or enter a home if a child was thought to be in danger.
1899	Illinois passed the first law setting guidelines for handling those in the justice system under the age of 16, including issues of separating adults and children in prisons and confidentiality.
1904	National Child Labor Committee formed aggressive national campaign for federal child labor law reforms.
1909	President Theodore Roosevelt chaired the White House Conference on Dependent Children, a two-day meeting to explore the issues faced by impoverished and neglected children.
1912	The U.S. Children's Bureau was established to address foster care, adoption, and child care standards. It remains in place today as part of the Department of Health and Human Services.
1920	The Child Welfare League of America, the nation's oldest child welfare organization, was established.
1930	President Hoover's White House Conference on Child Health and Protection produced the nation's first "Children's Charter," asserting the right of all children to have safe home and school environments and to receive medical care.
1935	The new Social Security Act established aid to dependent children and child welfare services.
1946	President Truman signed the National School Lunch Act to fight child hunger. In its first year, the federally assisted meal program served a half-billion meals to 7.1 million children.
1961	*Battered child syndrome*, a term introduced by Dr. C. Henry Kempe to describe children who are abused by their caretakers, was recognized as a medical condition.
1973	Children's Defense Fund, a national advocacy organization for children, was founded.
1975	The National Organization of Victim Assistance (NOVA) was founded.
1981	Title XX of the Social Security Act was amended to include the Social Services Block Grant to provide child protective services funding to states.
2002	All children 18 and under living below the poverty level could receive health care through Medicaid.

FIGURE 1.1

Timeline: A History of Addressing Child Maltreatment in the U.S.

bureaus, juvenile court systems, and funding for maternal and infant care. Legislation in the 1930s and 1940s addressed economic needs of young children by providing money for unemployed families with young children and a federal lunch program for low-income children in schools.

Prior to 1974, there were no child abuse reporting laws (Helfer, Kempe, & Krugman, 1997). In 1961, during the American Academy of Pediatrics Conference on Child Abuse, the first model child abuse law was drafted. The original intent focused on finding abuse and neglect cases and identifying deterrent punishment, but soon it was apparent that the whole family was often involved in the "battered child syndrome" (p. 23). **The Child Abuse Prevention and Treatment Act** or **CAPTA** (Public Law 93-247) was passed on January 31, 1974; its passage established a National Center on Child Abuse and Neglect (NCCAN), provided money to states for identification, investigation, prosecution, and treatment of child abuse and neglect, and established a minimal definition of child abuse and neglect.

The role that government plays in the protection of children from abuse and neglect has received increased attention during the recent past in individual states. In the 1960s, every single state in the United States passed legislation mandating that all cases of suspected as well as known child abuse and neglect be reported to a designated agency. Some states developed statewide approaches to child protection; others gave jurisdiction to counties. Across the country, several thousand different agencies are charged with the responsibility, and therefore various "official" approaches to protecting children exist (Melton & Flood, 1994).

Child Abuse Prevention and Treatment Act (CAPTA).

In 1974, the federal Child Abuse Prevention and Treatment Act (CAPTA) passed and required states to enact child abuse reporting statutes if they were to receive federal money under the act. It established a national research and demonstration grant program and required the Secretary of the Department of Health, Education, and Welfare to publish annual data on the incidence of child abuse and neglect. As reports of child abuse rose, the pressure to investigate the reports rose as well. Recognizing the growing crisis, Congress passed an amendment to CAPTA in 1988 that created the U.S. Advisory Board on Child Abuse and Neglect (Helfer, Kempe, & Krugman, 1997). By 1990, the advisory board labeled the child maltreatment situation "a national emergency" (Melton & Flood, 1994). CAPTA has been amended several times; most recently it was reauthorized, on June 25, 2003, as the Keeping Children and Families Safe Act of 2003.

CAPTA is in support of prevention, assessment, investigation, prosecution, and treatment activities. It also provides grants to public agencies and nonprofit organizations for demonstration programs and projects. Within the minimum standards set by CAPTA, each state is responsible for providing its own definitions of child abuse and neglect (Newton, 2001). States also have to ensure through a certification that the state is operating a statewide program relating to child abuse and neglect, or has in effect a state law that mandates such action. States are required to classify as abuse or neglect any act or failure to act that results in serious harm, including emotional harm, or death. Acts or failures to act that place children in immediate risk of serious harm, as well as all sexual abuse, must also be classified as abuse and neglect (National Clearinghouse on Child Abuse and Neglect, 2000).

Most states recognize four major types of maltreatment: neglect, physical abuse, sexual abuse, and emotional abuse (Davidson, n.d.). Although any of the forms of child maltreatment may be found separately, often they occur in combination. Not all state definitions include similar examples of abuse, and individual state definitions may cover additional situations (Child Welfare Information Gateway, 2006). Individual state statutes may be found online. (For direct, up-to-date links to these sites and more, please visit our website at www.cengage.com/education/hirschy.)

Native Americans and Child Welfare Legislation

The plight of Native American children in the United States historically was a tragic one. The attitude that Native American culture was inappropriate and that children needed to grow up away from that environment led not only to the boarding schools of the late 1800s and early 1900s, but also to a disproportionate number of Native American children being placed in foster care and adoptions. The Bureau of Indian Affairs (BIA) Division of Welfare was formed in part in the 1940s to provide social workers for the tribes who became concerned about the number of Indian children in long-term foster care or boarding school placements. Adoptive homes did not appear to be available for these children. In 1958, although opposed by many tribes, a joint adoption project of the BIA with the Child Welfare League of America (CWLA) placed Indian children in non-Indian homes, often hundreds of miles from their native reservations (Besaw et al., 2004).

The government became very concerned when it was recognized that not only were Indian children being placed in foster care in large numbers, but also 80–90% were being placed in non-Indian adoptive placements (Jones, 2007). The inappropriate handling of these cases led to the **Indian Child Welfare Act of 1978.** The Indian Child Welfare Act promoted the stability of the Native American family by requiring that certain standards be met before a child could be removed from a home and that, if removal is necessary, children be placed in Native American homes when at all possible.

The mistakes made in the treatment of Native American families can easily occur when a dominant culture seeks to impose its standards on all groups. Neglectful situations do not always mean a child is purposely maltreated. Cultural practices, such as the washing of children or supervision issues, may be considered neglectful in the United States but not in another country. The community may be a lower socioeconomic community where it is considered normal for very young children to wander alone or to be hungry. These factors indicate that a family is in need of information or assistance, not punishment. When a family fails to use community resources and is lacking education and awareness of children's needs and development, and a child's health or safety is at risk, Child Protective Services may need to intervene.

How should societies respond to child maltreatment? It seems clear that even though the media, politicians, and the public would like to believe that quick fixes can be found, the nature of child maltreatment, the depth to which it is ingrained in our society, and the complexity of the problem all defy simple solutions. If progress is to be made, we need to better understand family dynamics and relationships, children's development, and cultural influences on child maltreatment. A further look into theories that attempt to explain development, family relationships, and the evolution of child maltreatment will assist us in that understanding.

THEORIES RELATED TO CHILD ABUSE AND NEGLECT

Have you ever read an account of abuse and neglect and wondered: *How could someone do that to a child? Why does abuse and neglect occur to a child like Joey in our opening scenario? What influences people to become abusive? Why do families continue to abuse children? Why does a child sometimes want to stay in an abusive situation?* Understanding why child maltreatment occurs is something everyone, including the experts, struggles to grasp. Experts from major theoretical frameworks have posed possible answers to why abuse and neglect occurs, and to how it can be prevented. Looking at some of these perspectives can give insight to the how and why of child maltreatment. We will examine a few: behavioral and social learning theories, family systems theory, bio-ecological systems theory, biological/medical theories, attachment theory, and psychodynamic theory.

Behavioral and Social Learning Theories

Behavioral theories focus on how a stimulus in the environment creates a response from the individual receiving the stimulus (Skinner, 1953). Such

U.S. Legislation on Child Welfare and Maltreatment

1836	The first state child labor law was passed by Massachusetts that required children working in factories to attend a minimum of three months of school during the year.
1916	The Keating-Owen Child Labor Act of 1916 became the first federal child labor law. It limited working hours of children and established penalties.
1921	The Sheppard-Towner Act provided funding for maternal-infant health to protect infants and established state-level Children's Bureaus.
1935	The Social Security Act established financial aid to dependent children and set up child welfare services.
1936	The Walsh-Healey Act required the government not to purchase goods made by underage children.
1938	The Fair Labor Standards Act outlawed full-time work for those under 16.
1946	The National School Lunch Act provided a meal program to serve children whose families were unable to provide adequate food.
1974, 1978, 1992, 2003	The Child Abuse Prevention and Treatment Act (CAPTA) was the first comprehensive law on abuse and neglect. It required states to identify and prevent abuse. It also set up the National Center on Child Abuse and Neglect under the Department of Health and Human Services. It was amended in 1978, 1992, and 2003.
1978	The Indian Child Welfare Act was passed to regulate child welfare agencies and programs serving Native American children and families.
1980	The Adoption Assistance and Child Welfare Act was passed to change the foster care and adoption system.
1981	The Social Security Act was amended to provide child protective services funding to states. This became the major source of states' social service funding.
1986	The Child Abuse Victims' Rights Act gave child victims of sexual exploitation a civil damage claim.
1988	The Abandoned Infants Assistance Act provided funding and programs for foster care and abandoned children.
1991	Congress passed the Victims of Child Abuse Act to improve the investigation and prosecution of child abuse cases.
1997	The Adoption and Safe Families Act became law, creating timelines for moving children into permanent situations and also providing adoption bonuses for states.
2000	The Children's Internet Protection Act required schools and public libraries to equip computers with antipornography filters.
2000	The Child Abuse Prevention and Enforcement Act of 2000 provided funding and requirements for states to receive funding for child abuse.
2003	The Prosecutorial Remedies and Other Tools to End the Exploitation of Children Today (PROTECT) Act strengthened law enforcement's ability to stop violent crimes against children and codified the Amber Alert as a national method of tracking missing children.
2006	The Adam Walsh Child Protection and Safety Act of 2006 established a National Registry of substantiated child abuse cases and protections for children from sexual exploitation.

responses are shaped by rewards, punishments, or lack of reward or punishment. According to behavioral theory, a person might abuse a child because of a stimulus, such as the child's crying. The parent's response may be to spank the child, and the parent may feel some sort of reward, such as emotional release. This positive feeling may influence the parent to repeat the behavior. If children refuse to pick up their toys, adults may yell at them; and then when the children pick up the toys, the yelling is reinforced and repeated as a way to get the reward of the children picking up the toys. Physical and verbal violence and neglect are reinforced by children's behavior or by adults' feelings of being rewarded or punished. For example, a severely depressed mother may ignore her young children and not feed them because she feels that she, the mother, deserves the punishment of seeing her children hungry.

Social learning theory developed by Albert Bandura (2002) adapts behavioral theory to take into account the effects of relationships with other people and with the world on behavior. Imitation is an important concept in social learning theory. A person sees someone else abusing a child or is abused as a child and, according to social learning theory, may imitate or model the behavior. Bandura conducted hundreds of studies, which allowed him to establish concrete steps involved in "modeling." First, he emphasized **attention**, the ability to watch someone's behavior. Second, **retention**, the ability to be able to remember and/or imagine what was seen, occurs. Third, the child or adult has the ability to **reproduce** the behavior by acting out what was seen and heard repeatedly. Fourth, **motivation** then encourages the person to repeat the observed behavior on a continuing basis. Bandura's research indicated that aggressive behavior can be developed through imitation. This aggression may later be expressed in cases of child maltreatment. Behavioral and learning theories are often criticized for not taking into account internal attributes and the effects of larger influences, such as society and culture, on behavior.

Family Systems Theory

Family systems theory was developed by Dr. Murray Bowen in the 1950s from a general theory that looked at any type of system that existed in nature. It was adapted particularly for use in family therapy as a way of explaining the unique relationships in the family. The theory looks not at the individual but at family interactions. It focuses on how each person is part of a whole system and on how each family member affects all other members (Christian, 2006). Some of the major concepts include: patterns and rules, boundaries, roles, and equilibrium.

Patterns and Rules. There are predictable patterns that families establish. If a child is the focus of abuse by one parent, the other parent or

Behavioral and Social Learning Theories

1. Provide parents with parenting videos where they can observe and model appropriate guidance skills.
2. Model for children calm and appropriate methods for dealing with conflict.
3. Help parents develop coping techniques that they find rewarding, such as taking a soothing bath or the 7-11 technique of breathing in for 7 seconds and letting the breath out to the count of 11 when they are stressed.

siblings may develop patterns of behavior that allow them to ignore or justify the abuse of the child. Every family has rules; some are obvious and discussed, while others are not mentioned but are known by all. For example, children may know without being told that they are not to discuss with other people the abuse of a brother or their father's drunkenness.

Boundaries. Boundaries are established in each family and relate to communication and openness to new people, programs, or ideas. Families can have open and closed boundaries. They may be so open to new people that children are put at risk, such as when a mother dates a variety of men and leaves her children with them. They may be closed to using community resources, which could result in child neglect or injury. Some families become **enmeshed**, or overly involved with each other, where they have limited communication with those outside the family and are totally self-involved. This can lead to severe stress, such as when a mother of several young children, who has no friends, child care, or help with her children, abuses out of frustration.

Roles. Each family member adopts certain roles in the family. A child may become the caretaker, doing the housework or providing the emotional support for a parent. A father may have a role as the punisher, and any childhood disobedience is reported to him for discipline. Think about the roles in your family. Are they fair and appropriate? Every family member takes on roles, and sometimes abuse and neglect can be avoided by examining these roles and changing them to be more appropriate.

Equilibrium. Families strive to maintain a balance in the family and to keep things the same (**homeostasis**). All families prefer to avoid change in the family, as change can be frightening, even if it is for the better. Often

THEORY TO PRACTICE

Family Systems Theory

1. Encourage parents to talk to their children about family rules and consequences.
2. Model good communication skills with both the children and those who parent the children.
3. Listen carefully to family members as they talk to one another without interruption.
4. Consider how you in your classroom try to maintain balance. Is it healthy? Are there unspoken rules that create a negative atmosphere?

families who have experienced abuse will go to counseling, change the patterns of behavior, and six months later return to their old habits. Understanding this tendency can help professionals and families maintain the progress they have made.

Family systems theory offers many insights into how families function and into how to work with families that experience abuse and neglect. Educators and others who work with children can apply these ideas as they try to help families overcome abusive relationships.

Bio-Ecological Systems Theory

Bio-ecological systems theory was developed by Urie Bronfenbrenner (1979) to explain the impact of the child's environment and biology on the child's growth and development. Bronfenbrenner identified a series of influences on the child:

1. *Microsystems:* Those things that directly affect the child
2. *Macrosystems:* Those things that influence the child indirectly by impacting teachers, parents, or others who directly affect the child, such as the parent's workplace, the community and its resources, and religion
3. *Exosystem:* Those things that influence society, and therefore the child and family generally, such as laws, government, media, and culture
4. *Chronosystem:* The impact of time, the child's growth, and the historical setting on the child
5. *Mesosystem:* The relationships between people and things in the child's microsystems or other systems and their effects on the child. If a child has been abused by someone outside the family, the parent may contact the teacher and they can work together to help the child. This is an example of

THEORY TO PRACTICE

Bio-Ecological Systems Theory

1. Make families aware of community resources and how they can help the family.
2. Develop a positive relationship with parents, as it affects the parent's relationship with the child!
3. Be aware and cautious of outside influences on children, such as the Internet and those in the community who may have access to the child.

the mesosystem. The teacher and parent's working together will be affected by the child and the child's response to them. If the child does not like the teacher, that will affect the relationships between child and teacher and teacher and parent. (See Figure 1.2.)

This theory is particularly helpful when looking at abuse and neglect. Why parents abuse can be influenced by the way they were raised (family), by the culture, by stresses from their workplace, and by the age of the child. Abuse can occur as a result of the ability of an abuser to make contact with a child through the computer (media). The ability of a perpetrator to abuse repeatedly is influenced by the laws and the ability of institutions, such as a welfare services programs, to provide services to the family (Tomison & Wise, 1999).

Biological/Medical Theories

Are children abused because of the perpetrator's experiences or because of actual changes in that person's brain, perhaps caused by their abuse and neglect as a child? Could there be an abuse gene—a genetic tendency toward abuse? Biological/medical theories address these issues. The evolution of technology and science has provided new pathways to understanding the interrelationship of biology, psychology, and aberrant behaviors, such as abuse and neglect. Biological theorists believe that there is a biological component to abuse and neglect in some perpetrators. Studies with macaque monkeys (Maestripieri et al., 2006) have indicated that infant monkeys abused and neglected by their mothers had lower levels of critical neurotransmitters and hormones. These infants in turn grew up to be abusive and as adults had lower levels of these chemicals in their brains than nonabusive mothers. Studies on rats have shown that those lacking a certain gene neglected their infants no matter what type of environment, role model, or intervention was provided (Brown, Ye, Bronson, Dikkes, & Greenberg, 1996). Correlations have been shown between abusive

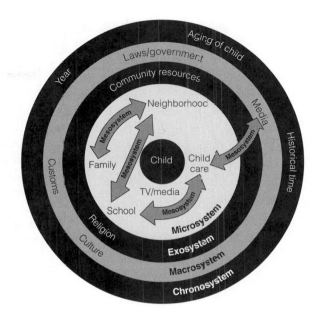

FIGURE 1.2

Bio-Ecological Systems Theory

Things can change! The microsystem has a direct effect on the child; other systems, an indirect effect. If a child does not go outside or get directly involved with the neighborhood, the neighborhood is in the child's exosystem, not the microsystem. If a child watches TV daily, TV is part of the child's microsystem. It could also be part of the exosystem if the child's parents watch TV and use parenting techniques they see there, or part of the macrosystem if the TV portrayal of families changes laws and attitudes of society.

Each of the systems have a profound effect on the child. Anything within one system can either directly or indirectly affect the child and can be found in another system. For example, media could be part of a child's microsystem if he watches it daily and acts out what he sees. But the legal system has adopted regulations on TV show ratings, such as PG which affect which shows his parents allow him to see and so media is part of the macrosystem.

behavior in humans and post–traumatic stress disorder (PTSD), depression, and even irritable bowel syndrome (Kendall-Tackett, 2000).

There appears to be connections between biology and abuse and neglect. But does a connection mean physiological differences cause abuse and neglect? What about environmental factors? We do know that when a person suffers from PTSD, depression, irritable bowel syndrome, or other biological disorder, it does *not* mean the person will become abusive. Many people suffer from these disorders without abusing and neglecting their children. Does biology predispose a person toward being abusive and neglectful? Or do factors in a person's life and personality, such as stress or isolation, that predispose a

THEORY TO PRACTICE

Biological/Medical Theories

1. When you are aware of health problems in parents, reassure the child and provide the parents with ideas for positive activities with the child.
2. When children have been abused, help them to learn prosocial skills, such as conflict resolution and problem solving, so they can have alternatives to violence now and in the future.

person toward abuse and neglect also happen to be the same factors that contribute to disorders such as PTSD and depression? It is a mistake to state causality or to determine that biology alone causes abuse. Environment, personality, and choice must also be taken into account. But researchers hope that by identifying possible relationships, new and effective forms of treatment for those who abuse and neglect children can be found.

Psychodynamic Theory

Psychodynamic theory, developed by Sigmund Freud, addresses abuse and neglect (Muris, 2006). The theory states that people's childhood experiences are internalized and filtered through the **id**, or the internal, instinctual drives such as hunger and sex, and through the **superego**, or conscience. The **ego** is the central force that balances the id and superego and integrates these into the personality. According to psychodynamic theory, when children are abused or neglected, their egos may not function properly and they may develop personality aberrations that, as adults, will not allow them to respond appropriately to their own children and that, in turn, can lead to abuse and neglect. Psychodynamic theory is used often in explanations of sexual abuse,

THEORY TO PRACTICE

Psychodynamic Theory

1. Teach children to learn to handle their fears and emotions by encouraging them to talk with you about them.
2. Help children develop healthy attitudes toward their bodies and an understanding of appropriate touches by providing parents with information on how to teach children about sex and body parts and by helping them to feel positive about all of their bodies!

where it is believed that adults who did not resolve sexual conflicts internally as children may express this in sexually abusive behaviors.

Attachment Theory

Attachment theory has its roots in both biological and psychodynamic theories. John Bowlby (1988) first formulated the idea that there are critical periods in a child's development during which the child must become securely attached to another human being or have difficulty forming future relationships. Mary Ainsworth joined Bowlby in his research, developed several methods to test Bowlby's theory and contributed to its development.

Bowlby followed the work of Konrad Lorenz, an **ethologist** whose work with animals demonstrated a critical period in which some infant animals and birds must form an attachment with their mother in order to develop appropriately. Bowlby felt that this is also true of humans. Both Ainsworth and Bowlby were trained in psychoanalysis, but they believed it ignored the importance of the mother-child relationship and focused too much on internal fantasies and factors in the development of dysfunctional relationships. Bowlby and Ainsworth had a particular interest in the relationship of attachment to abuse and neglect.

Attachment theory (Ainsworth, Blehar, Waters, & Wall, 1978) states that, during the first year of life, infants must form a secure attachment to a caregiver. Children who do not develop a secure attachment to an adult, usually the mother, have difficulty throughout their lives forming healthy relationships with peers, family, and others in their lives. These children are also at risk for disorders such as failure to thrive syndrome and subsequent personality, social, and learning disorders. Much research has been done on the development of attachment. Studies show a strong relationship between mothers who do not develop a secure attachment with their children and child abuse and neglect. Although much evidence indicates that attachment can play a significant role in abuse and neglect (Morton & Browne, 1998; Perry, 2002), we also see many children who

THEORY TO PRACTICE

Attachment Theory

1. Encourage mothers and fathers, especially those of infants, to visit the classroom of their children often and to interact with their children.
2. Provide ideas for fun and easy activities that parents can do with their children to deepen their relationship.

grow up without this secure attachment and yet who do not abuse and neglect children. Environment and other relationships also play a critical role.

Contributions of Theories

Theories provide a framework for our understanding of human behavior. No one theory explains development and behavior, but each theory offers us insights into why child maltreatment occurs and how it can be treated and prevented (Newberger, Newberger, & Hampton, 1983). It is important to use

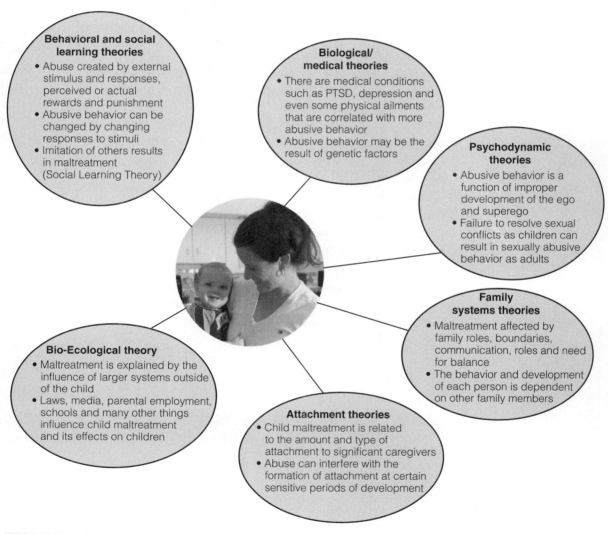

Behavioral and social learning theories
- Abuse created by external stimulus and responses, perceived or actual rewards and punishment
- Abusive behavior can be changed by changing responses to stimuli
- Imitation of others results in maltreatment (Social Learning Theory)

Biological/ medical theories
- There are medical conditions such as PTSD, depression and even some physical ailments that are correlated with more abusive behavior
- Abusive behavior may be the result of genetic factors

Psychodynamic theories
- Abusive behavior is a function of improper development of the ego and superego
- Failure to resolve sexual conflicts as children can result in sexually abusive behavior as adults

Bio-Ecological theory
- Maltreatment is explained by the influence of larger systems outside of the child
- Laws, media, parental employment, schools and many other things influence child maltreatment and its effects on children

Family systems theories
- Maltreatment affected by family roles, boundaries, communication, roles and need for balance
- The behavior and development of each person is dependent on other family members

Attachment theories
- Child maltreatment is related to the amount and type of attachment to significant caregivers
- Abuse can interfere with the formation of attachment at certain sensitive periods of development

FIGURE 1.3

Contributions of Theories to Understanding Child Maltreatment these theories in an integrated way to understand and explain the behavior of parents and children involved in abuse and neglect (see Figure 1.3).

CHILD ABUSE AND PROFESSIONAL STANDARDS

Many professional organizations, including the American Academy of Pediatrics, the Council on Exceptional Children, and the Child Welfare League of America, and many educational organizations have issued statements and standards on the causes and prevention of child abuse. The National Association for the Education of Young Children in 1996 issued a position statement entitled "Prevention of Child Abuse in Early Childhood Programs and the Responsibilities of Early Childhood Professionals to Prevent Child Abuse." This statement targets early childhood educators but is also very useful for anyone who works with families and children, including social workers and medical personnel.

This book utilizes the standards of the National Association for the Education of Young Children (NAEYC) as a framework in addressing the issues of child abuse and neglect. A copy of the standards can be found in Appendix C, and we will refer to it whenever possible.

SUMMARY

This chapter has reviewed what constitutes abuse, historical foundations of abuse and neglect, laws related to child maltreatment, and how theories can help us understand abuse and neglect. Abuse and neglect has many dimensions and can be defined differently according to time, culture, and law. History seems to indicate a harsh treatment of young children in the past, and yet this treatment must be viewed in the context of the culture, family life, and economic needs. No one theory can explain why children are abused and how to treat it, but all theories can help us understand what leads to abuse and give us ideas and methods for assisting families and children through prevention.

Application: When Working with Children

- Understand the culture of the family. Children may wear certain clothes, or practice hygiene differently from you, due to cultural differences. Read about the culture of each child in your classroom, and try to work within the cultural needs of the family. Also, try to make families from other cultures aware of guidance strategies used in the United States by sending home articles or information.

- Ask yourself: *Why is child abuse prevention important? Is it to protect society and families or because each child is valuable?* The answer may seem obvious, but think about how you respond to children and their families in this context.

- Learn your state laws regarding abuse and neglect.

Application: When Working with Families

- Build strong relationships with parents. Send home a questionnaire to obtain more information about family interactions (see Appendix G).
- Ask parents and children to share information about their unique cultures. All families have a culture and cultural scripts—Southern, Jewish, Hispanic, Asian, African American. All these identities give certain traditions and attitudes to individuals. Ask family members to come and share information with classes. When working with a child, ask the parents about things that influence their parenting.
- Encourage positive parent interactions with children through modeling of behavior, sending home activity ideas, and having regular discussions with them about their children.

Projects/Activities

1. Watch three family comedies, at least one of which is currently on television, and at least one from 10–30 years ago, such as "Leave It to Beaver" or "Home Improvement." Summarize what you see, and compare and contrast how families were portrayed differently in the past than they are now. How might these shows reflect parenting attitudes of their time, and how might they influence parents in their parenting practices? Would abuse and neglect have been viewed differently in the past than it is now? Use ecological theory as part of your explanation.

2. Read *Applying Family Systems Theory to Early Childhood Practice* at http://www.journal.naeyc.org/btj/200601/ChristianBTJ.asp. Give five ways that you could use this information to help a child who is experiencing stress in the family.

3. Research your state's laws on child abuse. Compare and contrast the state definition to the federal definition of child abuse.

4. Locate a law, bill, or case in your community or state regarding child abuse. Track its path from the beginning to the present, and note where it is in the governmental process. Write to an elected official regarding your position on this legislation as it applies to children and families.

5. Find a nursery rhyme or fairy tale that demonstrates child maltreatment. Give a summary of the rhyme or tale, how it demonstrates child maltreatment, and the subtle impact you think it could have on children and parents.

Questions to Consider

1. Are abuse and neglect only dependent on culture and time?
2. Is there an absolute definition of abuse and neglect?
3. Does any one theory explain child abuse and neglect? Does one explain it better than others?

Websites for More Information

For useful websites, visit www.cengage.com/education/hirschy

CHAPTER 2

Recognizing and Identifying Child Abuse and Neglect

VIGNETTE

Mrs. Rellas works in a child care facility for at-risk families. She is often confronted with situations in which she is not sure whether abuse and neglect is present. Sometimes Annie arrives with a bruise on her face, and Juan comes in with torn clothing and hungry. Ellen is often rubbing at her bottom and has an odor. Are these things signs of abuse and/or neglect? Mrs. Rellas is not always sure.

WHAT YOU WILL LEARN

- Statistics regarding child maltreatment
- Different types and categories of abuse and neglect
- Signs, symptoms, and characteristics of specific forms of abuse
- Effects of child maltreatment

INTRODUCTION

Abuse and neglect—what is it? Each state is required to have its own legal definition of abuse and neglect. The *Keeping Children and Families Safe Act of 2003,* an amendment to the federal *Child Abuse and Treatment Act (CAPTA),* requires that states at a minimum include the following: "Any recent act or failure to act on the part of a parent or caretaker which results in death, serious physical or emotional harm, sexual abuse or exploitation; or An act or failure to act which presents an imminent risk of serious harm" (U.S. Department of Health and Human Services [USDHHS], 2007a, p. xiii). We stated in Chapter 1 that **child abuse** is *the endangerment of a child's physical or emotional health and development by actions or failure to act.* This chapter identifies five major types of abuse: physical abuse, emotional abuse, sexual abuse, neglect, and child exploitation. We will explore each of these forms of maltreatment, including definition and identification issues.

ABUSE STATISTICS AND DEMOGRAPHICS

The best source of data on the maltreatment of children is the National Child Abuse and Neglect Data System (NCANDS), developed as a requirement of the CAPTA legislation. The system collects data from all 50 states, Puerto Rico, and the District of Columbia. However, due to variations in specific reporting requirements of each state, data is not available every year. The most current data is for 2006. In 2006, there were 3.3 million reports made to child protection agencies of possible abuse and neglect that involved about 6 million children. About 30% or 905,000 children were determined to be victims of child maltreatment (USDHHS, 2008). The predominant type of maltreatment in the United States is neglect, followed by physical and then sexual abuse (although this can vary according to area) (see Figure 2.1). Although psychological abuse is the least reported and verified abuse, most professionals recognize that it underlies all types of abuse and may actually be the most predominate (Crosson-Tower, 2002; Hines & Morrison, 2005).

Children of all ages are abused. Children under eight are less likely to defend themselves, less likely to tell someone before abuse becomes severe, more needy and vulnerable, and thus make up the largest group of maltreated children. In fact, victimization rates for children under three are 38.6 per 1,000 children versus 10.8 per 1,000 children for children ages 8–11. The number of abuse and neglect victims has decreased slightly in the past five years, from 12.3 victims per 1,000 children in 2002 to 12.1 per 1,000 in 2006 (USDHHS,

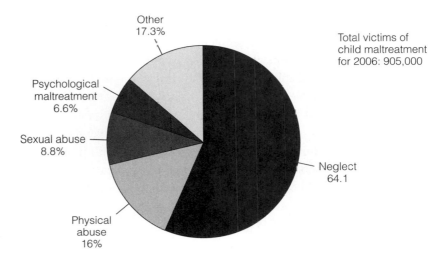

FIGURE 2.1

Types of Abuse and Victims, 2006
Source: Child Maltreatment, U.S. Department of Health and Human Services, 2008.

2008). This change may be due to better reporting and treatment, which would lead to fewer repeat cases, or it could be due to differences in definition of abuse and neglect.

PHYSICAL ABUSE

According to government definitions, physical abuse is any physical injury that is nonaccidental and "can include striking, kicking, burning, or biting the child or any action that results in a physical impairment" (Child Welfare Information Gateway, 2007b, p. 2). It can also include "punching, beating, shaking, throwing, stabbing, choking, hitting with a hand, stick, strap, or other object" (Goldman & Salus, 2003, p. 12).

In most states the definition also refers to things that "threaten the child with harm and create a substantial risk of harm" (p. 2). Physical punishment of a child, such as spanking, is usually not seen as abusive unless it creates visual damage or impairs the child, such as leaving bruising, or places the child in harm, such as denial of food for a long period. The definition of physical abuse can be vague and dependent on the background and beliefs of the person defining the abuse.

It is difficult to identify the rate of abuse due to definitional differences and different methods varying states use to count abuse cases (Barnett, Miller-Perin, & Perin, 2005). We define **physical abuse** as *any type of injury to a child that is physically inflicted or causes physical harm*. Physical abuse is the second most common form of abuse, but also the least likely to be repeated (Hines & Morrison, 2005).

Many types of physical abuse are seen in children. The phrase used initially in modern literature was the **battered child syndrome** (Kempe, Silverman, Steele, Droegemueller, & Silver, 1985). The term was coined to refer to multiple fractures in differing states of healing that were observed in children as a result of the ability to use x-rays. **Fractures and skeletal injuries** are usually breaks in bone that occur as a result of severe trauma to a child from an instrument, body part (e.g., hitting with a hand or kicking with a foot), or from being thrown against an object or the ground. They can be very small and can easily go undiagnosed. Infants and toddlers often present with multiple small fractures (Jenny, 2006). **Abdominal and internal injury trauma** is found more often with younger children and has a higher death rate than other types of trauma (Kellogg, 2007).

— Fast Fact —
"Bruises are the most common manifestation of physical abuse" (Dubowitz & Bennett, 2007).

Bruising

Bruising is a normal part of growing up. Every child sustains bruises while learning to walk, run, and play. **Bruising** is the physical injury seen most often in abuse (Dubowitz & Bennett, 2007). However, defining bruising as abuse is dependent on several factors. Bruises on infants who are not sitting up or rolling

Types of Physical Abuse

Skin Injuries	Bruises	Patterns or shapes of bruising such as a cord or fingers Bruises in various healing stages Clusters of bruises in areas Bruises in areas unlikely to be accidental Infant bruising
	Bites	Human teeth marks Bites in unusual locations Bites that break skin
	Abrasions/Cuts	Unlikely areas such as genitals Gums and inner mouth areas Lips, eyes, ears of infant
	Burns	Burns with recognizable pattern such as curling iron Lower half of body from bath water Cigarette burns Burns in clusters, such as small round burns from matches Rope burns Scalding from tap water or boiling liquids or grease Burns from fireplace
Internal Injuries	Muscle, Joint, and Skeletal Injuries	Broken bones and fractures Separation of bone from joint Sprains Swollen joints from being jerked and pulled Muscle injuries from being hit or pulled
	Organs and Internal Tissue	Stomach and intestinal injuries from punching, kicking Blood vessel rupture and damage
	Drug and Alcohol Exposure	Fetal alcohol syndrome Addiction Birth defects Learning disabilities
Sensory/Head	Teeth	Teeth missing or loose
	Eye Injuries	Injuries to eyes not easily explained or suspicious Bleeding or bruising in and around eyes and scalp
	Hair	Bald spots in hair
Failure to Thrive	Infant Growth	Child does not eat Listless or unresponsive Significantly behind in development with no obvious reason Height or weight substantially below norm or loss
Shaken Baby Syndrome	Eyes, Brain, Internal Organs	Retinal detachment Bleeding, swelling, and bruising in the brain Neck broken Internal organ, tissue damage

Bruising Stages

Child's skin color often makes timeframes and coloring difficult to determine.

Length of Time from Start of Bruise	Color
immediate	red
6–12 hours	blue
12–24 hours	black-purple
4–6 days	green tint, dark
5–10 days	pale green to yellow

over should be viewed with suspicion. However, many infants exhibit **mongolian spots**, a congenital mark that looks like bruising and is often seen on young children, especially young children of color. Ask the parents about any suspicious mark you see on an infant.

When are bruises not normal? How can you tell? Certain parts of the body will be bruised from active play, such as the elbows, knees, forehead, and shins. Bruising that is the result of abuse is usually found in places on the child's body that would not typically show marks. For example, you normally do not see bruises on the upper back between the shoulder blades, under the arm, on the backs of the legs, or on the neck. Think about areas that are impacted when a child falls. Is the bruising in that area? How easy is it to get a bruise between the shoulder blades or on the upper inside thigh area? Not very easy. Bruises in unusual locations or without adequate explanation are signs of concern. (See Figure 2.2.)

Bruises that are caused by objects used on the child often have a specific outline or pattern, such as a belt buckle or cord. Another indicator of abuse is bruising that is in different stages of healing. Many things may affect the color of a bruise, including time since injury, depth of bruise, and the child's skin sensitivity

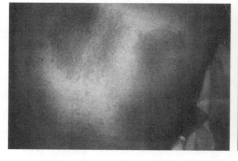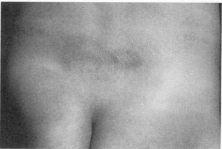

Mongolian spots on infant (left) and two-year-old (right).

(Dubowitz & Bennett, 2007). A bruise that is purple and near others that are various colors of yellow or red, or are almost gone, could indicate an ongoing case of abuse. Bruising associated with child abuse is often seen in clusters, with several bruises together in an area (Maguire, Mann, Siber, & Kemp, 2005).

Skin injuries such as **abrasions, cuts, bites, and burns** that are inflicted purposefully on a child can be caused by a body part (e.g., a hand or foot) or an instrument (e.g., a knife, curling iron, or hot pan). Skin injuries should be suspect when they are on parts of the body where an accident would be unlikely to cause the injury, when marks are from instruments that the child would be unlikely to be able to get, when large areas of a child's body are covered by the injury, or, in the case of bites, when the skin injury shows teeth marks larger than a child's would be.

Drug Exposure

Drug exposure is another form of abuse that is usually seen in children with parents who are addicted to drugs. Exposure can be from a parent using drugs prenatally (e.g., a pregnant cocaine addict), which affects the child. Such exposure is often seen as abuse if the child is born addicted to the substance. Although some question exists about whether a child born to a parent who is addicted to drugs is actually abused and neglected, protective services is usually

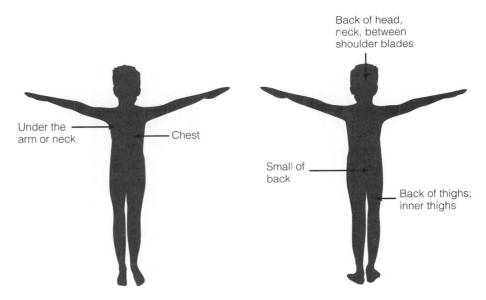

FIGURE 2.2

Suspicious Areas of Bruising

contacted and becomes involved when the child is born showing evidence of addiction or damage (Smith & Test, 2002).

Another form of drug exposure abuse that has become all too common is the child whose parents are producing drugs in the home, such as methamphetamines. The children experience abuse through ingestion of chemicals used in drug production. They are often exposed to parents or other adults who are using drugs, who may abuse or neglect the children, and are often hurt as the result of accidents in the drug labs (Messina, Marinelli-Casey, West, & Rawson, 2007). Abusive parents also sometimes give children street drugs as a means of calming them and getting them to sleep or to be quiet.

Fetal Alcohol Spectrum Disorders

Fetal alcohol spectrum disorders are developmental problems caused by the mother drinking alcohol. Milder forms could include learning disabilities or slight physical abnormalities. The most severe form is known as **fetal alcohol syndrome**, or **FAS** (Wattendorf & Muenke, 2005). Fetal alcohol syndrome symptoms include abnormal facial features such as a flat, wide bridge on the nose, thin upper lip, pointed nose, smaller head circumference, and small abnormalities in the hands and ears (see Figure 2.3). The syndrome also includes damage to the central nervous system. These children often experience learning disabilities and difficulty in reasoning and judgment, and can be mentally retarded. The damage is caused not only by heavy drinking. There is evidence that even small amounts of alcohol in pregnancy can affect a baby. The evidence is so strong that in 2005 the Surgeon General issued an advisory on the use of alcohol during pregnancy in which he stated, "when a pregnant woman drinks alcohol, so does her baby. Therefore, it's in the child's best interest for a pregnant woman to simply not drink alcohol" (USDHHS, 2007a). Although most evidence points to fetal alcohol syndrome being caused by the mother's consumption of alcohol, there is also a small body of evidence indicating that a father who drinks heavily before conception may contribute to the child's development of the syndrome as well (Abel, 2004).

Munchausen by Proxy Syndrome

Munchausen by Proxy Syndrome is a rare form of child abuse. It occurs when a parent purposely makes a child ill or falsifies tests and child histories so that the child is subjected to hospitalizations and testing that are either unnecessary or brought on by the parent's behaviors. Often it appears that such parents want

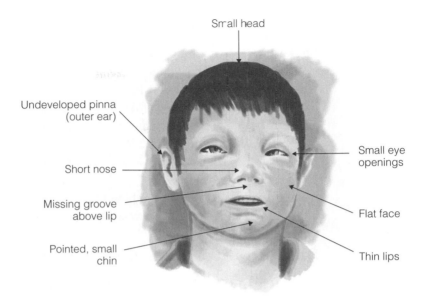

FIGURE 2.3

Physical Characteristics of Fetal Alcohol Syndrome

the attention they receive from medical personnel, and often these parents are seen as very caring. They receive positive reinforcement from medical personnel for being such good parents. Sometimes the health problems are already present and simply exaggerated by the parent or perpetrator; other times they are caused by them so that medical help will be needed. Munchausen by Proxy Syndrome is extremely difficult to diagnose but is one of great concern to the medical community (Stirling, 2007).

Failure to Thrive

Failure to Thrive (FTT) is a condition in which an infant or child fails to gain weight or loses weight in a significant manner and usually not corresponding to height gain (Block & Krebs, 2005). Often a psychological component exists in which the baby or child is listless or unresponsive to adults. Failure to Thrive can be the result of illness or disease, and not the fault of the parents. It also can be caused by neglecting, through lack of resources or understanding, to provide the child with adequate nutrition or by intentional withholding of food from the child (Block & Krebs, 2005). Failure to Thrive also results from the caregiver failing to provide emotional support and stimulation to an infant, which can result in the infant not eating. Failure to Thrive is a very serious form of abuse that must be dealt with immediately, often through hospitalization in order to prevent death or permanent injury.

Shaken Baby Syndrome (SBS)

Shaken Baby Syndrome (SBS) involves severe head trauma caused by violent shaking of a child. The common outcomes of the syndrome involve injury to the retina, sometimes causing bleeding, retinal detachment, and blindness; bruising of the brain as a result of tearing of veins and tissue; and bleeding and swelling. There is a high incidence of death and permanent injury as a result of SBS. According to Salehi-Had, Brandt, Rosas, and Rogers (2006), "Head trauma in small children resulting from shaking injury is associated with a much worse neurologic outcome than direct blunt head trauma" (p. 1039). They found that while Shaken Baby Syndrome has commonly been thought to only occur with young children under two, older children can also show signs of the syndrome as a result of shaking.

Sudden Infant Death Syndrome (SIDS)

— Fast Fact —
Ninety percent of SIDS deaths occur prior to six months of age (Sheehan, 2006).

Sudden Infant Death Syndrome (SIDS) is the most common cause of death between the ages of one and six months. It involves the sudden death of an infant during sleep without any obvious explanation, even after autopsy has been performed. There was historically a belief that SIDS was actually physical abuse. However, it is estimated that **infanticide** (the killing of an infant) occurs in less than 5% of the cases identified as SIDS (Hymel, 2006a). Those cases that are identified as infanticide are usually the result of smothering a child.

Reading the Signs of Physical Abuse

Physical abuse of children can sometimes be easily recognized. A child's swollen face, inability to walk, or burns all over a child's body can be identified by most people as signs that should be explored further. But often physical abuse is more subtle. Bruises may be hard to identify as abuse, and not just the result of a fall. Pain can be caused by many things, not just physical assault. How do you identify physical abuse?

The child that has been physically abused will often complain of pain. Children with stomach injuries may have nausea, vomiting, or swelling of the abdominal area. A child may show signs of having been bitten. Children who have self-inflicted bites usually have them on their hands or lower arms. Bites that are larger, in unusual areas, and repeated over time should be of concern. Children can burn themselves accidentally, but burns that are symmetrical, or have patterns and shapes, must be examined. Impetigo, a skin infection, can look like cigarette burns, although impetigo lesions are usually different sizes (Dubowitz & Bennett, 2007). Children who have difficulty putting weight on an extremity or who complain of pain and nausea may be experiencing a fracture. Any suspected fracture should be examined by a physician. A child with bruising or scarring around the mouth may have experienced physical abuse (Kellogg & Committee, 2005). Forcing spoons or instruments into a child's mouth can cause severe pain and injury. A child can also have eye damage by head trauma (e.g., having been hit in the head).

When evaluating physical abuse watch for:

- Unusual locations and shapes of injuries
- Repeated and multiple injuries
- Unusual injuries for the child's age
- "Accidental" injuries with unusual or unrealistic explanation
- Explanations of an injury from parent and child conflict

The checklist for evaluating physical abuse found in Appendix B has more possible signs.

Behavioral/Emotional Signs of Physical Abuse. Children who have been physically abused usually manifest behavioral symptoms as well as physical ones. Some children are withdrawn and fearful. Sometimes they cringe when an adult comes near or act as if they fear being hit. They may be very aggressive and angry all the time. These children often develop patterns of coping that interfere with learning and development. They may appear unintelligent or have severe learning disabilities. Loud voices and touching may cause them to shrink away or hit. Some explain injuries by making up stories or tell different stories at different times about an "accidental" injury.

EMOTIONAL ABUSE

Emotional abuse is known by many names, and includes aspects of neglect as well as abuse. Psychological or emotional maltreatment are terms often used (Glaser, 2002; Schneider, Ross, Graham, & Zielinksi, 2005). **Emotional neglect** usually involves not meeting a child's emotional needs through neglectful rather than intentional withholding of affection or verbal and emotional actions. **Emotional abuse** is more purposeful, involves intentional emotional harm and is easier to identify (Simeon, 2006). "Children who are emotionally abused often do not qualify for child protection intervention because the chronic, long-term abuse they experience is not classified as significant harm or risk of harm" (Sheehan, 2006, p. 41). Emotional abuse and the concept of harm are very difficult to quantify. If children endure fussing or are belittled (e.g., by being told they will never be as smart as a sibling, or that they are worthless), at what point does this become emotional abuse?

Do we define emotional abuse by the outcomes for the child or by the behaviors of the perpetrator (Barnett, Miller-Perin, & Perin, 2005)? Most emotional abuse occurs with the primary caregiver, although teachers can also be emotionally abusive and neglectful. According to Glaser (2002), an overall definition of emotional abuse and neglect should include the following:

- There must be a "relationship" with a child—not just a single event.
- The harmful behaviors toward the child dominate the relationship.
- The "interactions" create harm now or in the future for the child psychologically and/or emotionally.
- The maltreatment includes "omission as well as commission."
- The behavior toward the child "does not involve physical contact."

This book will define **emotional abuse** as behavior toward a child that is not physical, but which harms the child's psychological capacity and/or abilities as evidenced by changes in the child's emotions, abilities, or behaviors now or over time. Emotional abuse can be found separate from other forms of abuse, but many argue that all forms of abuse have at their foundation elements of emotional maltreatment (Crosson-Tower, 2002). Different categories have been established to identify specific forms of emotional abuse and neglect (Barnett, Miller-Perin, & Perin, 2005; Miller-Perin & Perin, 2007), but those established in 1985 by the American Professional Society on the Abuse of Children have been most commonly used (American Professional Society on the Abuse of Children, 1995). They are:

1. *Rejection.* This can include verbal and nonverbal hostile and/or rejecting behaviors (e.g., telling a child continually that the child is not loved, refusing to provide affection, picking out the child continually for criticism or belittling). A child might be told he is worthless, or that the parent wishes he had never been born. A child might be used by the family or a teacher as a scapegoat, so that everything wrong in the family or classroom is blamed on her.

2. *Terrorizing.* It is characterized by continual threats of harm to a child, his possessions, or people about whom the child cares. Subjecting a child to being around spousal abuse can fall into this category. Examples would be threatening to kill a child's dog if the child does not get good grades, or continual threats to beat the child with a chair or other objects when the child does not obey.

3. *Exploiting/corrupting.* This is actually two types of emotional abuse. The first, exploiting, involves the use of the child in some way, such as forcing children to participate or excessively pushing a child in an area to meet a parent's needs or unfulfilled dreams. This is demonstrated by parents pushing a child to achieve in sports or music to the point that it is overwhelming for the child. The other, corrupting, involves the child being taught antisocial behavior not in keeping with basic moral values. This

might include encouraging a child to smoke or do drugs, or teaching a child prejudice and hatred for a racial or ethnic group. "[C]hildren taught to hate are prevented from incorporating the desirable virtues of tolerance, reverence for life, respect for individual differences, and mutual understanding" (Katzman, 2005, p. 147).

4. *Denying emotional responses.* Children who are ignored, interacted with rarely, and shown little nurturing and positive emotions by the caregiver fall into this category. A child who does not receive emotional stimulation and does not have people around him who are responsive to his needs and feelings is emotionally neglected and abused. A child who attends school and the teacher never says her name, never speaks to her individually, and ignores her when she asks questions could be experiencing this form of emotional maltreatment.

5. *Isolating.* Many news stories have been about the most spectacular of these cases, for example, when a child is locked up in a closet and given food and essentials but not spoken to by the general family. Children who are isolated may not be allowed to speak with or spend time with family members or with those outside the family.

6. *Mental health/medical/educational neglect.* Medical and educational maltreatment are addressed later. Mental health neglect is not providing a child with needed mental health resources. This category would include a child who needs counseling but does not receive it, or a child who needs medication to control anger and to function and concentrate in a classroom but does not get it because the parent either refuses to provide it or is inconsistent in providing it. These children are emotionally neglected.

7. *Bullying.* Bullying can include physical and/or emotional maltreatment. It is increasingly becoming of more concern in schools today.

Bullying

Bullying can be defined as physical and/or verbal aggression, or withholding of friendship toward a child, usually by one or a group of other children who are trying to gain power over the individual, take property from them, or gain status in some way (Espelage & Swearer, 2003). Bullying can occur at any age, even among preschoolers.

One form of bullying that is showing a dramatic increase is **online victimization**, where a child *is harassed by* one or more children online in chat rooms, instant messages, e-mail, and on websites. Threats, lies, or confidential details of a child's life are shared virtually, often leading to humiliation and loss of friendships, and in some cases to suicide. One in eleven children report online harassment (Wolak, Mitchell, &

Finkelhor, 2006). This form of bullying is often easy because it can be done anonymously and does not require face-to-face contact.

Bullying usually occurs over a period of time. Children who bully are more likely to have experienced other forms of child maltreatment. Children who have been abused and neglected are also more likely to be victims of bullying (Shields & Cichetti, 2001). Bullying can happen at any age. Children can be bullied by siblings, older children, groups of children, or even by adults. Not only does bullying affect self-esteem, but it can impact children's intellectual and physical functioning as well.

Emotional abuse can take many forms. It is difficult to identify, and it is difficult to accurately attribute causality to a perpetrator. But it can be the most devastating form of abuse for children. Sometimes its effects are seen immediately; sometimes they are not apparent until decades later.

Reading the Signs of Emotional Abuse

Emotional abuse is very difficult to define, identify, report, and prosecute. Emotional abuse may be verbal (e.g., a person yelling and screaming). It can be coercive (e.g., forcing a child through psychological control). Emotional abuse uses fear, sometimes threats, and arguing. Emotional abuse can also involve withdrawal of love and support or no provision of physical affection. Withdrawal, depression, and acting out are all common indicators of emotional abuse. But they can also indicate many other problems. Emotional abuse, unlike physical abuse, cannot usually be seen physically in a child.

Although emotional abuse may be the most difficult form of abuse to identify, it is also the form of abuse that may be most damaging. According to the American Academy of Pediatrics, "it may have more adverse impact on the child and on later adult psychological functioning than the psychological consequences of physical abuse" (Kairys, Johnson, & Committee, 2002, p. 1). Children who are emotionally abused usually have a very negative view of themselves. A young child may feel guilty, and believe that the abuse is his fault. A child may show anger toward adults, or may act very withdrawn; she may be an overachiever, or may be an underachiever who does not feel she has any control over how well she does. All of these symptoms can be the result of severe emotional abuse. Appendix B contains a checklist of symptoms of emotional abuse.

NEGLECT

Neglect is the most prevalent form of child maltreatment. There were 567,787 confirmed cases of neglect in 2006 (USDHHS, 2008). It is the most reported form of maltreatment, primarily because the concept is an extremely difficult one to define. People disagree about what neglect is. Most agree that **neglect** is "failure to provide for a child's basic needs" (Barnett, Miller-Perin, & Perin, 2005, p. 135). But what are a child's basic needs? Certainly food and shelter are included, but how much and what type? Is education a basic need? Supervision is a basic need, but how much and at what ages? Medical care might be a need, but how much and how often? Are sanitation and hygiene a basic need, and what exactly do those terms mean? Some children receive baths once a day, others once a week, and in some countries, because of unhealthy water conditions, children may receive few baths in their childhood. A home may have mouse droppings and roaches, and yet the children may appear to be healthy. Is this neglect?

Failure to provide is also a nebulous concept. If a child misses a meal, few would call that neglect. How many meals must a child miss to constitute neglect? If a child has chronic cold or allergy problems and the parent does not take the child to the doctor, is that neglectful? The law does not define neglect in specific terms, and so it often "remains a matter of personal and professional judgment whether a particular circumstance is described as 'neglect' or not" (Turney & Tanner, 2001, p. 194). The definition of neglect must also take into account such issues as culture, consequences of the neglect, and how long and how often the neglect occurs (Barnett, Miller-Perin, & Perin, 2005). Professionals have great difficulty in deciding exactly what neglect is and therefore, while it is the most prevalent of child maltreatment cases, neglect is often ignored or not treated (McSherry, 2007).

Professionals have used different approaches to further define the concept of neglect. Most of them use an ecological approach that not only identifies family factors that create what some may term as neglect, but also examines such systems as the culture, media, laws, and so on that further create the definition. There is a common misunderstanding inherent in the definition of neglect: that poverty equals neglect. Although a clear association between poverty and child neglect exists, the type of relationship is not clear. What is clear is that many interrelationships affect both poverty and neglect (see Figure 2.4). A parent lacking a job may experience poverty that creates situations in which the parent leaves the child for long periods of time while looking for work, which may be neglectful. The parent may lose extended family support for child care, which may require the parent to leave the child alone for extended periods. The parent may have just emigrated and cannot afford medical care or adequate clothing. Parenting practices that lead to neglect may also be the same internal characteristics that lead the parent into poverty (McSherry, 2007). Many states differentiate between neglect that is caused by poverty and neglect that is not in defining the neglect as child maltreatment (Goldman & Salus, 2003).

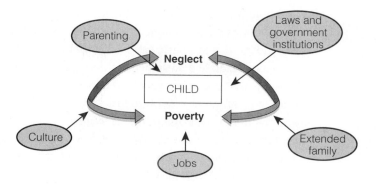

FIGURE 2.4

The Interrelationship Between Neglect and Poverty from the Bio-Ecological Systems Perspective

The major subtypes of neglect are physical neglect, supervisory neglect, emotional neglect, educational neglect, and medical neglect (DePanfilis, 2006).

Physical Neglect

Physical neglect includes anything that results in a child's physical needs being unmet. This type of neglect can include not providing proper hygiene for a child, such as a child who never seems to have a bath. It includes a child who has inadequate clothing, or whose physical needs are constantly ignored. Physical neglect may include not providing a child with an adequate place to sleep, as well as lack of food or lack of appropriate food. However, clothing and sleep arrangements, and sometimes appropriate food, can be perceived as inadequate due to cultural differences, not neglect. For example, a child may receive only rice and fish for meals; in some cultures, such a diet would be considered adequate, while in others it would be considered neglectful because it lacks variety. Or suppose a child is given only chips, soda, candy, and fried food for meals. Is that diet neglectful? Care must be taken to examine whether these things are really harming the child, or whether they are just different. Many cultures feel it is very important that an infant sleep with its mother. Our culture advises against this due to concerns over sudden infant death syndrome. An infant sleeping with a parent is not neglect. However, a child who is left sleeping on a hard floor with no cover and heat during the middle of winter might be neglected.

One area that is suggested as possibly neglectful is that of child obesity (Gallagher, 2005). While there are many causes of obesity, lack of parental supervision or parental authority to provide and insist on healthy eating habits are major factors in the obesity epidemic in children today, and some parents have been accused of neglect for failing to control a child's eating to the point where the child becomes dangerously obese. A disregard for a child's safety, such as leaving a child in a car alone for long periods of time, would also be considered physical neglect.

Physical neglect includes environmental factors, such as raising a child in a neighborhood that is known for violence and drugs, and exposing children to toxins, such as lead. While there may be no intent to do harm, such exposures create a threat to the child and are sometimes identified as neglect (DePanfilis, 2006).

Janine Wiedel/Digital Railroad

Neglect is the most prevalent form of child abuse.

Supervisory Neglect

Supervisory neglect is leaving children alone or with someone unable to adequately supervise the child. Whether or not leaving a child is neglect depends on the age of the child left alone, the age and ability of a person left supervising the child, the length of time the child is left and how often, and the location of the child when unsupervised (Hymel, 2006b; DePanfilis, 2006). Supervisory neglect includes leaving a child in child care with adequate supervision but not returning for the child in an appropriate amount of time. For instance, if the child care program closes at 6:00 P.M. but the child is not picked up by 7:00 P.M., the program may contact authorities who would take the child into protective custody.

What is the appropriate age for a child to be alone? The legal age depends on the state. Texas (like most states), for example, has no specific age at which a child can be left unsupervised, while Illinois gives the age of 14 as the age at which a child can be left alone. Deciding whether a child is ready to stay alone should be dependent on age, maturity, and circumstances (Hymel, 2006b). A checklist for determining if a child is ready to be left alone is provided in Appendix A.

Adequate supervision must be maintained not only by parents and family members but also by caregivers and educators. It is critical that child care providers maintain state-mandated guidelines for adult-child ratios for children. The best guidelines for adult-child ratios are those provided by the National Association for the Education of Young Children (NAEYC). Teachers in public schools must also provide supervision to the children in their care. Recently a child in kindergarten was sexually assaulted by another child in the bathroom, which was down the hall from the classroom. The teacher often sent children alone to the bathroom prior to this assault, as she had a roomful of children and no assistance. Did that constitute supervisory neglect?

Emotional Neglect

Emotional neglect is the lack of provision of a nurturing emotional environment or emotional deprivation that results in changes in the child's emotions, abilities, or behaviors now or over time (Child Welfare Information Gateway, 2007b; Spertus, Yehuda, Wong, Halligan, & Seremetis, 2003). Emotional neglect can be more devastating than any other form of neglect (DePanfilis, 2006), and yet it is the most difficult one to identify because the symptoms of emotional neglect are not always outwardly seen. Emotional neglect differs from emotional abuse in that it is more acts of omission than commission. Adults fail to provide support, nurturing, and affection to the child rather than purposely doing things to emotionally injure. Emotional neglect is often the result of parental depression, parental drug use, inadequate parenting skills, and spouse abuse (Crosson, 2005).

Educational Neglect

Educational neglect involves not ensuring that children receive an appropriate education. All states have mandatory school attendance laws for children. **Absenteeism** is not attending school for a period of time, while **truancy** is when a child has an unexcused absence from school, often without parental knowledge (Teasly, 2004). Children are sometimes kept at home to help with younger siblings or to assist in a family business. Educational neglect is associated with chronic absenteeism and truancy of the child from school. Children that are chronically absent from school and truant tend to come from families where other signs of neglect are evident (Teasly, 2004).

Some parents do not value education and allow children to miss whenever they wish. Other children refuse to attend school, and the parents feel powerless to enforce attendance. Yet other parents do not believe there is value in the child attending school. Educational neglect can also be the result of a parent's failing to support a child's education by not working with teachers, attending conferences, responding to teacher requests of help, or not encouraging homework or other home activities that contribute to educational success.

Another area that can be considered educational neglect focuses on teachers. Although little has been written on this topic, it is worth considering that a teacher who does not provide appropriate guidance, teaching strategies, and assistance to a child in the classroom could also be committing educational neglect.

Medical Neglect

Medical neglect is not providing adequate mental health, medical, and dental care for a child. Medical neglect can include delaying or denying children health care due to waiting too long to take them to the doctor when they are sick, failing to provide preventive care (e.g., immunizations), or not giving prescribed medications in an appropriate manner. Medical neglect is often dependent on time and severity. For instance, is it neglect if a parent forgets an occasional dose of an antibiotic? What if a parent consistently does not give an antibiotic when the child has been ill for weeks and keeps getting worse? Is it neglect if a child with a cold does not get taken to the doctor? What about if the cold has gone on for weeks and now the child cannot sleep or eat well?

One area of medical neglect that often is reported in the media is that of parents who refuse medical care for their child based on religious beliefs. The

United States is built on the idea of separation of church and state, and there is much concern about government interference in the practice of religion. The CAPTA has no requirements for parents to provide medical care not approved by their religion, and encourages each state to consider such cases on an individual basis (DePanfilis, 2006). Medical neglect also can be defined as a failure on the part of medical personnel to provide adequate care for a child who is brought to them.

Reading the Signs of Neglect

The most prevalent form of child maltreatment is neglect (DePanfilis, 2006). It is sometimes very obvious, such as the child who is starving, cold, and without proper clothing. The child left alone for days and the four-year-old left for several hours to watch an infant are also recognizable forms of neglect. But others are less obvious. The child who receives no positive attention and the child who lives in a home that is filthy may or may not be obvious victims of neglect. Neglect is often defined by the culture. Families in many cultures routinely leave very young children to care for siblings or put them to work. Cleanliness standards differ according to cultures and tradition, and some cultures believe that too much bathing is a source of health problems (and in some developing countries without pure water, it could be).

Neglect is primarily recognized by the behavior of the child. If the child seems developmentally delayed, unhappy, withdrawn, aggressive, or is continually asking for food, there is cause for concern. If the child appears adequately supervised, fed, clothed (even if the standards are not what many prefer), healthy, and reasonably adjusted and happy, then even if there are some concerns, neglect may not be the issue. Use the checklist in Appendix B, and consider carefully the signs of neglect. If a counselor or caseworker is available to you, a referral for community resources could provide economic, social, or parenting support for the family that will alleviate the neglect that may be observed. If, however, the signs are severe, the neglect should be reported.

SEXUAL ABUSE

Child sexual abuse (CSA) is an internationally recognized problem, and the past 20 years has seen a surge of research on its consequences (Graham, Rogers, & Davies, 2007). One estimate of CSA suggests that 3–30% of males and 6–62% of females have been victims of child sexual abuse (Baker, 2002; Reynolds & Birkimer, 2002). In 2006, 27.2% of the identified victims of child maltreatment experienced sexual abuse. Sexual abuse involves both boys and girls, but the vast majority involves girls between the ages of 8 and 15 (USDHHS, 2008).

Many states have their own definitions of sexual abuse. Sexual abuse is defined by the 1984 amended Child Abuse Prevention and Treatment Act as:

> The term sexual abuse includes: (i) the employment, use, persuasion, inducement, enticement, or coercion of any child to engage in any sexually explicit conduct (or any simulation of such conduct) for the purpose of producing any visual depiction of such conduct, or (ii) the rape, molestation, prostitution, or other form of sexual exploitation of children, or incest with children, under circumstances which indicate the child's health or welfare is harmed or threatened thereby. (CAPTA, as found in Crosson-Tower, 2005, p. 123)

We will define **sexual abuse** as *any involvement of a child in sexually related activities*. Sexual abuse or exploitation can include:

- Penetration or genital contact orally, genitally, or anally by a penis or other object
- Fondling (touching) of child's private parts or having the child fondle an adult
- Exposing a child to sexual acts through verbal description and discussion, Internet, video, or other media
- Exposing to a child the adult's private parts or pictures of sexual activity or pornography
- Lack of supervision of a child's sexual activities, even if the child consents
- Use of the child for sexual exploitation, including prostitution and pornography

The most common type of sexual abuse is **incest**, or sexual maltreatment among family members (Goldman & Salus, 2003). **Rape** is sexual intercourse that usually involves violence toward the child. **Child pornography** is the creation of sexual materials, usually for the purpose of sale, although it is also used to initiate children into sexual activity (Crosson, 2005). **Voyeurism** involves watching children perform sexual acts in which they are forced to participate, or having children watch as sexual acts are performed. **Pedophiles** are usually men who are sexually aroused by children (Hall & Hall, 2007). They often act on this through child sexual exploitation or child pornography.

Children are often prepared for sexual activity by the perpetrator through a process called grooming. In the **grooming** process, the perpetrator develops a relationship with the child to create comfort and trust and gradually moves along a continuum before initiating sexual activity with the child. Grooming may include becoming friends, giving presents, rubbing the child's back and arms, showing the child pornography, disrobing, fondling, and ultimately intercourse.

Janine Wiedel Photolibrary/Alamy Limited

Children who experience sexual abuse experience trauma for a lifetime.

Grooming ultimately uses activities to gain a child's trust, and then that trust is used to bring the child into sexual activity.

Today many parents ask how much exposure to sexual content is appropriate for young children. Is it okay for them to watch a show rated PG-13 with sexual content? What about television shows where characters partially disrobe or simulate sexual activity? It is important to be aware of age and understanding of children, as many sexual acts seem extremely violent to young children.

There is also concern about cultural definitions of sexual abuse (Barnett, Miller-Perin, & Perin, 2005). Many cultures have practices such as children sleeping with parents, viewing sexual activity, child marriages, fondling of very young children's genitals as a method of soothing them, and relaxed nudity around young children. These practices may or may not be sexually abusive, but must be examined carefully when trying to interpret abusive behavior. One extreme form of sexual abuse is female circumcision, which is practiced in many third-world countries (Lalor, 2004a). **Female circumcision** involves the surgical removal of the clitoris or sewing up of the vaginal opening and is often done with very crude instruments and little or no anesthetic. Some cultural practices can also lead to sexual abuse. Witchdoctors and folktales in Africa, for example, encourage sexual intercourse with a virgin to rid one's self of AIDS, to gain luck, or to attain wealth (Lalor, 2004b).

Many cultures practice arranged marriages, which are often arranged at very young ages, although usually consummated after the girl begins menstruation. These forced marriages and the subsequent consummation underage may be considered by many groups as sexual abuse. It is common in many areas in Africa for girls to be married as children or young teens. However, in the United States this is usually considered sexual abuse, and most states have laws that set the age at which a girl can be married at 18 without parental permission and 16 with a parent's permission. A case in the United States involved a 14-year-old girl forced to marry a 19-year-old by the leader of a polygamist group. The leader was found guilty of being an accomplice to rape (Dobner, 2007); however, the religious group felt that she was not forced and that it was in keeping with their religious practices and freedoms. In 2008, more than 400 children were removed from a polygamous compound in Texas and placed in foster care because of concern over teen marriages and pregnancies. Most of these children were subsequently returned due to lack of proof, but questions remained. Many cultural contradictions exist when examining child sexual abuse. How would you define sexual abuse?

Child prostitution is a global problem. Children who are used sexually for profit can be found all over the world. Some children sell themselves in an effort to make money for their families or to gain enough money to buy food for them. Other children are forced into prostitution by parents or other adults. The issue of child prostitution is a serious one. A large percentage of runaways and children who are living on the street utilize child prostitution as a means of support (Pederson & Hegna, 2003). It is estimated that 293,000 children under 18 in the United States are at risk for child prostitution (End Child Prostitution [ECPAT-USA], 2003). Most children in prostitution find themselves in forced situations where they are kept in slavery and are dependent on an adult who arranges sex for hire.

One final area that has become important in the examination of child sexual exploitation is that of online victimization. Online sexual victimization is the maltreatment of children using the Internet as a source. It involves sexual solicitation and approaching, where the child is brought into online sexual activities or sex talk. Unwanted exposure to sexual material, where the child is exposed to nudity and sexual acts while using e-mail, the Internet, instant messages, or other forms of online communication, also falls under this

THEORY TO PRACTICE

1. Be familiar with other cultural practices.
2. If you do not understand a culture, ask open-ended questions of the family to help you learn about the child and family.

category. Online victimization, also known as cybersex, can include the use of children in child pornography to create online sexual videos and pictures that are sold, posting pornographic materials for children to view online, and the solicitation of sex from a child by online predators.

One in seven children will encounter sexual activity online (Sher, 2007). One in three will be exposed to unwanted sexual material, and one in eleven will be harassed online (Wolak, Mitchell, & Finkelhor, 2006). Parents and educators can take precautions and teach skills to protect children from online predators by monitoring online usage, teaching children about Internet safety, and setting rules about how the Internet will be used.

Reading the Signs of Sexual Abuse

Children who have been sexually abused are often very afraid to reveal any information. Some have been slowly indoctrinated to see it as the way adults show affection. Such children may not display any overt signs, although they or the adults may seem overly attached. Other children may complain of pain in their genital area or exhibit pain in walking, toileting, or sitting. Only a doctor can determine if such pain is the result of a physical condition or illness or the result of sexual abuse. Often the child will show no physical signs of sexual abuse, especially if it occurred awhile before or has been chronic. Children who have not been sexually assaulted may still have been forced to watch sexual encounters, look at or touch an adult's genitals, or have been in some way exposed to inappropriate sexual activities. These children may be withdrawn, use sexual terms, or act out sexual behavior in their play.

If a child acts out sexual encounters in play, ask the child for more information about how the child knows about this. Ask open-ended questions and be careful not to lead the child into saying something that may not be true. Keep your tone matter-of-fact. Often children have seen sexual encounters on television or in movies and repeat the behavior without understanding. Some families have little privacy, and in some cultures it is considered normal for children to sleep in the same room with parents where they often hear or see sexual encounters. This is not typically seen as sexual abuse unless it is done purposely toward the child. However, if a child talks about such behavior and is concerned, those feelings and information on what is culturally appropriate in this country should be shared with parents. Review the signs of sexual abuse checklist in Appendix B.

CHILD EXPLOITATION

Child exploitation involves the use of a child by an adult to achieve some tangible benefit. Children can be used economically through illegal adoption, slavery, child labor, selling of organs, prostitution, or even in advertising.

Children can be used politically, as soldiers. **Child trafficking**, according to UNICEF, is "the recruitment, transportation, transfer, harboring or receipt of a child for the purpose of exploitation. Exploitation shall include, at a minimum, the exploitation of the prostitution of others or other forms of sexual exploitation, forced labor or services, slavery or practices similar to slavery, servitude or the removal of organs" (Innocenti Research Center, 2005, p. 3). Although child trafficking is seen as slavery by many, other cultures perceive the selling of children or their services as an economic necessity to maintain the life of the children and their families in the face of extreme poverty and violence. In fact, in some countries, child trafficking is a tradition that is seen to benefit both children and families (Innocenti Research Center, 2002).

Child trafficking or exploitation is difficult to define in numbers. There are estimates of one to two million children worldwide (Beyer, 2004). The United States recognized the severity of the problem by passing the **Trafficking Victims Protection Act** in 2000 which monitors and sanctions countries that allow trafficking, and provides penalties to traffickers and protection services for adults and children who are victims (USDHHS, 2004). Child exploitation is the result of larger ecological as well as individual factors. Poverty, corrupt political environments, HIV/AIDS with resultant large numbers of orphans, wars and armed conflicts, and changes in family structure (the move from extended family including grandparents, cousins, aunts, uncles, etc., to the current nuclear parents[s]-and-child family system) have all set the stage for large-scale use of children for individual benefit (Mulinge, 2002).

Baby Trafficking

Baby trafficking, the illegal sale of infants, has become an increasingly significant international issue. More birth control options and greater accessibility to these options, as well as the relaxing of moral conventions against a single person having and raising a child, have contributed to fewer babies available for adoption. Many areas of the world have baby trafficking, but there are particular concerns in the United States and Europe where more people are able to pay large sums for children. Mothers of such children are often tricked, bribed, or forced into giving their children to baby traffickers who sell them for large sums (Kitsantonis & Brunwasser, 2006).

Child Labor

Child labor is the "economic exploitation of children through the performance of any work that is likely to be hazardous or to be harmful to the child's health or to interfere with the child's education, or to hamper physical, emotional, mental/intellectual, moral, or social development" (Mulinge, 2002, p. 1119). Although the numbers of children involved in child labor are impossible to determine, as most of it is kept secret, they are probably in the millions. Significant numbers of children in the United States are involved in illegal child labor (Manheimer, 2006).

Children have worked beside their parents since history began, and such work has usually been recognized as good and healthy. When does it become exploitation? Federal law allows for children as young as 10 to be employed on farms, and most states allow those 12 or 13 to work in nonhazardous conditions for a few hours a day with parental consent (Child Labor Coalition, n.d.). However, the law is very strict about the ages and types of work that children can do. Many young children have paper routes, help around the house, or babysit, but exploitation occurs when children are used for another's economic gain. This type of exploitation is most often found in agricultural work; estimates indicate that 70% of child workers labor in that area (Venkateswarlu, Kasper, Reis, Lacaopoino, & Wise, 2003). Children also are found in sweatshops—places where products are produced, often by hand, and where the environmental conditions are often dangerous.

Child labor is a difficult issue. While the mortality rates for child laborers are extremely high and education low (Estevan & Baland, 2007), child labor in some areas of severe poverty is an economic necessity that may provide other benefits to children, such as protection from domestic abuse and even some education (Iversen, 2002). What if the survival of a family depends on the few pennies a child brings into the family by working on a local farm? What if an orphaned child with nowhere to go is taken into a labor camp? The situation internationally is not clear-cut. Perhaps the area of greatest concern is not the laboring of children but rather the treatment of the children who are performing labor, including pay, conditions, and age.

Media Exploitation

An interesting area of exploitation is the use of children by the media. The United States has enacted laws in past decades to protect children who are actors and models by defining the length of time per day they can work and the educational needs that must be met and by putting some restrictions on how their money is used by parents. However, there is still rampant use of children by parents and talent agents for economic gain (Sand, 2002). Concerns about these children include their lack of privacy and the type of childhood they have. There is also illegal use of children in child pornography, and increasing concern about the use of children in adult-oriented films with adult-themed content. A film called *The Kite Runner* that involved the sexual assault of a young boy raised significant controversy regarding its use of children and the lack of information about the film provided to their parents. Other films have portrayed rape, prostitution, and extreme physical abuse using child actors. Children are also used in sexually suggestive ways for modeling, commercials, and films. Do these efforts to use children to entertain constitute exploitation? The question is a troubling one.

Children and Warfare

Children are killed or maimed as a result of war, and children in war zones are often psychologically and economically affected. During the 1990s, an estimated two million children died and six million were severely injured or disabled as a result of war (Myers-Walls, 2003). More than 300,000 children may currently be found serving as child soldiers (Derluyn, Broekaert, Schuyten, & Temmerman, 2004). Children (boys and girls) are often abducted from their homes or taken after their parents are killed and brought into camps in which they are indoctrinated and taught how to kill (Singer, 2005; Ung, 2001). These children are often very young and accept killing as a natural part of their lives. In Rwanda, for example, 486 boys younger than 14 were suspected of taking part in mass killings (Singer, 2005). Many child soldiers are purposefully addicted to drugs to make them more aggressive and dependent on the military forces for which they fight. They have little understanding of moral conduct and the value of life (Ashby, 2002). Such children often are killed in battle or grow up with a host of physical and mental scars (Derluyn et al., 2004).

Reading the Signs of Child Exploitation

Child exploitation can take the form of sexual slavery, child labor, or even use or involvement of children for illicit drug runs or other illegal activities, as well as the use of children as soldiers. Human trafficking of young children in the United States for purposes of work or sex is estimated at 14,000–18,000 (*Child Victims,* 2007). Some children describe running down to the local dealer for their parents to purchase drugs, helping in a drug lab, or working in their parents' stores for hours at a time.

Child exploitation occurs when a child is used for labor in hazardous work or in work that is beyond the child's abilities, or when the child's labor is used for the parent's gain. The checklist on indicators of child exploitation in Appendix B can provide a starting point if you have concerns about a child being exploited. Observe the child, develop a trusting relationship, and ask general questions about the child's life—where the child lives, what the child does when not at school or child care, and so on. Ask open-ended questions. Do not ask for

John Warburton-Lee/Danita Delimont Agency/Digital Railroad

This young boy carries an AK47 assault rifle.

too many details that could "lead" the child into answers that may or may not be true. If you suspect the child is being exploited, report it and let investigators ask more detailed questions.

SUMMARY

The definitions of child maltreatment are many, but they all can be distilled into one: harm of a child either by omission or commission. The definitions in this chapter must be examined in context. Yelling at a child once for spilling milk is not the same as screaming at the child daily, or telling the child that he is worthless and not wanted. An arranged marriage that allows the couple to get to know each other and is not formalized until the couple is of age is different from a child marriage where forced consummation occurs when the girl reaches menstruation. Each act must be weighed both in terms of harm to the child now and in the future, and in terms of severity and frequency. Such acts also must be weighed in terms of the prevailing law. Some acts, such as prostitution or breaking a child's arm, are not open to interpretation and are always abuse.

Understanding definitions of abuse is critical to the ability to identify and work with children who are abused.

Application: When Working with Children

- As children enter the classroom, facility, or home, perform a quick body and health check to notice bruising, abrasions, or any new marks on the children.

- Practice writing observations on children, at least one per week on each child, remembering to be objective, accurate, descriptive, and clear. Keep notes on children's appearance and behavior.

- Use role-play to question children about bruises, scratches, and other marks on their bodies.

Application: When Working with Families

- Invite a caseworker, police officer who works with abuse and neglect, health care professional, school nurse, or licensing representative to speak to parents about guidelines, laws, and practices regarding maltreatment issues.

- Organize a picnic in a park. Invite parents to bring a cultural dish to share with others. Plan fun activities that provide a model for parents.

- Distribute a survey for parents asking them to list a variety of concerns, dreams, and goals they have regarding their children.

- Send home checklists of signs of abuse and articles on what abuse is and how to avoid maltreating children.

- If allowed, make home visits to the children in your classroom.

Projects/Activities

1. Identify possible types of abuse in the following case studies by comparing these situations with the definitions in the chapter.
   a. Suzy has difficulty in class with following rules and thinking through situations. She seems to have an extra space along the bridge of her nose.
   b. Andre has sores on his arm that constantly ooze and never seem to heal. He says they are from bug bites.
   c. Jenehah is new to class and says she has been in many new schools. She says she misses her mommy and daddy, but her uncle says they are gone. She also says she is afraid to go home with her uncle, but will not say why.
2. Locate federal laws or your state laws on abuse and neglect. What definitions are used in the laws? How do they compare with the definitions

provided in this text? Write a two-page paper or create a chart demonstrating and describing the similarities and differences.

Questions to Consider

1. How can I tell the difference between maltreatment and accidental injury?
2. Who do I call or discuss my concerns with regarding the appearance or behavior of a child in my care?
3. What are the warning signs in children who may be maltreated, abused, and neglected?

Websites for More Information

For useful websites, visit www.cengage.com/education/hirschy

CHAPTER 3

Assessing and Reporting Child Maltreatment

Wadsworth/Cengage Learning

WHAT YOU WILL LEARN

- How to recognize and assess when a child is abused and neglected
- Your role in assessing and reporting abuse and neglect
- To whom, how, and where to make a report
- What to say when you report abuse and neglect

INTRODUCTION

What do you do when a child like Jamie comes into your life? Every state has mandatory reporting laws (Crosson-Tower, 2005). Most states require school and child care personnel, mental health workers, medical personnel, social workers and police to report. Some states require clergy, photo processors, and others to report (U.S. Department of Health and Human Services [USDHHS], 2005). A few states require all citizens to report suspected abuse and neglect. Most states have penalties for failure to report that can include fines or even jail time.

Many mandated reporters do not report abuse. There are many reasons why teachers, medical personnel, and others who work with children do not report child abuse:

- They want to give the parent the benefit of the doubt.
- Often professionals believe they can help and handle the situation themselves.
- They fear reporting something that may be untrue.

VIGNETTE

Jamie, six, was small for his age but always had a bright smile. He seemed older than the other children in knowledge of the world and often looked confused as he watched the other children in regular play, as if it was something he did not understand. His efforts to make friends did not go well, but he kept trying. Some days he came to school and said he was hungry, that he had not had enough time to eat, so I gave him a breakfast bar. Other days he was filthy and had an odor, and I was sure it had been awhile since he had a bath. I often sent notes to remind his mother (a single parent) to send a coat, to return a form, or to request a conference, which were never answered. One day he told me laughingly about watching his mother and aunt sit at the table and use needles to "shoot up." I knew it was time to do more than just contact his mom.

Mandatory Reporting Requirements: A Sample of States (U.S. Department of Health and Human Services, 2005)

Arizona	Peace officers, clergy, or Christian Science practitioners Parents, stepparents, or guardians Physicians, physician's assistants, optometrists, dentists, behavioral health professionals, nurses, psychologists, counselors, or social workers School personnel or domestic violence victim advocates Any other person who has responsibility for the care or treatment of the minor
Delaware	Physicians, dentists, interns, residents, osteopaths, nurses, or medical examiners School employees Social workers or psychologists
Florida	Physicians, osteopaths, medical examiners, chiropractors, nurses, or hospital personnel Other health or mental health professionals Practitioners who rely solely on spiritual means for healing School teachers or other school officials or personnel Social workers; day care center workers or other professional child care workers; foster care, residential, or institutional workers Law enforcement officers or judges
Hawaii	Physicians, physicians in training, psychologists, dentists, nurses, osteopathic physicians and surgeons, optometrists, chiropractors, podiatrists, pharmacists, and other health-related professionals Medical examiners or coroners Employees or officers of any public or private school; child care employees; employees or officers of any licensed or registered child care facility, foster home, or similar institution Employees or officers of any public or private agency or institution, or other individuals providing social, medical, hospital, or mental health services, including financial assistance Employees or officers of any law enforcement agency, including, but not limited to, the courts, police departments, correctional institutions, and parole or probation offices Employees of any public or private agency providing recreational or sports activities
Idaho	Physicians, residents on hospital staffs, interns, nurses, or coroners School teachers or day care personnel Social workers or law enforcement personnel
Illinois	Physicians, hospital administrators and personnel, surgeons, physician assistants, osteopaths, chiropractors, genetic counselors, dentists, coroners, medical examiners, emergency medical technicians, nurses, acupuncturists, respiratory care practitioners, or home health aides School personnel, directors or staff of nursery schools or child day care centers, recreational program or facility personnel, child care workers, or homemakers Substance abuse treatment personnel, crisis line or hotline personnel, social workers, domestic violence program personnel, psychologists, psychiatrists, or counselors Social services administrators, foster parents, or field personnel of the Illinois Department of Public Aid, Public Health, Human Services, Corrections, Human Rights, or Children and Family Services Truant officers, law enforcement officers, probation officers, funeral home directors or employees Clergy members Commercial film and photographic print processors
Kentucky	Physicians, osteopathic physicians, nurses, coroners, medical examiners, residents, interns, chiropractors, dentists, optometrists, emergency medical technicians, paramedics, or health professionals

	Teachers, school personnel, or child care personnel Social workers or mental health professionals Peace officers
Maryland	Health practitioners Educators or human service workers Police officers
Texas	A professional, for purposes of the reporting laws, is an individual who is licensed or certified by the state or who is an employee of a facility licensed, certified, or operated by the state and who, in the normal course of official duties or duties for which a license or certification is required, has direct contact with children. Professionals include: Teachers or day care employees Nurses, doctors, or employees of a clinic or health care facility that provides reproductive services Juvenile probation officers or juvenile detention or correctional officers
Washing-ton (state)	Practitioners, county coroners or medical examiners, pharmacists, or nurses Professional school personnel or child care providers Social service counselors or psychologists Employees of the State Department of Social and Health Services Juvenile probation officers, law enforcement officers, personnel of the Department of Corrections, or placement and liaison specialists Responsible living skills program staff, HOPE center staff, state family and children's ombudsman, or any volunteer in the ombudsman's office Any adult with whom a child resides

- They are concerned that reporting abuse will affect their jobs or that they will not be believed.
- They fear the possibility that reporting will make things worse and the child will be abused more.
- They worry about how the parents will react toward them as the reporters.
- They think someone else will report it.
- Administrators, superiors, and even colleagues may discourage reporting.

The responsibility of every professional, teacher, caseworker, nurse, or anyone who works with children is to report abuse and neglect that they *suspect,* not just that which they know is happening. Every state has a law requiring certain professionals—usually teachers, child care providers, doctors, and so on—to report suspected child abuse (Child Welfare Information Gateway, 2007a). The National Child Abuse and Neglect Data System identified more than 2,295 child fatalities in 2006 (Child Welfare Information Gateway, 2007b). In at least some of these cases, people suspected child abuse. If they had made a report, that number could have been reduced. But it is not the number that matters, is it? It is the children who will not grow up and live their lives. If a report is found to be unsubstantiated, then a mistake was made and the person accused will be cleared. But if a report is not made, a child may die or be irreparably harmed.

ROLES OF PROFESSIONALS IN ASSESSING AND REPORTING CHILD ABUSE

All professionals have a responsibility to report child abuse themselves. But what additional responsibilities do those who work with children and their institutions have? Primarily, these responsibilities consist of protection and prevention.

Role of Schools and Child Care Programs

Schools and educational facilities are the most trusted of institutions. Although many parents will disagree with specific aspects of educational programs, they still leave their children each day in these environments and most do not worry excessively while their children are there. Society expects schools and child care programs not only to educate children but also to protect them and prevent violence against them. What are the primary roles of schools and child care programs in dealing with abuse and neglect?

1. *Provide a safe environment.* Children and their families should be safe at school. Safety includes an environment free of physical hazards and protection from other children and adults who would do them harm.

2. *Prevent abuse and neglect.* Adults should be aware of signs of abuse and neglect and reporting procedures. Schools and child care programs should provide policies, procedures, and supervision for employees so that opportunity for abusive behavior is limited. Parents should have access to schools and to their child's classroom. Parent communication should be open and resources should be provided for parents who are at risk.

3. *Educate about abuse and neglect.* Children should be taught safety curricula that encompass what they should and should not allow, who to tell if they are being abused, and how to avoid victimization. Personnel in schools and child care should be taught to watch for signs of possible neglect and abuse. Parents should also be educated on how to recognize and prevent abuse and neglect.

4. *Report suspected abuse and neglect.* Every state has some requirement for educators to report abuse. The largest group of professionals reporting abuse and neglect are educators (USDHHS, 2008). Teachers, child care, and school personnel spend more time with children than anyone except parents and are in the best position to provide information on suspected abuse. Yet many never report their suspicions. Mandated reporters in many states are given 48 hours to report suspected abuse.

Teaching basic safety and protective curricula can begin very early.

Role of Medical, Legal, and Social Service Programs

All states require medical personnel to report suspected abuse and neglect. Most states require caseworkers and police to report as well. Medical personnel may include doctors, nurses, mental health professionals, medical assistants, dentists, and medical technicians. Social service personnel may include program administrators, caseworkers, and office personnel. Police include support personnel and police officers who are not on active duty. Auxiliary staff, such as secretaries and custodial staff, also need to be aware of and alert to signs of abuse and neglect.

The role of medical personnel in working with abuse and neglect often includes diagnosis and treatment of the abused child. Many state statutes allow doctors to diagnose and treat abuse, as well as take photographs without the consent of parents (Kellogg, 2007). Social service personnel and police often see evidence of abuse and neglect in the course of their work. A caseworker who is working with a family to locate a job or qualify for food stamps may see that a child has severe bruising or encounter a baby who appears to be malnourished. A police officer who stops someone for drunken driving may find a child in the car, or an officer called out on a domestic dispute may see a child with a bruised face.

Prevention of Child Abuse in Early Childhood Programs and the Responsibilities of Early Childhood Professionals to Prevent Child Abuse (NAEYC, 1996)

1. Early childhood programs should employ an adequate number of staff to work with children and to provide adequate supervision of program staff and volunteers.
2. The program environment (both indoor and outdoor areas) should be designed to reduce the possibility of private, hidden locations in which abuse may occur.
3. All program staff, substitutes, and volunteers should receive preservice orientation and refresher training at regular intervals.
4. Centers, schools, and homes should have clear policies and procedures for maintaining a safe, secure environment.
5. Teachers and caregivers should be supervised by qualified personnel on an ongoing basis, and parents should be encouraged to spend time in the program.
6. Programs should not institute "no-touch policies" to reduce the risk of abuse, as these policies are misguided efforts that fail to recognize the importance of touch to children's healthy development.

 THEORY TO PRACTICE

1. Be aware of your role with children to provide a role model in establishing healthy relationships.
2. Work together with parents to institute policies in schools and the community to provide safety for children.

Medical and social service personnel often worry about client confidentiality issues. However, the role of professionals in regard to identification and reporting of abuse is clear. Again, it is not the job of the teacher, administrator, physician, or police officer to prove abuse before reporting. *All* suspected cases must be reported.

ASSESSING ABUSE AND NEGLECT

The assessment of whether or not abuse and neglect has occurred is not easy. A child's bruises may have been caused from a fall. A child who seems hungry all the time may have a very high metabolism. A four-year-old girl who is afraid of bathrooms and constantly pulling at her panties may have a fear of falling down the bathtub drain or a skin irritation from not wiping properly. But even though some behaviors may be normal, we often explain away circumstances that should be carefully examined. Child abuse and neglect should be considered a possible cause of problems for a child, but not assumed to be the cause (Burrows-Horton & Cruise, 2001).

The best way to avoid unjustly exposing families to wrongful accusations is to become aware of the signs and symptoms of different types of abuse and neglect, discuss the situation with an administrator or other professional, and then report if you still suspect that abuse and neglect has occurred. It is also important to take into consideration cultural issues when identifying abuse and neglect (see Chapter 9). "While no child should be abused and every suspected case must be reported, families should not be reported to authorities simply because their child-rearing and other social practices differ from the mainstream" (Hagen, 1999, p. 56).

Child Observation and Assessment

Adults who work with children need to continually observe and assess the behavior and appearance of each child. When children arrive, they should be greeted by name and a quick appraisal should be conducted. Teachers and professionals should talk to each child throughout the time together in a positive way and establish trust and rapport. Jamie's teacher in the beginning of this chapter showed concern for him, talked to him, and created trust so that he was able to share with her experiences from home. It takes time and individual interaction to establish a relationship of trust. Teachers, doctors, caseworkers, school nurses, even school custodial and nutritional staff can become crucial supports for children and may be the first to recognize the signs of abuse and neglect or be the first to experience an outcry—a child's asking for help.

Informal Assessments. All teachers should perform routine health and well-being appraisals on children. Anyone can observe a child for the following:

- Cleanliness
- Obvious cuts and bruises that look unusual or are in locations that would not normally bruise

Sample Questioning Techniques When Determining Possible Abuse by Developmental Stage

Toddlers	Very simple and general questions are appropriate, such as "How did you get your booboo?" (or whatever term the toddler uses). Toddlers cannot usually express verbally what is going on, but sometimes they can show you using a doll. Most of the information for toddlers needs to come from observation and questions for parents.
Preschoolers	Ask general, concrete questions, such as "Tell me about what you did when you were at home after school" or "What happened to your arm?" Be sure not to lead the child by saying, "Did someone hurt you?" Just let the child tell you. Sometimes you can give the child a family of dolls and ask the child to show you what happened. Act very matter-of-fact, and do not show concern or alarm at what you are told. Just write it all down.
School-Aged Children	General, concrete questions are still best. If a child says he was hit, you can ask, "Can you tell me more about what happened?" rather than "Who hurt you?" School-aged children are often afraid and will ask you not to tell anyone. Tell the child that he can trust you to do what is best to protect him. Again, do not try to get details. A trained interviewer can get better information that will be more helpful in court or in working with the family. Sometimes in wanting to help, our facial expressions or comments can influence the child's story.
Parents	General questions are still a good idea. "I noticed Ellen's back had some bruises. What happened?" Do not say "Did she fall?" Let the parent tell you what happened. Listen carefully for inconsistencies. Does it sound like something that could happen? You may want to ask the same question a couple of days later in a different way, such as "That bruise is a pretty bad one. I've been trying to remember . . . what happened?"

- Signs of hunger or malnourishment
- Signs of sadness or pain when moving or touched
- Excessive fear or withdrawal
- Obvious developmental delays

Teachers are in a particularly good position to do a daily assessment. These can be done as the children enter the classroom. Any professional, however, can greet a child, touch her arm, look into her face, and appraise for signs of problems. The Health and Well-Being Assessment found in Appendix D can be used on a daily basis or anytime to identify possible problems and provide documentation.

Documentation. Child abuse and neglect is usually identified over a period of time after seeing multiple indicators. It is critical that documentation be made of all that is observed with the child. When you first become concerned about a child, but feel unsure about whether abuse or neglect may be occurring, record your concerns, including dates, times, behaviors, appearance, and any conversations that lead you to be suspicious. If a child states that he did not receive breakfast, quickly write this on a card or a form kept for this purpose. A Classroom Concern Form is included in the Online Appendix. Some people prefer to keep 3 x 5 cards for the purpose of quickly recording the name of the child, the date, and the concern or conversation. These forms or cards can be kept routinely for all the children in the classroom and can assist you in parent conferences and other types of assessments as well.

What seems unimportant or minor once may show a pattern of abuse and neglect in documentation over time. The Classroom Concern Form can be posted on the inside of a cabinet so that a quick note can be jotted down. This can be used for concerns about abuse and neglect but also for specific issues, such as curriculum needs. Some programs send home daily summaries or reports of children's behavior or well-being. If you suspect that abuse and neglect may be occurring, make copies and keep all the summaries for the child in a file. Many different forms of documentation can be kept on a child. Often it is difficult to decide whether the concerns you have are really signs of abuse and neglect. In such cases, child abuse checklists can help.

Child Abuse Checklists. One of the best methods for assessing child abuse and neglect is through the use of checklists. Checklists for the major forms of abuse and neglect can be found in Appendix B. When child maltreatment is suspected, going through such a list will narrow down suspicions. Remember, there are many reasons for each behavior and characteristic that is found in a checklist. Even when a child exhibits several of the identified behaviors, there may be legitimate explanations. Examine the information as a whole. Look at the list and decide if several of the behaviors are exhibited and if there are good explanations for what has been observed.

How many of the identified characteristics should be exhibited before you call? There is no answer to that question. When you are confident that abuse or neglect *may* be occurring (not *is* occurring) and have documentation on the checklists that back up your suspicions, it is time to report your suspicions and let those who are trained take over. If you think a child is in danger or your suspicions are strong, do not wait! Documentation is appropriate when you are still unsure about whether to call, but when you really think abuse is there, call immediately!

Document any unusual behavior or marks on a child that you see.

REPORTING ABUSE AND NEGLECT

Most professionals are required to report child abuse. It is the law, and there are penalties for not reporting. One principal in Texas was convicted and sentenced to jail as a result of not reporting an abuse case that a child had reported to him because he knew the family and believed that nothing like that could be happening.

Although every state has mandatory reporting laws, they vary in regard to the definitions of abuse, what type of abuse and neglect must be reported, who is a mandatory reporter, reporting standards, and inclusion of the reporter's name in the report (USDHHS, 2005). Check individual state child abuse reporting laws to understand exactly what is required. Many administrators believe it is their responsibility, and not that of teachers or those under their supervision, to report abuse and neglect. Many administrators think the teacher should not report if the administrator feels it is not warranted, even if the teacher disagrees (Hagen, 1999). But laws are clear, and teachers or other professionals who suspect abuse should report to the appropriate authorities even if their administrators do not go along. Several studies have indicated that teachers usually make reports to administrators, and that administrators expect this (Hagen, 1999). However, in most states, it is still the teacher's or professional's responsibility to make the report.

Will the parents know who reported? Most states have privacy laws that provide reporters with anonymity, but in truth, parents often think they know who the reporter is, or they will try to guess. If such a parent confronts you after you have made a report, an appropriate response would be to say, "This must be a terrible trial [or time] for your family," "I will do anything I can to be supportive," or "This must be very hard on you!" without actually admitting anything. Usually, many different people are aware of the situation and might have called in the report, so do not assume the parents know for sure who made the call.

How to Report

Once a professional has decided that a report of *suspected* abuse should be made, it is wise to discuss it with another professional. If you are a teacher, talk to a counselor, administrator, the school nurse, or a trusted colleague. Remember that this information should be kept confidential. You have an ethical obligation to share this information only with those who must know. Also, you can never be sure whether someone with whom you share the information has a connection to this family and you will lose your anonymity. Use the reporting checklist in Figure 3.1. If the report is being made about a fellow professional or teacher, you will want to use the same checklist and document the behavior you have observed. Then make the call!

There is a national telephone number where you can reach counselors who can answer questions, provide counseling, help you make your referral, suggest resources for those who want to report abuse, talk with children who are being

THEORY TO PRACTICE

1. Write clear, precise accounts of everything you have heard or observed related to an abuse incident.
2. Make certain that you do not allow your judgments to interfere with your observations.

Child Abuse Reporting Checklist

□ If you feel the child is in immediate danger, call the police!

□ Gather all documentation of possible abuse and neglect including daily reports, anecdotal records, and forms.

□ Share the information with your supervisor or the school counselor. Some states require you to call in the report and others allow the supervisor to call, so check your state rules. If the supervisor or counselor will not call in the abuse allegation, but you still have a reasonable belief that abuse or neglect is occurring or has occurred, then you should call. Most states require you, the person who suspects the abuse, to call. If in doubt, call the Childhelp® National Child Abuse Hotline at 1-800-4-A-CHILD (1-800-422-4453). They have counselors to help you.

□ Fill out a "Child Abuse Reporting Form" (see appendix) and call. Write on the form the names of people you speak to, time and date of report, and what is said.

□ Ask the person you speak with when someone might contact you, and if they will be able to tell you the results of the investigation. This will differ state to state and agency to agency. Ask them for a case number for the report.

□ Recognize that you have done all that you can, and don't worry—it is not your job to prove abuse, just to report suspected abuse!

FIGURE 3.1

Child Abuse Reporting Checklist

abused, and help you decide if you should report. The Childhelp® National Child Abuse Hotline can be contacted at 1-800-4-A-CHILD (1-800-422-4453).

Where to Report

You should contact your state child abuse reporting authority. Some states have websites where reports can be made, and some have 800 numbers; but all states have some method of contacting authorities to report abuse. State child abuse reporting numbers are in the Online Appendix of this book. Federal jurisdictions such as tribal lands and military bases may have different agencies responsible for abuse and neglect and may have different reporting requirements. However, reporting is mandated for most professionals on federal lands. If you are in an area that has federal jurisdiction, you can contact the state number for a referral to the appropriate agency, or you can ask local law enforcement about the procedure and who should be contacted.

Frequently Asked Questions (FAQs)

1. *Should I speak to the parents before I report?*

   If you are unsure about whether abuse or neglect has occurred, it can be appropriate to ask the parents about an injury by saying, "I noticed that Johnny had a bruise on his face this morning. What happened?" If a child has told you about a fall, then ask the parents to tell you about it and see if their story matches the child's story. Do not accuse the parents or ask questions that make them feel like you are interrogating them. That is not your job, and it could cause conflict.

2. *Should I speak to my supervisor before reporting?*

   It is usually best to inform your superiors when you are making a report. It may be that others have come to them with similar concerns or that they have additional information. If your supervisor does not want you to report and you still believe that there is a need, go ahead. You know the child better than your supervisor, and you have a responsibility to protect the child. In many states, it is you, the person involved with the child, and not your supervisor, who is required to report.

3. *Should I give my name or report anonymously?*

   Most states allow anonymous reporting of abuse and neglect. This may seem to be the easiest method. However, caseworkers often need to ask questions and get more information in order to determine if abuse has really occurred. It is in the child's best interest for you to share your name and contact information when you call. The agency to which you report will not share your name with the perpetrator.

SUMMARY

Identifying possible abuse and neglect can be difficult. The same symptoms that are caused by abuse and neglect can occur when there are changes in a family situation, health problems, new schools, changes in the child's environment, or accidents. When you are unsure, it is best to keep a record of the things that concern you, with dates, times, and a summary of what you have observed. Such records will allow you to decide if your suspicions are strong enough to do something about; they do not have to provide proof, but just support for your concerns. When you feel that you need to report, do so. Even if you have no records but believe danger is imminent for the child, make the call.

Once you decide to report, call the child abuse hotline and share your concerns. Make sure you write down names, the time of the call, and any information you are given. If a parent confronts you, be concerned and sympathetic, but do not acknowledge that you were the reporter. Remember that reporting of *suspected* abuse and neglect is required by law! This is about a child's life—a child whose life you may save by your report!

Application: When Working with Children

- Get to know each child with whom you work. Ask about their interests. Become an advocate, a trusted adult, for each child.
- Let children know that they can share things with you and that you will not tell unless you need help in protecting them. Encourage them to be open about their problems.
- Know how to conduct informal health and well-being assessments while greeting children.
- Keep child abuse checklists handy and record concerns you have about children.

Application: When Working with Families

- Greet parents when they bring children and pick them up. Ask the parents about their jobs and interests; develop a relationship with them.
- Send home a family questionnaire or have the parents fill one out at your office. Find out how the family spends their time, where the children sleep, foods they enjoy, what they do for fun, and any concerns the parents may have.

Projects/Activities

1. Call a child abuse hotline. Ask them:
   - What things are needed in a report?
   - What is the best way to decide if abuse or neglect should be reported?
   - What is one thing you wish people would do before they call?

   Write down the answers and report to your class on the results.
2. Call a protective services agency and ask to interview a person who is in charge of investigating abuse and neglect. Ask about their job, how they came to do this kind of work, their education, and what courses or course of study in school would have helped them to better prepare for this work. Write a two- to three-page summary of your findings.
3. Search a minimum of four websites and develop a checklist for identifying one of the forms of abuse or neglect: physical, social, emotional, sexual, or

child exploitation. Write a summary of the information you found and list your websites. Remember to develop your own list, and not just copy theirs or one from this textbook!

4. Use a web search to explore child abuse reporting requirements for tribal lands and the military. Write a two-page report on your findings.

Questions to Consider

1. When should suspicions of abuse and neglect be reported?
2. How should they be reported?
3. How can I identify abuse and neglect if it is not apparent?

Websites for More Information

For useful websites, visit www.cengage.com/education/hirschy

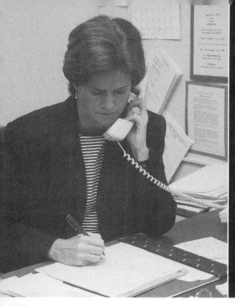

CHAPTER 4

What Happens When Abuse and Neglect Have Occurred?

VIGNETTE

Alicia Rodriguez, a teacher for four years, called a child abuse hotline as her director encouraged after Alicia noticed that Reggie had bruises all over his arms and legs, and he said that his mother's boyfriend got mad at him for not taking out the trash. That afternoon a caseworker came to see her, asked for more information, and spoke to Reggie. A caseworker came several hours later and took Reggie with her. The next day Reggie did not return, and a couple of weeks later, Alicia heard that he was now in foster care. Another child in her classroom, Amy, had also been reported as being neglected, but Amy was at home and things had gotten better. Amy said that lots of people were helping their family. Alicia wondered why the cases were handled in such different ways.

WHAT YOU WILL LEARN

- How is abuse and neglect investigated
- Who investigates abuse and neglect
- The roles of Child Protective Services, the police, and the courts in investigation and disposition of abuse and neglect cases
- What happens when abuse or neglect is verified
- How families can receive help
- What happens when children are removed from their homes

INTRODUCTION

How are abuse and neglect cases handled? What made the difference between the way Reggie and Amy's cases were handled? When child abuse is alleged, every state has an agency that investigates. Most states maintain a toll-free number (see Chapter 3) for a child abuse hotline where initial reports can be made. Every state has an agency that is mandated to accept and screen child abuse reports (Crosson-Tower, 2003; Winterfeld & Sakagawa, 2003). Most states charge their Department of Protective Services, often an agency within a state family services or protection division, with the intake of reports and investigation of abuse and neglect. However, some states, such as Florida, assign those responsibilities to local law enforcement. Law enforcement is always involved if there is a death or serious injury and in many states when any allegation of sexual abuse occurs. Most states share information between law enforcement and child protection agencies (Winterfeld & Sakagawa, 2003).

INVESTIGATION OF ABUSE AND NEGLECT

Child abuse and neglect investigation is a multiple-step process: (1) intake: the intake of the original allegation; (2) assignment and investigation: the assignment to the appropriate agency for investigation; and (3) adjudication: determination of abuse, and how confirmed cases will be processed and handled (Jones, 2006).

Intake

When a report is received the agency must determine:

1. Does the information provided qualify this as a possible case of abuse and neglect? A person who calls in because they are divorced and they were not allowed to see their child on the appointed visitation day would probably be told that their report would not qualify.

2. Is the child in immediate danger? If so, the intake professional will immediately contact the appropriate agency and someone will intervene quickly.

3. What level of danger is there for the child? If the case is one of neglect involving the condition of the home, it might be assigned a lower priority and it may take days or even weeks to be investigated. If it is severe abuse, it will be assigned highest priority and it will be only a matter of hours until investigation.

When the case qualifies, the intake professional will find out as much as possible about the case from the caller, including addresses, names, phone numbers, and specific information about why the caller is reporting the incident. They will then try to determine again if it qualifies under state guidelines as possible abuse and neglect, and also will try to establish the credibility of the person calling to be sure the report is valid (Goldman & Salus, 2003). Angry parents who are divorced and neighbors or relatives looking for vengeance of some type sometimes call in false reports. Although professionals, and in some states everyone, are required to report abuse, most states also have penalties for those who knowingly turn in a false report of abuse and neglect.

Assignment and Investigation

The intake worker then determines the priority level of the case and sends it to the appropriate agency. Top priority is usually given to cases where physical or sexual abuse is alleged, where the child appears to be in imminent danger, and where the child is in danger of family flight due to the call. All states specify the maximum amount of time available to caseworkers to investigate cases. Top priority cases, usually those involving sexual abuse and significant physical abuse, are investigated typically within 24 hours, while less serious cases may take longer.

Law enforcement is often involved in the investigation process. Many child abuse reports originate from police who have been called into a different type of crime scene, such as robbery or drugs, and have found evidence of child abuse or neglect as part of the investigation. Police officers are also involved in interviewing and gathering evidence regarding abuse and neglect when the possibility of the case becoming a criminal case exists. Most child abuse cases are not criminal cases, but are handled under noncriminal courts such as family courts. Criminal cases are usually those that involve sexual abuse or severe physical abuse. Law enforcement can also provide protective custody for a child in cases of immediate danger. Medical professionals are often used to determine whether abuse has occurred and may gather evidence regarding sexual or physical abuse (Hershkowitz, Fisher, & Lamb, 2007).

The investigation process is multifaceted. The caseworker (or law enforcement official in some states) will gather as much information as possible. The person who reported may be contacted and asked questions. The child may be interviewed at school or at an agency. The parents will be contacted and questioned. Neighbors, relatives, and others with knowledge and information about possible abuse or neglect may be contacted. The purpose of the investigation is to get as clear a picture as possible of the allegation so that an appropriate determination can be made.

When children are interviewed, the interview is often done by a **forensic interviewer**, a person who is specially trained to ask nonleading and appropriate questions of children. A forensic interview is a legally justifiable interview done at the request of the police or protective services to gather facts and investigate. A forensic interviewer will usually interview the child in a room without distractions. They often videotape the interview, and law enforcement, medical, or counseling professionals may watch through a one-way mirror and request that the interviewer ask certain questions to facilitate the investigation. The children are often asked questions to determine if they can differentiate truth from nontruth (Hanson, 2008). Children, such as Reggie in our case study, are sometimes interviewed by a caseworker, attorney, counselor, medical practitioner, or law enforcement official at school, child care, or at home. The interviewer typically follows a protocol for questions that includes establishing rapport with the child, keeping the questions open-ended, and asking questions based on the child's developmental level (Hershkowitz, Fisher, & Lamb, 2007):

1. *Establishing rapport with the child.* Interviewers often begin with general questions about the child, such as things she likes to do and her favorite TV shows, and will sometimes share their own favorite things. The interviewer will try to reassure the child that she is not in trouble and that the questions are being asked so they can better understand what has happened and be better able to help the child. The children are reassured that they are safe and that they will be protected. The interviewers use body language to convey concern and encourage discussion.

2. *Asking open-ended questions.* Interviewers ask children questions that do not have a one-word answer, for example, "Tell me about your arm" rather than "Did someone hit you on the arm?" The interviewers avoid leading children's answers by asking as few questions as possible and encouraging the children to talk. The interviewers work to get children to be very specific if they are describing incidents, including small details of the environment, clothing, and experience.

3. *Asking questions based on the child's developmental level.* Children who are three are interviewed differently from children who are twelve. Younger children may be interviewed using props such as dolls. Older children may be asked for more details. Asking questions related to emotions seen from the child is important. A child may say that nothing has happened, but then begin to hug himself tightly and rock. Questions about such actions often reveal additional information.

Cultural issues often become an important issue in the investigation. Parents or even the child may not speak English and an interpreter may be necessary. In addition, cultural practices may not be understood by the investigator and may be misinterpreted as abuse and neglect. Caseworkers and other investigators should gather information about cultural background before making a determination so that the family and child-rearing practices are better understood (DePanfilis & Salus, 2003).

THEORY TO PRACTICE

1. When reporting maltreatment, be cognizant of the culture of the family and report this to Child Protective Services.
2. Make informed statements that integrate your knowledge of the situation, including the culture.

Adjudication

A case under investigation is usually completed in one of three ways:

1. Substantiated, and a case is opened and action is taken

2. Unsubstantiated, where there is not enough evidence to indicate abuse and the incident is closed

3. Indicated, where child maltreatment cannot be substantiated but there is still reason to suspect, and a case is opened (Goldman & Salus, 2003)

Some states require all information regarding the allegation to be erased from the records if it is unsubstantiated. However, many states keep the record for a period of time in case another report is received (Winterfeld & Sakagawa, 2003). When the case is indicated or substantiated, a case is opened. If the case involves a criminal issue, it is referred for criminal proceedings and for casework for the child and family. Most cases of child abuse and neglect that require legal procedings are not handled as criminal cases, but as civil cases through family or juvenile courts. Each state has laws that determine how cases are to be handled and who has jurisdiction.

Most cases of abuse and neglect are not handled through court systems but through the Child Protective Services (CPS) agency for the state. Caseworkers are assigned, sometimes one for both the child and family, and sometimes one for the child and one for the family. One caseworker usually acts as a case manager, providing coordination of services for the family (Goldman & Salus, 2003). The Adam Walsh Child Protection and Safety Act of 2006 was enacted by Congress to establish a national registry of individuals who have substantiated child abuse cases. This registry can provide law enforcement and protective services with the opportunity to identify perpetrators who have moved to different locations.

THE COURT SYSTEM

The court system becomes involved in the abuse and neglect of a child for a variety of reasons. Courts are usually involved when there is removal of a child from the home, abandonment of a child, placing of a child in foster care, sexual abuse, severe abuse and neglect, death, or noncompliance with and refusal or reluctance of parents to work with child protective agencies. Custody issues must be determined by the court. Custody is the legal responsibility for the child, although the term is also used to denote who has physical charge over a child. Temporary custody is often given to protective services so that they can have the legal right to make decisions and placements for children. This is usually given for a specific amount of time and must be reviewed by a judge or the court system. Permanent custody, which means that a person or the state is

Juvenile and family courts often provide more comprehensive assistance for families and children involved in child maltreatment.

given full legal custody of the child and the rights of the parents are severed, requires a court system.

Different courts have jurisdiction (authority) over different types of cases. There are many different types of courts, and each state has its own judicial system with its own court structure. Laws in each state mandate what type of case is heard in which court. The primary court system is divided into criminal courts and civil courts. Most cases of abuse and neglect handled by the court system are handled in civil court. Most civil court procedings involve a judge but not a jury. Civil courts can include family court, probate court, and juvenile court, as well as other types. A few states have family courts in which issues related to children and familes are handled. They tend to coordinate services for families and work closely with case managers to provide more comprehensive services and assistance to the family. Some states handle abuse and neglect through their probate courts. Most states place child abuse and neglect cases in their juvenile court system (Jones, 2006).

When a case is tried in a court, the process involves three steps—**petition, hearing**, and **adjudication and disposition**:

1. *Petition.* A petition is a complaint or allegation of child abuse or neglect. The petition will state the allegation and may request removal of a child.

Abuse and neglect petitions are usually focused on the welfare of the child and state in the document "in behalf of the child," instead of being filed against the parents (Crosson, 2005).

2. *Hearing.* A hearing is held as soon as possible to determine if a child is to be placed in substitute care, to appoint counsel for parents who do not have a lawyer and an attorney or guardian ad litem for the child, to order assessments and services for families and children, and to define expectations for the parents and what needs to happen next. Sometimes the case ends after the hearing if the parents are cooperative and Child Protective Services sees no need to proceed further.

3. *Adjudication and disposition.* The court system may go through several other types of hearings to determine the outcome of the petition. Hearings may be held to review evidence, to hear testimony, to issue orders, to place a child in temporary or permanent custody, to sever parental rights, and to make a disposition of the case (Jones, 2006). Civil court proceedings do not usually have specific guidelines and penalties as criminal courts do. They have the ability to be creative and to make stipulations regarding the best interests of the child. A court may, for example, require parenting classes or employment seminars as conditions for the parents to maintain custody of the child (see Figure 4.1).

Both parents and Child Protective Services will usually utilize the services of an attorney for advice or representation in court.

The Child Abuse Prevention and Treatment Act (CAPTA), the federal law governing grants for abuse and neglect to states, requires that a guardian ad litem (GAL) be appointed for a child who is going through the court system. A

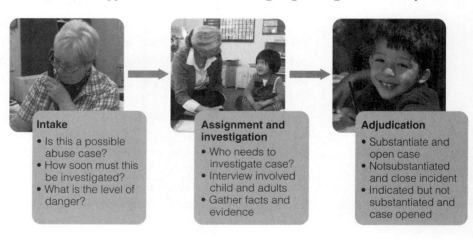

Intake
- Is this a possible abuse case?
- How soon must this be investigated?
- What is the level of danger?

Assignment and investigation
- Who needs to investigate case?
- Interview involved child and adults
- Gather facts and evidence

Adjudication
- Substantiate and open case
- Notsubstantiated and close incident
- Indicated but not substantiated and case opened

FIGURE 4.1

Photos courtesy of Wadsworth/Cengage Learning

guardian ad litem is a person appointed by the court to serve as a special advocate just for the child. The GAL does not represent parents or agencies involved, but only the child. The GAL gets to know the child, does an independent investigation of the case, and makes sure that courts and social service agencies are meeting the child's best interests and that the case is resolved as quickly and painlessly as possible (Goldman & Salus, 2003). The Court Appointed Special Advocates (CASA) program often provides volunteers who serve in this capacity. Sometimes attorneys and other professionals are appointed by the courts to serve as guardians ad litem.

When abuse is severe, sexual abuse occurs, or death results, the case is sent to the criminal courts. Law enforcement and prosecution departments become responsible for gathering evidence and for disposition of the case. Such cases are usually heard by a jury and penalties are often set by state law. Criminal cases must rely heavily on evidence and therefore often require testimony of the child and other professionals regarding the injuries and the abuse and neglect that occurred. Testifying in court can be very traumatic for a young child. Most courts only require the child to appear in court for a minimum amount of time; some allow children to appear through remote broadcast so they are not traumatized by having to face the perpetrator. Many courts allow the child's testimony to be submitted by videotape. The use of videotaped testimony as opposed to putting a child on the stand in court is advocated by many children's organizations including the American Academy of Pediatrics and Prevent Child Abuse America.

CHILD PROTECTIVE SERVICES

When an allegation of abuse or neglect has been substantiated or indicated, a case is opened by the local protective services division, which usually assigns a case manager to coordinate services to the family and child (DePanfilis & Salus, 2003). Child Protective Services (CPS) identifies services that will prevent or alleviate abuse and neglect in the family, assist the family in getting needed services, and monitor the family situation. The large number of cases that require investigation means that CPS is usually understaffed and overworked (Hines & Morrison, 2005).

Family-centered services focus on building the strengths of the family so that they can provide a healthy and safe environment for children. These services provide the family, and not the individual child, with the ability to function well. Family-centered services are usually categorized as either **family support** or **family preservation** (Crosson, 2005). Family support services are preventative services, aimed at strengthening the family. Family support services are for families who have not experienced abuse and neglect but who are at risk, such as teen parents. Family support services also can be provided to anyone who wishes to build a stronger family and provide a safe and optimal home environment for the children and adults who are part of the family. Family preservation services are those given to families who have been identified as being abusive or neglectful but who are believed capable, with the services, of keeping the child in the home (Crosson, 2005). Family-centered services are covered in more depth in Chapter 11.

Amy, the child at the beginning of this chapter, was in a family that received family preservation services. Family preservation services may be the same services as those offered for family support. Caseworkers may work with teachers and others who are providing support and education to assist the child and family. These services include intensive visitation and involvement by a CPS caseworker who will monitor the situation in case it deteriorates and intervention to protect the child is necessary. When intervention is necessary, the caseworker, in most states, will petition the court for temporary removal of the child from the home and for temporary custody. Some states allow for removal without a court order (Winterfeld & Sakagawa, 2003). The child is then placed by CPS in foster care.

FOSTER CARE

Reggie, the little boy in the vignette at the beginning of this chapter, was placed in foster care. Foster care is the temporary placement of a child outside the home, usually with a relative, foster home, group home, therapeutic home, or special institution for children. Approximately 324,000 children were removed from their homes and placed in foster care in 2006 (U.S. Department of Health and Human Services [USDHHS], 2008). However, more than 500,000 children were in foster care during that year (U.S. Children's Bureau, 2007), and only slightly over 200,000 children actually left the system that year. The average stay for a child in foster care was more than 28 months (USDHHS, 2008). Around 20,000 of the children who left the system reached the age of adulthood and were put out of the system (Geenen & Powers, 2007).

Foster care is an important resource for children who are in danger of victimization or revictimization; however, children who are in foster care generally suffer academic, emotional, social, and even physical problems while in care and afterward (Drapeau, Saint-Jacques, Lepine, Begin, & Bernard, 2007; Geenen & Powers, 2007; Ooserman, Schuengel, Slot, Bullens, & Doreleijers, 2007). Therefore, foster care should be a last resort for caseworkers who are working with families. While in foster care, children receive a variety of support services as needed, such as counseling, academic, and medical support.

Relative care, the placement of the child with a relative other than the custodial parent or relative, provides children with known caregivers who

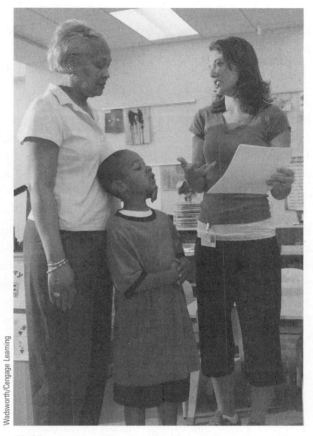

Children are usually placed with grandparents or other relatives instead of foster care. The teacher will want to develop a partnership with the person who has custody.

already have a relationship with the child. However, relative caregivers tend to be older, less educated, and more economically distressed (Bass, Shields, & Behrman, 2004). Although some states provide funding subsidies for relative care, others do not, which can place additional burdens on the family. Relatives can also find it difficult to limit the parent's ability to interact with the child as specified by the terms of the placement. There have been incidences of child deaths and additional abuse as a result of an aunt or grandmother not following placement instructions and allowing the parent open access to the child. Nevertheless, relative care can provide a very positive placement with someone who already knows and loves the child. Relative care may be an informal agreement with CPS and the parents for the child to live with the relative, or it may be formalized by CPS or the relative taking legal custody of the child.

Nonfamilial foster homes are those in which families not related to the child are identified for child placement. Nonfamilial foster homes make up 48% of the

— Fast Fact —
Forty-six percent of children in foster care are in nonfamilial foster homes (USDHHS, 2006a).

placements of children out of the home (USDHHS, 2008). Most of these families are not acquainted with the child or parents but are recruited, trained, and monitored by CPS or a private agency. Many churches and nonprofit organizations recruit and supervise foster parents. Most are paid a stipend by the state to cover basic expenses and costs of the child. Foster parents are people who care about children and agree to provide shelter and care. Although foster parents can usually specify numbers and ages of children, the need for foster care often requires caseworkers to ask foster parents to be flexible. Foster parents usually go through a lengthy training process, as well as criminal background checks and lengthy home studies and interviews, before they are accepted and utilized.

Group homes and institutional care provide options for those children who do not fit into a home situation. Children who are older, who require specialized care, who may be available for adoption but are not adopted, or who have not been successful in a foster home are usually placed in group homes or institutional care. Many of these programs provide a trained staff and specialized care that can provide structure and rehabilitation for the child (Crosson, 2005).

Foster care provides a temporary solution to child maltreatment, but federal law requires each state receiving funding to set timeframes for terminating parental rights if the parents have not been able to demonstrate competency in getting their children back. The court system can sever parental rights due to abuse and neglect. Most states have laws that allow the severing of parental rights in cases of severe abuse or death of another child in the home. In addition, when parents are unable or unwilling after one or two years to demonstrate the ability for the child to return, rights can be severed, and the child is made a ward of the state and becomes available for adoption (Humphrey, Turnbull, & Turnbull, 2006). Teachers and other professionals can assist children who have been placed in foster care by being sensitive to their needs and recognizing the trauma in their lives.

— **Fast Fact** —
Most children are adopted by a relative or their foster care home (Cowan, 2004).

ADOPTION

Prior to 1980 many children were staying for prolonged periods of time in foster care while their parents were unable or unwilling to take them back. The Adoption and Safe Families Act was passed by Congress in 1980 and revised in 1997 to end this practice. It states that a child who has been in foster care for 15 out of the past 22 months and whose parents have not met the requirements for having their child returned to their home can and must be placed for adoption (Humphrey, Turnbull, & Turnbull, 2006). When parental rights are terminated due to child maltreatment, children are placed for adoption. If they are white infants with no physical problems, many adoptive parents are waiting for them. If they are a sibling group, older, or have physical, emotional, intellectual, or developmental problems, their road to adoption is not easy. Most of these children who are adopted are adopted by relatives or by their foster parents (Cowan, 2004).

Most adoptions due to child maltreatment are handled by a Child Protective Services office or a nonprofit entity, such as a religious organization or children's home. Many states operate statewide databanks of children available for adoption. One such system, the Texas Adoption Resource Exchange, provides a website where children waiting for adoption can be seen and where information such as age, interests, and possible disabilities is provided. (For direct, up-to-date links to this website and more, please visit our website at http://www.cengage.com/education/hirschy.) Adoptions involving children whose parents voluntarily give up rights are sometimes handled by attorneys.

Parents who seek to adopt children who have been maltreated go through a process similar to those who want to be foster parents. Most states require them to go through parenting training, as well as interviews, case studies, and home visits. Parents who adopt children who have been abused and neglected must be aware of the special needs of these children. Many of these children have emotional, physical, intellectual, and social problems, which we explore in more detail in Chapter 6. Adoptive parents must be patient and flexible when dealing with the unique challenges of these children.

COORDINATED RESPONSES TO ABUSE AND NEGLECT

The intake, investigation, and treatment process of children and families involved in maltreatment is very complicated. It is often hard for agencies and professionals to determine boundaries, and they often conflict in their desire to do their jobs and help children. Some agencies and programs are family focused and their philosophy is first to preserve and protect the family unit, while others are child focused and their philosophy is focused first on the child. Other agencies are concerned with enforcing the law and legal statutes. Differing areas of focus and duplication of efforts can cause conflict between agencies and can be detrimental to the well-being of the child and the family. Many have recognized that the best approach is a coordinated, collaborative approach to the investigation and intervention of child maltreatment (Winterfeld & Sakagawa, 2003).

Child Advocacy Centers

One method of coordination that has been very successful is the development of Child Advocacy Centers. Child Advocacy Centers (CACs) have been developed in hundreds of counties and communities across the county. There are more than 500 Child Advocacy Centers. These CACs promote the coordination of agencies in their work with child maltreatment. The centers are usually funded by a combination of public and private funds. The focus of the CACs is on the child. They provide:

- A child-appropriate facility where children can be brought and interviewed and receive services
- A multidisciplinary team of caseworkers, police, therapists, and other professionals who support the child
- Advocacy for victims through legal assistance and abuse prevention programs for the community, and often legislative advocacy on behalf of maltreated children
- Forensic interviews conducted by trained interviewers
- Medical team assistance for identifying and treating abuse
- Multidisciplinary case review and tracking so that services and evidence can be coordinated

Collin County Child Advocacy Center

Collin County Child Advocacy Center
Courtesy of the Collin County Children's Advocacy Center, Plano, TX

The Collin County Child Advocacy Center is located in Plano, Texas. Law enforcement officers from four local cities who work with abuse and neglect, Child Protective Services employees, and agency staff all work together in the same location. While the focus of the Advocacy Center is the child, they also work with community organizations to provide services for families as well as children. The investigation of child abuse occurs in a collaborative environment where all information is shared.

Interviews of children are conducted by trained forensic interviewers employed by the Advocacy Center in rooms with one-way mirrors so that law enforcement, protective services, medical staff, and district attorney personnel can observe the interviews and feed additional questions to the interviewer. One room is set aside with complete medical equipment to conduct investigations regarding sexual or sometimes physical abuse of a child. These are conducted by specially trained nurse practitioners and doctors who are on call to the Center.

Formal and informal staffing of cases and cross training on issues of child abuse and neglect occur. The staff supports one another and finds that by working together, the outcomes for the child are more positive. Each group has its own responsibilities. Law enforcement handles the investigation and development of criminal cases, protective services makes decisions and provides direct services related to supervision of families and child placement, and the Advocacy Center provides specialized

Bright colors and fun areas to play soften the trauma for children who come to the Advocacy Center.
Courtesy of the Collin County Children's Advocacy Center, Plano, TX

New clothes, toys, and food are available at any time for children in need.
Courtesy of the Collin County Children's Advocacy Center, Plano, TX

investigative staff, support services, and therapy for children and families. One family member not served by the Center is the perpetrator. However, the other family members can receive therapy and assistance.

The Center provides a room with new clothing, toys, and materials for children who are suddenly moved into a foster care placement or are in need. A room in the entry is filled with stuffed animals, and each child who comes to the Center can pick one to take home. The Center is bright, cheery, and child-friendly. Rooms where parents and children can have supervised visits are also provided. The Collin County Child Advocacy Center is a positive role model for the collaboration and coordination of investigation and disposition of abuse and neglect (Etheridge, 2007; Winterfeld, & Sakagawa, 2003). (For direct, up-to-date links to their website and more, please visit our website at www.cengage.com/education/hirschy.)

SUMMARY

When child abuse has occurred and is reported, many different groups take steps to investigate the allegations. These groups include law enforcement, Child Protective Services, and the court system. If a case is substantiated, child protection becomes the focus. When possible, children are kept in their home and services are provided to assist the family in becoming more protective and avoiding further maltreatment. When children must be removed from the home, foster care provides alternatives. Children of families who cannot or will not protect them can be placed for adoption.

The agencies and services discussed provide both intervention and prevention for maltreated children. Intervention occurs when a child is at risk for or has been abused or neglected. Prevention involves methods used to keep child maltreatment from happening or from being repeated. The agencies discussed in this chapter do mainly intervention but their ultimate goal is prevention, and usually they employ methods to address both.

Application: When Working with Children

- Be sensitive about school activities where families are involved.
- Assign school projects such as family trees in a way that allows children to include foster, birth, and adoptive families in the same visual.
- Be sensitive to the grieving process children experience when removed from their homes.
- Communicate with the foster family or caseworker when you see behavioral changes in a child under protective services.

Application: When Working with Families

- Ask adoptive parents how comfortable they are with your sharing this information in the classroom and respect those wishes.
- When a child in your class is placed in foster care and remains with you, provide the foster parents with as much information as you can about the child.
- Support families who are working with protective services by giving them information, support, a positive attitude, and a listening ear.

Projects/Activities

1. Interview an adult who has been adopted and one who has adopted a child. Ask them about their experiences, and have them tell you what they would want a person who is preparing to work with children to know about adoption.

2. Look up websites for your local Child Advocacy Centers and Court Appointed Special Advocates (CASA) offices. Find out what they offer and whom they serve.

3. Compare family and nonfamily foster care. What are the pros and cons of each?

4. Have guest speakers from Child Protective Services come and describe their work.

5. Explore your state's adoption resources, and see if they have a database of children who are awaiting adoption that you can examine.

6. Explore your state's listings of adoptive children. Most states have photographs and information about children in the state who are available for adoption, and you can find them by doing an Internet search with the name of your state and the word *adoptions*. Alternatively, you can view Texas, California, or New York children waiting for adoption by using their adoption websites. Then identify three children from the information you have read and pictures you have seen, and list reasons why it might be easy or difficult to find an adoptive family for each of them.

Questions to Consider

1. How can Child Protective Services, law enforcement, and the courts be more effective in supporting children who have been maltreated?

2. What are the most effective methods of building resilience in families who are at risk for abuse and neglect?

Websites for More Information

For useful websites, visit www.cengage.com/education/hirschy

CHAPTER 5

Perpetrators: Those Who Abuse and Neglect Children

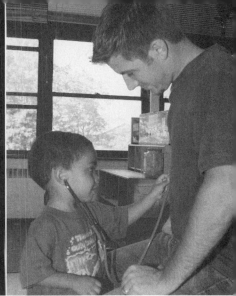

Wadsworth/Cengage Learning

WHAT YOU WILL LEARN

- Who abuses children in the community
- How teachers and other professionals commit child abuse
- Types of family members who abuse children
- Factors that contribute to family members abusing children

INTRODUCTION

Many ask, "How could someone abuse a child?" or state, "Only a monster could abuse a child." Sometimes that is true, but most often abusers are parents who are coping with ignorance, or with economic, emotional, or social issues that are overwhelming, and who do not have appropriate understanding of and skills with children. Many factors influence the behavior of perpetrators, or those who abuse children. Some perpetrators abuse out of ignorance—they were treated that way and do not know any better, or do not understand that their behavior is abusive. Some who abuse have emotional or psychological trauma or issues in their lives. Others are under severe stress, have few coping skills, lack parenting skills, or lack resources.

It must be clear, though, that abuse is not caused by a deficit or problem in the perpetrator's life. Many factors can contribute to or create conditions that might put someone at risk to abuse and neglect. But ultimately, abusing a child is a *choice* that someone makes. Neglect is a choice to do or not to do things that result in neglect. Unless a person is mentally incompetent, each individual has personal

VIGNETTE

Jenny was a caseworker working with two children who attended the Mendel Child Care Program. Jovana was seven and in the afterschool program, and her brother Micah was four. Jovana, who was in Mr. Smith's group, was very frightened of men. When she was younger she had been sexually assaulted by her soccer coach. Mr. Smith was very gentle and patient, but Jenny was concerned about the emotional appropriateness of Jovana being placed with a male teacher after school. Micah's teacher was Mr. James, a very loving and positive person. Micah had been physically abused by his stepfather. Jenny watched the interactions between Micah and Mr. James and noticed that Micah stayed very close to his teacher and seemed very attached to him. Jenny wondered how someone could have abused these sweet, innocent children and caused so much pain.

responsibility and can make those choices. For every person who has lost a job, lives in poverty, divorces, uses drugs, or lacks parenting skills and chooses to abuse a child, there are many, many more people in the same situation who choose *not* to abuse a child. Personal responsibility cannot be taken away just because of difficult circumstances.

Yet, those circumstances must be taken into account. It is so much easier for a person who has a good job, family who help with the children, and good examples of appropriate parenting skills not to abuse than it is for someone who is struggling to make enough money to feed the children, or who has never seen appropriate discipline of children, or who is a single parent with several children and no one to help. Individual responsibility cannot be dismissed, but empathy for and understanding of the perpetrator are important.

WHO ABUSES CHILDREN?

Most children are abused by family members. The following data from the National Child Abuse and Neglect Data System (Miller-Perrin & Perrin, 2007) provide a picture of perpetrators who abuse children: 83.4% of child victims were maltreated by parents acting alone or with another adult; other relatives accounted for 5% of abuse cases; and of parents committing child maltreatment, 4.3% of them were stepparents. It is clear from these statistics that children are at greatest risk from those they love the most (see Figure 5.1).

Who is the most likely to commit different types of abuse? Mothers are the primary abusers of children, followed by fathers and then by both parents. This

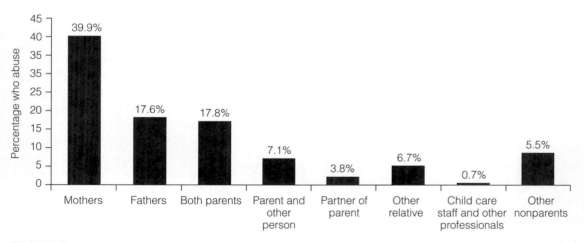

FIGURE 5.1

Those Who Abuse
Source: Child Maltreatment, U.S. Department of Health and Human Services, 2008.

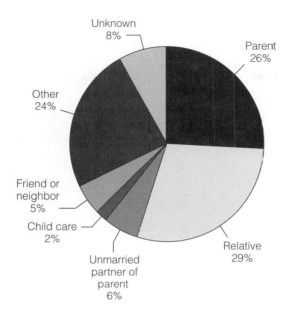

FIGURE 5.2

Perpetrators of Child Sexual Abuse

is a very different picture from the typical perception that abuse is from strangers. More than two-thirds of physical and psychological abuse and neglect of children is committed by parents. However, most sexual abuse of children is committed by relatives other than parents (see Figure 5.2).

Most abusers are women. According to recent data, 45.3% of them were younger than 30. Most perpetrators of abuse were white (53.7%), which is reflective of the majority population in the United States; only 20.7% were African American and 19.5% were Hispanic (U.S. Department of Health and Human Services [USDHHS], 2008). Perpetrators of abuse are primarily young white mothers. However, people who victimize children come in all ages, sexes, races, and walks of life. We will first focus on nonfamily perpetrators, and then explore family members who maltreat children.

ABUSE BY NONFAMILY

Most nonfamily abuse is committed as sexual abuse. A significant amount of sexual abuse is committed by the unmarried partner of the parent (6.2%), followed by a friend or neighbor (4.9%). Other perpetrators who are not family constitute 23.8% of sexual abuse of children (Miller-Perrin & Perrin, 2007). A significant amount of abuse occurs when children are left with friends, neighbors, or adolescent babysitters (Moulden & Wexler, 2007).

— **Fast Fact** —
It is estimated that 86–95% of sexual abuse is committed by someone who knows the child (Snyder, 2000).

One area of great concern recently has been institutional and professional perpetrators, those who work with children in capacities such as teacher, priest, minister, or coach. Gallagher (2000) and Wolfe, Jaffe, & Jette (2003) define institutional abuse as "The sexual, physical or abuse of a child (under 18 years of age) by an adult who works with him or her." The professional perpetrators employed in such positions use "either the institutions or organizations within which they work to target and abuse children" (Sullivan, 2002, p. 153). "Such perpetrators may be employed in a paid or voluntary capacity; in the public, voluntary, or private sector; in a residential or nonresidential setting; and may work either directly with children or be in an ancillary role" (Wolfe, Jaffe, & Jette, 2003, p. 181). Abuse that occurs within institutions such as schools, churches, and scouting and sports programs can be particularly traumatic for children and their parents. The abuse is worsened by the feelings of betrayal, shame and guilt that the child or parents somehow caused the abuse, fear of authority, and continual reminders of the abuse in settings in which the child may continue to be involved, such as school or religious settings (Wolfe, Jaffe, & Jette, 2003). There is a tendency in child care and educational environments to focus on men as abusers, but women also commit sexual abuse; and most cases of sexual abuse of preschool children in child care are committed by women (Moulden & Wexler, 2007).

Professionals who work in institutions with children are often in a position to abuse, as they typically have the trust of children and parents. They are usually of average or above average intelligence, and they work in fields that provide them with skills to build child and parent trust as well as access. Such abusers, particularly sexual abusers, exhibit certain patterns. Sexual abusers who are professionals abuse boys more than girls, while family abusers sexually abuse more girls. Professionals who abuse have a tendency to take a job partly because of their interest in sexually abusing a child. Usually these perpetrators' sexual interest in young children began during their teens, and the first episode of abusive behavior occurred either in their teens or early twenties, unlike family sexual abusers who often begin their assaults later (Sulllivan & Beech, 2004).

Educators and Caregivers Who Abuse

— **Fast Fact** —
People employed by schools are estimated to commit some form of sexual abuse (including sexual innuendo to students) with as many as 4.5 million students, over the course of their schooling (Irvine & Tanner, 2007).

Educators and child care providers are of particular concern. Recently, many schools and child care facilities have taken additional measures to protect children. Many child care centers have routinely set up surveillance cameras in classrooms; schools often require all adults to enter through a secured door after being checked; and children are only allowed to leave with an adult who has been identified by the parent. However, teachers and school employees are also in need of scrutiny. One survey indicated that within a five-year period, more than 2,500 incidents were reported of teachers having committed some form of sexual abuse on children (Irvine & Tanner, 2007).

According to the National Association for Child Care Resource and Referral Agencies (NACCRRA), full background checks that include checking child abuse and sex offender registries, fingerprints, and criminal history are done in only two states and the District of Columbia. Only 29 states do a fingerprint check, and only seven states require a sexual abuse registry check for child care employees (NACCRRA, 2007). Yet recidivism (repeating abuse and/or neglect of a child) of abusers is high (Way, Chung, Jonson-Reid, & Drake, 2001). Although 42 states require background checks for public school teachers, a much lower number require them for other school personnel, and only a handful require criminal background checks for nonschool youth sports personnel (Lohman, 2004). Many states are considering additional legislation and safeguards, as it is clear that more is needed (MacLaggan, 2007).

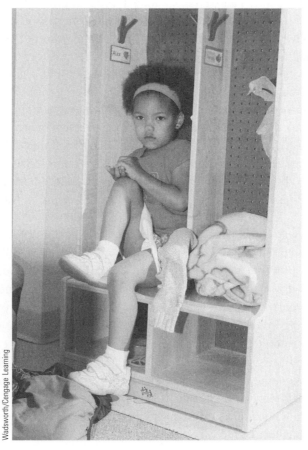

Wadsworth/Cengage Learning

Children sometimes do not feel safe and protected in school.

Although much of the publicity has focused on teachers and sexual abuse, a more pervasive issue is emotional abuse by teachers, something that has not been well explored in the literature. Emotional abuse such as shouting, humiliating, labeling, frightening, scolding, and the absence of supportive and nurturing environments for pupils has been common in many teaching environments (Shumba, 2002). When does reprimanding or pushing children to change behavior or do well become abuse? Think about those children in the classroom who never seem to do anything right. Imagine the second-grade teacher who moves a child's desk away from the other children, comments constantly on how poorly he did on this quiz or that project, and often tells him, "I don't know what I am going to do with you" or "You are never going to pass this class." Or picture the child care teacher who puts a three-year-old in time-out for spilling paint, and who repeatedly says things like, "Why can't you put away the blocks like Suzy? You are always leaving them out!" These behaviors cause pain for young children and, when continued throughout the year in a classroom, can lead to lifelong emotional problems for the child.

These children who never do anything right are the children the teacher always catches getting into trouble, and who get blamed and singled out no matter how many other children were involved. Such children endure this treatment daily for an entire school year. Will it affect their self-esteem? What about their future? Almost certainly, such behavior toward a child is a form of abuse. How many children can you remember from your own school years who had similar experiences? You probably knew more than one.

It is critical that teachers practice appropriate guidance techniques to prevent emotional abuse in the classroom. A checklist for teachers to use to guide them in thinking about their behavior with children (Am I at Risk to Emotionally Abuse? A Checklist for Teachers) can be found in NaNAppendix

The other abuse issue to be addressed with child care and school personnel involves the reactions of other professionals in the school or program. Children often feel unable to report abuse out of fear they will not be believed or out of fear of the abuser (Skinner, 2001). Children who report sometimes find that the teachers they tell are not sympathetic or are unwilling to believe the abuse has occurred. It is often difficult for a teacher to believe that someone they work with would commit such an act. Abuse can also occur when teachers in child care programs leave children temporarily under the care of another adult or an adolescent who is not employed by the institution (Moulden & Wexler, 2007). Licensing laws in each state address who and under what circumstances children can be left in the care of other adults. But some do not follow their state's standards. For more information on state licensing standards, contact your local child care licensing agency.

Teachers and administrators in child care, educational, religious, and recreational facilities must observe great vigilance in protecting children. Anyone who comes in contact with children in institutional settings should be required to have thorough background checks, and if they have not had such a check, they should not be left alone with a child or group of children.

It is interesting that, as a society, we are most concerned about and fear strangers as perpetrators of abuse and neglect, while they in fact commit a very small number of the abuse and neglect incidents that occur. Yet, so much of parent and teacher energies are focused on protecting and teaching children about stranger abuse. We need to focus more on children's understanding that abuse can come from anyone and that it is a crime no matter who commits the abuse.

ABUSE BY FAMILY MEMBERS

Child maltreatment is committed by family members more than 80% of the time (USDHHS, 2007a). Parents, stepparents, grandmothers, siblings, uncles, and aunts abuse children in the family. Parents commit the majority of abuse. What

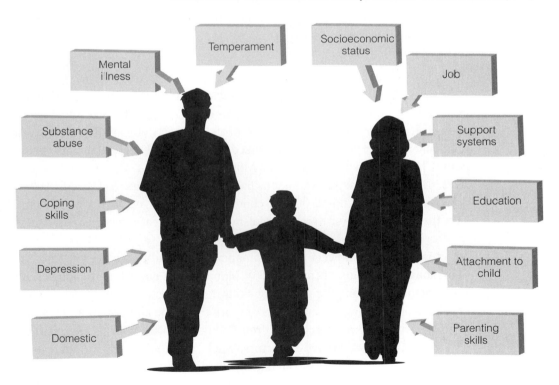

FIGURE 5.3

Factors Influencing Abuse

factors influence whether parents or family members will abuse their children? They can be divided into: parenting and personal factors, situational factors, adult self-abusive factors, and sibling abuse (see Figure 5.3).

Parenting Factors Affecting Child Maltreatment

Many parenting issues can contribute to abusive behavior. Whether an adult has been abused as a child, the type of parenting skills they have, and even the temperament and difficulty level of the child can influence abusive behavior.

Low self-esteem, stress, lack of external support systems, and fewer coping skills are seen consistently in parents who abuse and neglect their children (Berger, 2005; Crosson, 2005; Miller-Perrin & Perrin, 2007; Schaeffer, Alexander, Bethke, & Kretz, 2005). Parents who do not feel good about themselves and are depressed often neglect themselves and their child. Lower self-esteem may also be expressed through anger and aggression toward a child who is more vulnerable. Parents who lack support systems find themselves unable to cope at times. A grandparent who can take a child for the afternoon, a friend to tell about frustrations, or even Great-Aunt Agatha to call and ask for parenting advice provide support systems that can allow parents to cope without maltreating their child.

— **Fast Fact** —
Fewer than one-third of parents who were abused abuse their own children (Dixon, Browne, & Hamilton-Giachritsis, 2005).

Personal History of Childhood Abuse. The idea of intergenerational transmission of abuse, parents abusing because they were abused, has been one of considerable discussion and debate. The fact that a relationship exists between being abused as a child and abusing a child is supported by much research (Bifulco, Moran, Ball, Jacobs, Baines, & Cavagin, 2002; Dixon, Browne, & Hamilton-Giachritis, 2005; Pears & Capaldi, 2001). Some estimate that up to 30% of children who grow up in a violent home (whether child abuse or domestic violence) will maltreat their children (Hines & Morrison, 2005).

It is a mistake, however, to automatically assume that a person who has been abused will abuse (Corby, 2006). Many factors contribute to abuse. The same factors, such as poor parenting skills, low self-esteem, and psychological problems, that would put any parent at more risk to be abusive are often found in adults who were abused as children (Bifulco, Moran, Ball, Jacobs, Baines, & Cavagin, 2002). Protective factors, such as family support, education, socioeconomic status, and consistency in discipline seem to mediate the tendency toward child maltreatment for those who were abused (Bifulco, Moran, Ball, Jacobs, Baines, & Cavagin, 2002; Pears & Capaldi, 2001; Rossman & Rea, 2005).

Tips on Abuse Prevention for Those Who Have Been Abused

Working with Parents Who Were Abused	Working with Children Who Were Abused
Help with economic resources, such as job training, rental assistance, and medical coverage.	Provide basic education on child development and child guidance in middle school and high school.
Encourage support networks, such as support groups, extended family interactions, neighbor babysitting co-ops, and counseling.	Model guidance strategies for children by talking to them (alone and when they are calm) about why and how they are being disciplined, making choices, practicing appropriate behavior, and what constitutes inappropriate behavior.
Provide parent education, including articles, videos, and other information on child guidance and child development. Offer classes for parents on topics such as discipline and handling temper tantrums.	Be patient with children, and be calm when dealing with guidance issues.
Model appropriate guidance strategies for parents, and talk about how these techniques are like or different from what the parent does.	Encourage the parent to provide the child with counseling. Offer opportunities for the child to discuss feelings and concerns with a trusted adult.

Nevertheless, knowing that parents who were abused are at higher risk of abusing their own children, and that children who are abused are at higher risk of abusing their future children, is an important reminder to those who work with children and families. Professionals who work with parents should be aware of the need to encourage more parenting skill building, and to make sure that parents have access to economic resources and social supports.

Parental Satisfaction. Parenting is a job that sometimes seems to have few rewards. The pressure of providing food, clothing, and shelter, making sure that children are clean, fed, and supervised, and meeting emotional needs, helping with homework, and teaching a young child, on top of trying to meet parental and spousal needs, can be overwhelming. But most parents continue because they receive satisfaction from their role as a parent. A child's smile or hug is a reward that keeps parents going. But what about parents who find little or no satisfaction in their role as parents? The result can be abuse and neglect. Parental satisfaction is an important factor in child maltreatment, and parents who feel little parental satisfaction are more likely to be abusive (Carpenter & Donahue, 2006).

Parenting Knowledge. Parents at risk for abuse and neglect often lack knowledge of child development and have unrealistic expectations for children. They may, for example, not understand that a three-year-old regressing in toilet training following the birth of a new baby is a common occurrence. They may expect two- and three-year-olds to understand real versus pretend, or may punish them for not telling the truth, when these children may be unable to understand such concepts.

Wadsworth/Cengage Learning

Parents who find satisfaction in their role as parent are less likely to be abusive or neglectful.

Parenting styles identified by Diana Baumrind and others include *authoritarian, authoritative,* and *permissive* parenting (Baumrind, 1971; Rossman & Rea, 2005). **Authoritarian** parents require absolute obedience from the child without discussion. They often have unrealistic expectations of children. There are high demands toward children from parents, but a low response to the needs of children by parents. This style is rigid and controlling and often uses harsh discipline as a contolling measure. Research indicates that parents who are more negative, punitive, and controlling in their parenting are more likely to be abusive than parents who exhibit characteristics congruent with a more authoritative approach (Barnett, Miller-Perin, & Perin, 2005). Children in these homes tend to have lower self-esteem and do less well in school.

Authoritative parenting involves guiding the child through setting rules and standards, and through the use of discussion, persuasion, consequences for behavior, and consistency. Demand and response to children and parents is equally interactive and satisfying. Children in authoritative parenting situations tend to do better in school, be more emotionally stable, and have more positive outcomes.

Permissive or **indulgent** parents allow the children to do what they want as long as safety is not a factor. Such parents are usually very indulgent and accepting of any behavior of the children. They tend to be supportive but do not set rules and structure. There is low demand of children from parents, and a high response to the needs of children by parents. Children in homes where permissive parenting is used tend to have more behavioral problems and, later, delinquency.

Another parenting style that has been added to Baumrind's original list is the **uninvolved** or **neglectful** parenting style (Maccoby & Martin, 1983). These parents are so involved in their own lives that they ignore the children; the children receive very little support from the parents, and the parents exert little control (Gullotta & Blau, 2008). This form of parenting is neglectful and can result in very negative outcomes for the child.

Spanking and Child Abuse.

Spanking is usually defined as using the hand to hit a child on the buttocks, hand, or leg with the purpose of correcting behavior. Some states define physical abuse by excluding spanking as a cause of abuse unless it causes the death of a child. In 2003, 43% of parents used some form of hitting or spanking with their child, while 73% of parents felt there were times when spanking was appropriate (Bostrom, M., 2003).

Physical abuse is not necessarily spanking, or vice versa. But as we discuss in later chapters, abuse can be strongly related to spanking. Children who are spanked are more likely to be physically abused than those who are not (Gershoff, 2002). Many parents who abuse their child cite discipline as the reason for the abuse. However, spanking does not directly lead to child abuse. Although most researchers do not support spanking, some feel that the effects of simple spanking have been overstated (Baumrind, Larzelere, & Cowan, 2002; Paolucci & Violato, 2004). It is the position of the textbook authors that spanking is not the best form of guidance and that there is a strong enough relationship between spanking and long-term harmful effects on children that it should be avoided.

Child Difficulty

Children do not cause their parents to be abusive; however, some behaviors or predispositions of children tend to be related to higher incidences of abuse in families and in teaching situations. Children with temperaments that are

THEORY TO PRACTICE

1. Understand the policies and practices on spanking where you work.
2. Find alternative methods of discipline to spanking.
3. Recognize that many parents spank and feel it is an appropriate form of punishment. Do not criticize, but provide articles and information on other methods of discipline for them.

perceived by parents as difficult tend to suffer more abuse (Windham, Rosenberg, Fuddy, McFarlane, Sia, & Duggan, 2004). Parents who view their child as more aggressive are more likely to abuse or neglect the child. Whether the child's aggressiveness is only a perception, whether the child is naturally more aggressive, or whether the child's aggression is a result of parental aggression toward the child is often difficult to determine (Berger, 2005).

Temperament is the innate traits of a person that form a basis for behavior and personality. A child may be very active or very calm; may love new experiences and trying new things or like things to stay the same; may like noise, music, bright colors, and lights or like quiet, soft light, and pastel colors; and may want to eat, sleep, and do things at the same time and be very regulated or want to eat and sleep at different times and be hard to get on a schedule.

Temperament can affect child-and-parent (and child-and-teacher) relationships in many ways. Parents who have temperaments that prefer structure and schedules can be overwhelmed by a child who is spontaneous and cannot follow routines well. Some parents compensate by becoming more flexible while others become frustrated. The ability of the parent and child to adapt their different temperaments to meet one another's needs is referred to as **goodness of fit** (Thomas & Chess, 1977). Differing temperaments can trigger aggressive behavior in frustrated parents who cannot understand their child.

Crying has been seen as a critical trigger in some cases of child abuse, particularly in infants under six months. Often a child who cries incessantly or one who is colicky is frustrating for a parent who does not know how to comfort the child. It is not only the actual length of crying but also the parental perception that the child cries a lot that is related to abuse. Different parents have different levels of tolerance for crying and for different types of crying; for example, whining and high-pitched screaming might be handled in different ways by a parent. Some parents practice abusive behaviors such as shaking, hitting, and spanking when crying does not stop. When the parent lacks adequate coping skills, the crying of an infant can lead to abuse (Flaherty, 2006; Reijneveld, van der Wal, Brugman, Sing, & Verloove, 2004).

Situational Factors

Many factors can put a person at risk for child maltreatment. One major risk factor is becoming a parent as a teen. Parents who are very young when they have children are more likely to abuse their child (Dixon, Hamilton-Giachritsis, & Browne, 2005; Pears & Capaldi, 2001). Although many of the factors that go with being a teen parent, such as economic stress and lack of maturity, contribute to the risk of abuse, the mere fact that the parent is young in itself appears to be a critical factor in being at risk to abuse or neglect a child.

Unemployment, lower socioeconomic status, and lower educational levels correlate with child maltreatment by parents. Low income of the family and less stable parental relationships and housing situations combine with the tendency in these families to have more children, and more children with special needs. Such situations create stress. Education serves as a mediating factor, as parents

Parents who are young or with few resources or parental assistance are often stressed and at risk for abusive behavior.

with more education appear less likely to abuse (Berger, 2005; Crosson, 2005; Wekerle, Wall, Leung, & Trocme, 2007).

Divorce, Marital Satisfaction, and Single Parenting.

Children in single-parent households are more at risk of child maltreatment than children in two-parent families (Corby, 2006). There are more stressors in the one-parent home, including poverty, fewer supports, and fewer people to assume caretaking duties. Although stepparents do not appear to be at any more risk for committing physical abuse than biological parents (Miller-Perrin & Perrin, 2007), the addition of a stepparent in the household does increase the likelihood of sexual abuse (Corby, 2006). The maltreatment of children is a particular concern when there are additional nonparent adults in the home.

Cultural Factors

Child maltreatment is often interpreted according to culture. Some cultures practice the touching and rubbing of young children's private areas as a means of soothing them. Many cultures have differing views of when children should be unsupervised, ages at which they should work or watch younger siblings, and methods of discipline. Difficulties can arise when parents immigrate to this country from another culture or when they have been raised in an area where everyone is from a specific culture. Some of their cultural practices regarding child rearing may be at odds with our laws and traditions, and problems arise when those practices are continued.

A report on the adaptation of Liberian families who have recently arrived in the United States points out some of the difficulties in regard to cultural factors. These parents are used to having the community share parenting in areas such as supervision of children and discipline, and they may be seen as neglecting their children by not supervising them properly when they assume that others in the community are watching the children. "Assumptions that may be commonplace for many American parents, such as the importance of car seats and regular bed times for children, may be strange to refugee parents and may take some time to internalize" (Schmidt, 2005, p. 6). Some cultures practice very harsh forms of discipline that are considered abusive in the United States.

Adult Self-Abusive Factors

Drug, alcohol, and domestic abuse all create strong risk factors for child abuse and neglect. Children in homes where substance abuse occurs are at great risk for maltreatment (McNichol & Tash, 2001). Children are at risk from parents who may be under the influence of drugs or alcohol. They are also at risk from other adults who may be buying, selling, or using substances and from an environment where the substances are within easy reach of children or is contaminated due to processing of illegal substances (Berger, 2005; Messina, Marinelli-Casey, West, & Rawson, 2007).

Many studies have identified the correlations between domestic violence and violence against children (Barnett, Miller-Perin, & Perin, 2005; Berger, 2005; Corby, 2006; Dixon, Browne, & Hamilton-Giachritis, 2005; Schaeffer, Alexander, Bethke, & Kretz, 2005). Children in homes where domestic violence occurs are likely to experience the same abuse as their parent, or to suffer emotional abuse or neglect from the abused parent who is unable to cope with the trauma of being abused. Many children in such circumstances assume a parental role and try to protect the abused parent or experience severe psychological trauma from the domestic violence they witness.

Sibling Abuse

An area that has been described as "pandemic" is sibling abuse (Kiselica & Morrill-Richards, 2007). Children who grow up in families with domestic violence, inappropriate parenting, or controlling environments are at greater risk of sibling abuse. **Sibling abuse** occurs when a child becomes psychologically, physically, or sexually aggressive toward a sibling in a way that can cause consistent or permanent harm. Most siblings disagree, argue, fight, and name-call; but when the behavior is severe and consistent or when one or more children committing it continually targets the same sibling, then abuse may be occurring. Sibling abuse is perhaps one of the most underreported and most harmful forms of abuse.

SUMMARY

Closeness, touching, and caring are ways that families and friends find safety and security in their relationships. Parents are encouraged to love their children by showing physical displays of affection to them, as well as to other family members and close friends. Children trust their neighbors, ministers, teachers, coaches, and other adults around them. Most abuse is committed by family members, friends, and adults who are part of a child's everyday life. Children need to be made aware that there are people to whom they can confide if they are being abused and that abuse, even from a loving adult in their life, is not acceptable.

Application: When Working with Children

- Have children draw pictures of their family. Using open-ended statements or questions, ask them to explain their pictures to you: "Tell me about your picture. Who is in the picture? What are they doing?"
- Be aware when a child seems afraid of an adult or begins to talk obsessively about a certain adult in their family or in their life.
- Become aware of the temperaments of the children in your classroom and your own temperament. Do you find yourself being more negative with children whose temperaments are different from your own?

Application: When Working with Families

- Compile a list of people, organizations, and resource and referral agencies. Describe what each of them does, and get the name, title, and telephone number of a contact person at each. Obtain a brochure or flyer, business card, or some other written information. Keep this information in a file to share with families.
- Know the different parenting styles and use this knowledge to assist you when working with families.
- Alcohol abuse can instigate family violence. Become aware of other precursors to violent behavior, such as drugs, so that you can recognize signs of problems and learn how to cope with them.

Projects/Activities

1. Go to your state's child care licensing agency on the Internet. Find the state licensing standards. Write a two-page report on what these standards have to say about abuse and neglect, and supervision of children. Are they enough to protect children in a program? What should be changed?

2. Role-play a parent-teacher meeting with one student being the teacher and one student being the parent of a child who has been abused by a coach. You and the parent are trying to devise a plan to support the child as the child works though this situation. What were some of the difficulties for the teacher? For the parent? How easy or difficult was it to deal with your responses? What would you do differently?

3. You overhear a conversation between two children in a center about one of the children seeing her daddy's private parts. How do you handle the situation with the child? Write a page of dialogue indicating what the child might say and what you might say to better understand the situation. (Remember, this could be an innocent situation.)

4. Develop four scenarios of ways a teacher might speak to a child that could be considered abusive. Then demonstrate how the teacher's words and

actions could be changed to be supportive and not demeaning to the child.

5. Using the temperament checklist provided in Appendix H, determine your temperament and that of a child you consider challenging or difficult. Write a summary of how your temperaments are alike and different, and describe how temperament might contribute to your perception of the child as challenging or difficult. Include ideas on how you and the child could work together.

Questions to Consider

1. What are several societal contributors to the incidence of child abuse today?
2. Under what conditions do parents abuse their children?
3. How can you know if there is sibling abuse?
4. Describe the three styles of parenting. Which type is most beneficial to families?
5. What role does attachment play in relationships with family and friends?
6. What should parents do if they suspect that a professional, for example, a clergy member, friend, or coach, is abusing a child?

Websites for More Information

For useful websites, visit www.cengage.com/education/hirschy

Wadsworth/Cengage Learning

CHAPTER 6

Impact of Abuse and Neglect on Children's Lives

VIGNETTE

Amy was 12 months old and had just entered our child care program. Her brother, Allen, was six and came to us after school. Amy could not sit up well. She was small for her age and would not pick up or play with any of the toys we offered her. Allen had difficulty in showing any affection for anyone. He was often in trouble and said he didn't care. He was very small for his age and didn't get along with his peers. His face seemed flat and the bridge of his nose was wide. We were told the children were under protective services and were living in a foster home. I wasn't sure how to best help them, especially Amy, since she was in my class.

WHAT YOU WILL LEARN

- The immediate and long-term effects of maltreatment on children's development

- The immediate and long-term effects of child maltreatment on children socially, emotionally, physically, and intellectually

- Treatment and service options to assist a child who has been maltreated

INTRODUCTION

Child abuse and neglect does not have consequences only during childhood; it affects children when they become adults—their future family, workplace, and relationships. In fact, those who have suffered child maltreatment "have been shown to have problems in their financial, social, emotional, marital, and behavioral functioning" (Hines & Morrison, 2005, p. 100). There are consequences for a maltreated child's long-term health and well-being. Amy and Allen in our vignette have suffered severe impairments as a result of child maltreatment. Are these permanent? What are the long- and short-term consequences, and are treatments available?

SOCIAL/EMOTIONAL IMPACT OF MALTREATMENT ON CHILDREN AND ADULTS

Child abuse strongly impacts a child's ability to function socially and the child's emotional well-being. The child who has been abused may have difficulty forming attachments. He may not understand normal social cues that people give, such as how close to stand to people or how to carry on a normal conversation. He may feel under constant stress, something that often induces a more rapid heartbeat than that in the normal child (Perry & Szalavitz, 2006). The child may show extreme anger or behavioral problems or have very low self-esteem.

Many common causes of emotional disability in this country can be linked to maltreatment in childhood. Children who are abused often feel negative about themselves and about others as well. This can lead to difficulties in forming adult relationships, depression, and other health problems. In some cases, limited stimulation in life has slowed development. Maltreated children may suffer emotional trauma from abuse and neglect in the home or even from being removed from an abusive home. Past research on family systems has demonstrated that sometimes parents and children are more stressed by changes that are made in the original family system, such as placing a child in foster care, than they are when the family system stays intact (Fomby & Cherlin, 2007). Children who are abused and neglected often have unstable living conditions, continual family crises, and a variety of adults coming in and out of their lives, all of which can affect healthy emotional development.

Young children who have had several disruptions and continual crises in their lives do less well in school, are emotionally more maladjusted, and tend to be more disruptive in child care and school (Martinez & Forgatch, 2002). In the case of older middle and high school students, there is an increased chance of their dropping out of school.

Post–traumatic stress disorder (PTSD) has been recognized as a predominant effect of child abuse and neglect. **Post–traumatic stress disorder (PTSD)** may be defined as a cluster of emotional, psychological, and physical symptoms following an extremely stressful event. Those suffering from PTSD have overreactive stress response systems, which often makes them overreact to even small stressors (Perry & Szalavitz, 2006). Children who have been abused experience significant trauma and suffer from PTSD, exhibiting such symptoms as anxiety, dissociation, and behavioral problems (Mennen, 2004).

Psychological distress as an adult often takes place because of the experience of childhood **emotional neglect**. One research study involving male and female undergraduate students categorized them as being either neglected or not neglected by a male or female caregiver. This study found that those who reported being neglected by their primary female caregiver were experiencing significantly more psychological distress than either those reporting no neglect or those reporting neglect by a primary male caregiver (Wark, Kruczek, & Boley, 2003). Since most children experience the female caregiver in their lives as the one who provides most of the care and nurturing, neglect from the female caregiver can have long-lasting consequences.

The perceptions of an individual are what are real for that individual. Two individuals may have very different perceptions of the same experience. As noted in Chapter 2, attachment or emotional closeness with caregivers is fundamental to a child's psychological well-being. The lack of affection found in emotionally neglectful parent-child relationships has long-standing conse-quences for later psychological development.

Attachment

Uri Bronfenbrenner (1977) said, "Every child needs one person who is crazy about him" (p. 5). We know that attachment is critical to healthy development. According to Dr. Bruce Perry (2001), **attachment** is a special bond formed between an infant and primary caregiver that is enduring with that specific person; brings the child comfort, safety, and happiness; and the loss or implied loss of which distresses the child. Attachment develops as the result of bonding experiences that occur when the adult consistently provides affection, nurturance, food, shelter, and care for the child. There are sensitive periods in a young child's life when these bonding experiences need to be present in order for the brain to develop appropriately. Children who do not form appropriate attachments, particularly as a result of neglect or abuse, are at risk for failure to thrive, are often unable to form close relationships during childhood and into adulthood, and can experience significant social and emotional problems. There are also degrees to which children can have difficulty attaching. Children may be partially attached to an adult but due to maltreatment that attachment may not be secure. The long-term consequences and severity of impaired attachment depends on when it began, how long the attachment problems lasted, and the severity of the neglect of the child (Perry, 2001).

According to Perry and Szalavitz (2006), "Children who don't get consistent, physical affection or the chance to build loving bonds simply don't receive the patterned, repetitive stimulation necessary to properly build the systems in the brain that connect reward, pleasure and human-to human interactions" (p. 86). Even though attachment is very important, children who do not form healthy attachments in early childhood can still learn to function well in society. They

Young children who are neglected and left alone for long periods of time in cribs can suffer severe physical, mental, and emotional damage.

can form attachments later. But losing this opportunity in infancy usually means the child will have a very difficult job repairing the damage, and the child's relationships may never be the same as they would have been without this form of neglect.

Emotional Disabilities and ADHD

Children who have been abused are at much greater risk for emotional disabilities, including anxiety, depression, obsessive-compulsive behavior, suicide ideation, and other forms of emotional disturbance (Freeman & Morris, 2001; Kendall-Tacket, 2000; Onyskiw & Hayduk, 2001; Prosser & Corso, 2007). Maltreated children not only have a greater tendency to experience these difficulties immediately, but also are much more likely to experience them as adolescents and adults.

Children, particularly girls, who have been abused are also more likely to exhibit symptoms of attention deficit disorder (ADD) (Briscoe-Smith & Hinshaw, 2006). However, some symptoms of post–traumatic stress disorder often look the same as ADD. **Dissociation** is a state where the body and mind tries to protect the child by slowing the heart rate, and providing chemicals to the brain that kill pain and help the child to feel calm. In dissociation, the child's mind often retreats or creates an alternate reality so that the child can emotionally get away from the abuse that is occurring (Perry & Szalavitz, 2006). Teachers may see this as daydreaming, "spacing out," or ignoring behaviors in the classroom, when in fact the child is in some way feeling the trauma she has experienced and is protecting herself. Sometimes, instead of dissociating, children experience **hyperarousal** and become hyperactive as a coping mechanism.

Aggressive and Sexual Behavior

Children can develop aggressive or sexualized behavior if they have been maltreated. Such children may model what they have seen and what has been done to them by acting out toward others. Children who have been victimized sexually may act provocatively, attempt to touch the private parts of an adult or another child, attempt to engage in sexual activities, kiss on the lips, try to undress, stimulate themselves sexually, or attempt to victimize another child sexually. As such children mature, they may begin to act out sexually, become promiscuous, or have sexual problems (Price, Hilsenroth, Petretic-Jackson, & Bonge, 2001).

Children who have been maltreated are often more aggressive. This may be a protective reaction to keep them from further abuse, or they may be modeling behavior they have seen. One study (Bolger & Patterson, 2001) that focused on almost 2,000 early elementary children found that children who had been maltreated were significantly more aggressive and significantly more likely to be rejected by peers as a result of their aggressive behavior. This behavior tended to be repeated often and to continue as these children got older. Children who have been maltreated should be taught appropriate methods of expressing anger and aggressive feelings, as well as social skills.

Social Skills

Children who are abused and neglected tend to have fewer friends, and their interactions and relationships with friends, other peers, and adults are often inappropriate or lacking in prosocial skills. Children who have been maltreated have fewer social skills and are less likely to be liked by their peers (Bolger & Patterson, 2001). **Prosocial skills**, the set of skills that helps the child to get along with peers and adults in positive ways, are often missing in a child who has been maltreated. Many of these children through neglect have not been exposed to appropriate behavior. Many maltreated children find that their worldview has been skewed by abuse and neglect, and their perceptions and distrust of others interfere with prosocial behaviors. Moral development of children can also be impacted by child maltreatment. Children who have been abused and neglected exhibit more cheating, stealing, and lying behavior, are less giving, and exhibit less compliance to rules and less guilt than children who have not been maltreated (Koenig, Cicchetti, & Rogosch, 2004). These outcomes may explain in part why prison populations have an overrepresentation of adults who were maltreated as children.

PHYSICAL IMPACT OF MALTREATMENT ON CHILDREN AND ADULTS

Chronic child maltreatment can lead to physical changes in the body. The maltreated child may experience a more rapid heart rate on a regular basis, an increase or decrease in certain chemicals in the body, and some changes in breathing. The child also may suffer from nutritional deficits that result in impaired growth physically and intellectually. Children who are neglected often have poor teeth, which can cause other health problems, and may not receive immunizations or appropriate medical care for health problems, which can result in long-term disabilities or poor health. Maltreated children as adults may experience chronic illness and stress that originated in child maltreatment (Dubowitz, 1999; Gold, 2000).

Parental Drug/Alcohol Use and Children

Children can suffer physical disabilities of many kinds as the result of abuse and neglect. One area of growing concern is the outcomes in children of parent drug and alcohol use. In earlier chapters, we referred to **fetal alcohol syndrome**, a devastating syndrome that can cause a variety of physical, social, intellectual, and emotional difficulties for children throughout life. Children exposed to drugs experience similar consequences. A child born to a heroin addict will be born addicted to heroin and will experience lifetime difficulties in all areas of development. Children who are exposed to amphetamines and other drugs through parental drug use or the production of drugs in the home may experience drug exposure, accidental burns, death, or poisoning. They also often become addicted to the substances and are at increased risk of drug abuse when older (Messina et al., 2007). These drugs can affect growth, including brain development. Approximately 55% of children taken out of home-based methamphetamine labs had toxic levels of chemicals in their bodies (EPIC National Clandestine Laboratory Seizure System, 2003). Many caseworkers report that parent use of methamphetamines and other drug use exists in the majority of cases they investigate (Etheridge, 2007).

Failure to Thrive

Failure to thrive (FTT) is a term used to describe infants and children who do not grow, or sometimes even lose weight, and who are at the bottom 3–5% of children on a growth chart. It is believed that FTT patients probably account for 1–5% of pediatric hospital admissions (Gahagan, 2006). Failure to thrive can result from a genetic or physical problem of the child, such as inability to eat or digest food properly, or from a disease or developmental disorder (Block & Krebs, 2005). It also can occur because of neglect, and can worsen if the parent does not take advantage of community resources (Kessler & Dawson, 1999). If the neglect is severe, the child can die. Extreme cases of FTT often result in death. Historically, many children who lived in orphanages suffered from FTT as a result of inadequate care and feeding, and in some orphanages, large numbers of children under the age of one died.

Failure to thrive can result not only from inadequate food, but also from inadequate love and nurturing. One cause of FTT is inadequate parenting skills and knowledge, which may include a lack of understanding about appropriate methods of feeding a child. For instance, a family who routinely feeds their four-month-old biscuits, gravy, and cola would fall into this category. Failure to thrive may also result from neglect in which the child is left alone for long periods in a crib, or from rejection or lack of affection from the primary caregiver.

Teen parents, parents who have limited intelligence, parents who have been separated from the child for a long period, parents who are substance abusers, and parents who are socially isolated or involved in family violence may have children at risk for FTT. Failure to thrive also can occur in homes where the parents' careers become so pervasive that the parents do not have the physical and emotional reserves necessary to love and care for a child. Older as well as younger children can experience FTT, and children who show weight loss or severely limited weight and height may be at risk (Greenberg, 2002). Children suffering from FTT benefit from multidisciplinary teams, including medical specialists, nutritionists, and social workers, focused on treatment. Parent education, particularly home visitors, also is an effective means of treatment (Tittle, 2002). Resolving issues in parents' lives through counseling, support services, and other resources can benefit children who show symptoms of FTT.

Psychosocial Short Stature (PSS) or Dwarfism

Psychosocial short stature (PSS) is the failure to grow or delayed puberty that results in an extremely short stature. Usually it is associated with emotional neglect or abuse. This condition can begin at birth with failure to thrive, or it can begin when a child is older and has endured parental rejection or some form of abuse (Sirotnak, 2001). It is not known how many children might be affected by PSS from abuse and neglect, as it is extremely difficult to determine that abuse and neglect, and not a genetic or biological cause, are behind the shorter stature and other physical symptoms that are present. The diagnosis is usually made after abuse and neglect or emotional deprivation of the child has been identified (Northam, 2004).

Death

The ultimate outcome to an infant, child, adolescent, or adult who has suffered from severe child maltreatment is death. Death can come in a number of different ways to individuals who have suffered from abuse and neglect.

- Death can be a direct result of physical abuse or neglect.
- Death can be an indirect result of abuse or neglect, such as a child who dies from pneumonia after being left outside in the cold without adequate clothing.
- Death can occur when a child who has been abused takes her own life or follows a reckless lifestyle due to feelings of guilt, anger, or sadness following abuse.

During 2005, approximately 1,460 fatalities of children resulted from abuse and neglect (U.S. Department of Health and Human Services [USDHHS], 2006b).

Additional Health Consequences

The experience of childhood abuse and neglect is often accompanied by a number of physical health consequences for children after the abuse, and later as adults as well. A variety of physical health outcomes, including infectious diseases, irritable bowel syndrome, pain disorders, cancer, and heart disease, are seen in much higher rates among those who have been abused than in those who have not (Corby, 2006; Dube et al., 2003; Johnson et al., 2002). Much research indicates that children who experience abuse and neglect have many physical aftereffects.

People who have been abused as children often experience health risks as adults, as the result of coping behaviors. Adults who were maltreated as children tend to experience more alcoholism, more drug use, and more overeating, as well as other addictive behaviors (Rogers & Davies, 2007). Adults who experienced child maltreatment are also more likely to have additional physical problems that may be caused by changes in the brain and nervous system from the body's reaction to abuse and neglect.

INTELLECTUAL IMPACT OF MALTREATMENT ON CHILDREN AND ADULTS

Brain development, particularly during the first three years of life, is a dynamic process that is strongly influenced by genetic and biological processes. Equally affecting the brain are environmental influences and experiences. Parental neglect and abuse can cause critical changes and developmental issues in brain development (Glaser, 2000).

Brain Development and Changes from Trauma

The 1990s was referred to as "the decade of the brain." As the result of technological advances, we were suddenly able to see what the brain looks like in various states, how outside factors affect the brain, how the brain works, and how child maltreatment can alter the development of the brain.

Much research has focused on how trauma and abuse affects brain development. Many studies have clearly indicated that children who are abused experience significant changes to the brain, including changes in EEG readings and chemical changes (Glaser, 2000). Children who have been traumatized more often have smaller brains with abnormal structures than do children who have not suffered abuse (Beers & De Bellis, 2002). Changes that occur in the brain as a result of abuse can consequently manifest in a child's behavior as well.

The brain is a dynamic organ. It is constantly taking in information from each of our senses, and processing and organizing it. The brain forms connections to the millions of brain cells that exist. These connections allow us to process and store information. The more connections we have, the more "staying power" we have as we hold information until it becomes permanent and remains without conscious thought. These connections form the basis of our perceptions, emotions, and intellect. A child may see a picture of a cow and not remember it; but if the child sees, hears, and touches a cow and is exposed to the cow over long periods of time, "cow" becomes a permanent part of the child's brain and memory. Critical to the storage of this information are chemicals that transmit information throughout the brain. The brain also develops from simple to complex, with the parts of the brain that control bodily processes (the "fight-or-flight response" and other automatic responses such as breathing) developing first, and the areas of the brain controlling verbal ability, learning, and behavior developing later. When maltreatment occurs during the first year, the parts of the brain that deal with body control and emotional regulation may be affected. The body may also overproduce certain chemicals in the brain that can result in delayed or lessened development of the brain's higher functioning. Children who have been traumatized at early ages may have smaller brains and may have experienced reduced development of the more complex regions as well as overproduction of some neurotransmitters related to fight or flight. These children overreact to situations, are constantly watching and fearful, and may exhibit more learning and social difficulties as a result of these brain changes.

Perry (2000) describes the child who has been traumatized and sits in a classroom trying to concentrate on a lesson that he is learning. The child may be overly sensitive to movement and activity around him, which makes him overly concerned and aroused. He may have difficulty sitting still, taking in and processing information, and not reacting negatively to movement and comments by others. Such a child may require a quieter classroom or a teacher who can assist him in developing coping strategies.

Children who are maltreated often have different areas of the brain that are activated in social situations than children who have not experienced abuse. These children may miss social cues and misread facial expressions or physical stances, considering them as aggressive behaviors or not understanding their meaning. For instance, when a teacher looks such a child in the eye, the child may misinterpret that direct look, which is meant to show the teacher is paying attention, as one that means the teacher is angry or unhappy with the child. A lot of activity in the classroom may excite some children to learn, but children who have experienced abuse may find that this excitement activates the part of their brains that deals with "fight or flight," and they may become aggressive or fearful. Children who are learning information verbally require that large parts of the brain be in use, and the emotional factors that must be in place for this are often not there for the traumatized child (Boss, 2003).

These brain changes can create lifelong repercussions. Some have wondered if these changes in the brain may create more likelihood that the abused child becomes an abusive parent. Brain changes have been noticed in animals as a result of abuse that may indicate physiological changes that perpetuate abusive behavior. A study (Maestripieri et al., 2006) done with rhesus macaques indicated that abused infants showed chemical changes in their brains and that those mothers who abused their infants also showed the same types of chemical changes. While this study has not been replicated in humans, it is an indicator that chemical changes occurring in the brain as a result of abuse may tend to perpetuate abusive behavior.

Children who have been maltreated have higher rates of intellectual and academic difficulties (Noble, Tottenham, & Casey, 2005). Learning is impeded, learning disabilities are common, and failure in school happens as these children are unable to process information appropriately.

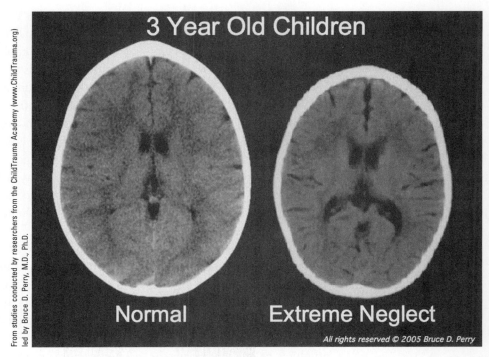

These images illustrate the negative impact of neglect on the developing brain. The CT scans on the left are from healthy three year old children with an average head size (50th percentile). The image on the right is from a series of three, three-year-old children following severe sensory-deprivation neglect in early childhood. Each child's brain is significantly smaller than average and each has abnormal development of cortex (cortical atrophy) and other abnormalities suggesting abnormal development of the brain.

LONG-TERM CONSEQUENCES OF ABUSE AND NEGLECT

Some studies show that the long-term consequences associated with abuse and neglect not only emerge in childhood, but also are evident in adults with histories of child maltreatment as well. Many of the behaviors that begin as a result of abuse in childhood will persist in adulthood and can contribute to the intergenerational transmission of abuse (Dixon, Hamilton-Giachritsis, & Browne, 2005).

Criminal and violent behavior, socioemotional difficulties, substance abuse, and alcoholism are just a few of the long-term consequences of abuse and neglect. There are negative physical and psychological effects for child and adolescent victims as well as for adults with childhood histories. The effects of child maltreatment last a lifetime, affecting not only the child but also the child as an adult and sometimes generations beyond.

As has been stated, of great concern is **intergenerational transmission of abuse**—when parents who were abused abuse their children. Many studies indicate a tendency toward an abused child becoming abusive as an adult (Pears & Capaldi, 2001), although this is not a foregone conclusion. In fact, less than one-third of parents who were abused abuse their own children (Dixon, Hamilton-Giachritsis, & Browne, 2005). As discussed in the previous chapter, a complex interplay of issues exists that can lead abused parents to continue abuse with their children. The likelihood of abuse is probably more a function of parents' parenting and social skills, financial resources, and other external factors, which are also influenced by how the children grew up, than just the fact that the parents were abused.

TREATMENT OF ABUSED AND NEGLECTED CHILDREN

How do you "fix" a child who has been maltreated? What methods are employed to help a severely traumatized child lead a normal, happy life? Can such children lead normal and happy lives? The answer is "yes," but often they need help. Research shows that maltreated children who receive some form of therapy have less long-term trauma and better outcomes than children who do not receive therapy (Hetzel-Riggin, Brausch, & Montgomery, 2007). Although abused children may not demonstrate, at any given time, symptoms that indicate they are not functioning in healthy ways, problems can appear later in adolescence or adulthood (Saunders, Berliner, & Hanson, 2004). Some children do well just talking about issues when they come up, but most children re-experience trauma from the maltreatment at various life stages, and often therapy can help them resolve this in positive ways.

A variety of maladaptive behaviors are seen in maltreated children, including extreme anger and aggression, problems with social skills, sexualized behavior, learning impairments, anxiety, post–traumatic stress disorders, trust issues, inability to read social cues and behaviors and to respond appropriately, poor self-esteem, depression, fear, and victimization by peers.

Treatment and Service Plan

A variety of treatment interventions work with children who have been maltreated. Some interventions are better adapted to certain types of problem behaviors, and treatment must involve a complete assessment of the child socially, emotionally, intellectually, and physically to determine the exact problems the child may be experiencing and their causes. A complete assessment of the parent or caregiver and sibling relationships, including personalities, family interpersonal relationships, family member temperaments, communication, and attachment and guidance history is critical before deciding which interventions will be best (Saunders, Berliner, & Hanson, 2004).

After a complete history is done, the professional sets goals for the child and develops a treatment plan. Goal-setting should be done with parents, if possible, or with the current caregiver. If caseworkers are involved, they should be a part of this treatment planning as well. Teachers and child care providers should be included in the planning and treatment process if the behaviors are causing problems in the classroom. It is also important to include the children in the planning process whenever possible so that they can have control over helping themselves to improve. Cooperation from the child is important to the success of any plan.

When establishing goals for a child's improvement, it is important to take into account:

- Availability of needed services
- Ability of parents to afford or gain access to the services
- Transportation costs and issues
- The child's schedule and whether services will interfere with routines
- Time factors, such as services that would take the child or parent away from work or school
- Whether the planned intervention is culturally appropriate

Types of Services and Treatment

Treatment and services should be focused around improving the child's life and giving the child tools to cope with internal and external stressors—providing the child with a toolkit to use in dealing with issues surrounding the abuse now as well as in the future. This toolkit might include:

- Skills to manage stress and anxiety
- Self-esteem building
- Social skills for dealing with peers
- Anger management
- Parent and other authority figure interaction skills
- Counseling to understand feelings regarding the maltreatment and appropriate ways to express them
- Problem-solving skills
- Development of an understanding of cause and effect
- Behavior management skills
- Protective skills, such as understanding of appropriate touches, stranger resistance, and how to get help if needed

How does a child develop this toolkit and learn to cope with his maltreatment? Parents can help children by receiving parenting skills training, counseling, and assistance with needed resources. Teachers and other professionals can help children by providing resources and helping them to build skills. Children who are scaffolded, or receive support, in developing their toolkit are more likely to have sufficient coping skills.

Any parent of a child who has experienced maltreatment from others would benefit from professional help in better understanding the trauma the child has experienced, and from being given specific parenting and guidance techniques that will help the child. Children can benefit from specialized and therapeutic group programs, including therapeutic foster and child care, special school programs, group therapy sessions, and art or music therapy. Activities such as new hobbies, athletics, and art or music classes help children develop feelings of control over personal situations and self-esteem. Individual or group therapy can help children understand what has happened and how to deal with their feelings. Such therapy can be specific to the abusive situation or it can revolve around larger issues in the child's life and the development of skills to deal with behavioral, emotional, and social issues.

Play therapy has proven particularly beneficial for young children. Play therapy involves the child and therapist in a playful situation. The play can include building, drawing, board games, dramatic play, blocks, or any form of play that the therapist thinks will assist the child in expressing and understanding her feelings and in learning skills to help her function in healthy ways. Play therapy can be done individually or in groups. Forms of play therapy are sometimes taught to parents and teachers to assist them in improving interactions and building skills with the child.

SUMMARY

Much research has been done about the impact of child abuse and neglect in children, adolescents, and families. The social, emotional, physical, and intellectual development of a child is always affected in some way by abuse and neglect. Many lasting consequences regarding a child's well-being result from child maltreatment. The impact of child maltreatment may be mild or severe, disappear after a short time, or last a lifetime, and victims are affected in different ways. Providing children who have been maltreated with a toolkit of skills to assist them in overcoming the short- and long-term effects is important to their improved functioning. Children such as Amy and Allen in our opening vignette can benefit from intensive intervention by the adults around them in overcoming the effects of child maltreatment.

Wadsworth/Cengage Learning

Play therapy can provide young children with the opportunity to understand and work through their trauma.

Application: When Working with Children

- Be aware of those children who may have been traumatized and provide support.
- Provide guidance in the classroom that is positive.
- Assist parents and therapists in any way they request in developing and administering treatment plans for a child.
- Provide a lot of nurturing to very young children in your classroom.
- Treat children as they are developmentally, not just according to age.

Application: When Working with Families

- Have a parent meeting with a speaker on brain development to assist parents in understanding how early experience creates lasting influences on the child's brain development.

- Provide parents with information on the importance of nurturing young children and skills that will help them do that.
- Be sensitive and listen carefully to what parents or caregivers tell you about the children, and document any information that you believe may be important for you to remember.

Projects/Activities

1. Personal Bubble: Choose a partner and have that person stand across the room from you. Then, standing still, have your partner slowly walk across the room to you until you feel uncomfortable with the closeness and say, STOP! Switch roles with your partner, and repeat the exercise. Discuss any differences in the distances each of you chose, and why those differences might exist.

2. Read more about brain development, and create a visual representation of how the brain develops.

Questions to Consider

1. How is social and emotional development impaired by abuse and neglect?
2. How has brain research helped us to understand children who have been abused and neglected?
3. What measures need to be taken to ensure the safety of our children against abuse and neglect?
4. What forms of treatment can help a traumatized child overcome abuse and neglect?

Websites for More Information

For useful websites, visit www.cengage.com/education/hirschy

rth/Cengage Learning

CHAPTER 7

Special Topics in Child Maltreatment

VIGNETTE

Jason was a social worker at a school in a poor, high-crime neighborhood. He was working with a first-grade teacher who was very concerned about several children in her classroom. Amy, the teacher, had Jason observe Justin, a child with special needs who had been integrated into the classroom. Justin came to school some days looking very frightened, and at times, he would be limping or holding his arm, sometimes bruised. While unable to express himself verbally, he often acted afraid of adults when they came close. Amy had asked the parents about the bruises and was told that falling was part of Justin's disability, although this was not observed at school. While Jason was observing in the classroom, he noticed Adam, who wore long sleeves, was very quiet, and seemed excessively fearful. Adam often cried when it was time to go home. Amy would just tell him to "be a big boy." Jason knew Consuela, another child in the class, quite well. He had worked with her family who had been severely neglectful with their children. Yet Consuela was happy and excelled in the classroom. The special issues and concerns in this classroom were enough to keep him busy!

WHAT YOU WILL LEARN

- The effects of culture, socioeconomic status, and religion on child maltreatment

- How the gender of a child affects whether the child is abused or neglected, and in what ways

- How the gender of the perpetrator is related to child abuse

- The effect on the ages and stages of development in child maltreatment, and the reaction of children to being maltreated

- How children with special needs are at risk for abuse, and how you can help

- What makes a child resilient and how to promote resiliency in children

- The different forms bullying takes, its effect on children, and how to combat it

INTRODUCTION

Child maltreatment affects children in so many ways. It can cause many physical problems, and often it is emotionally devastating. How strongly and in what ways it impacts a child depends on many factors. Culture, socioeconomic status, and religion all play a role in child maltreatment. The age and gender of a child often make a crucial difference in whether the child is maltreated, and in how maltreatment will affect the child. Even the age and gender of the perpetrator can make a difference in child maltreatment. Although many children who are abused and neglected suffer devastating and long-term emotional effects, some children do not. Some children seem to cope and weather even the most difficult of circumstances. What makes them so resilient? This chapter examines the role of culture, socioeconomic status, religion, age, and gender in child maltreatment, and discusses the issue of resiliency in children.

DIVERSITY ISSUES IN CHILD MALTREATMENT

The United States is a melting pot of diverse people. There are many types of diversity in the United States. Families can be nuclear, with just the children and parents, or extended, consisting of parents, children, grandparents, aunts and uncles, and cousins. Many different races, cultures, religions, and ethnicities are represented in our country. How does diversity impact abuse and neglect?

Culture and Ethnicity

Culture affects to a large degree how people think, feel, and behave. Culture is the geographic location, values, beliefs, characteristics, language, rules, traditions, rituals, artifacts, and ideas that one group of people hold in common. A **microculture** is "a social group that shares distinctive traits, values, and behaviors that set it apart" from the larger culture (Cushner, McClelland, & Safford, 2006, p. 62). Microcultures include the elderly, teenagers, conservatives, the poor, and the wealthy. **Ethnicity** includes many elements of culture, but usually involves a group of people with commonalities over time and often who have a geographic commonality or heritage either currently or from ancestry. These people tend to share attributes that have developed and have remained stable over time. People are usually born into an ethnicity, rather than choosing one. Although physical characteristics can be a part of ethnicity, they do not have to be. Ethnic groups include Hispanic, Southern, and Jewish. *Race* is a term that is often used but often misunderstood. **Race** is the identification of a group based on perceived physical characteristics, which may or may not be accurate. For example, a person who is Hispanic may have dark skin and hair or may have a light complexion and be blonde. People can belong to more than one subculture and ethnicity. What impact do ethnicity, race, and culture have on child maltreatment?

The rates regarding race and ethnicity in relation to child maltreatment (see Figure 7.1) indicate that African Americans, American Indians or Alaskan Natives, and Pacific Islanders all have higher percentages of child maltreatment

— **Fast Fact** —
There is a discrepancy between population representation of some racial and ethnic groups and child maltreatment.

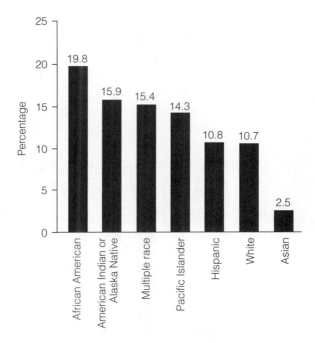

FIGURE 7.1

Race and ethnicity of victims, 2006

Source: Taken from *Child Maltreatment,* U.S. Department of Health and Human Services, 2008, p. 28. Rate per 1,000 children of the same race or ethnicity.

in relationship to their population than Hispanics, whites, and Asians (U.S. Department of Health and Human Services, 2007a). Why is there such a discrepancy between population representation of some racial and ethnic groups and child maltreatment? The answer is multidimensional. For example, race and ethnicity are often factors in poverty in a society where the predominant race holds power, and poverty is a risk factor for child maltreatment.

The definition of abuse and neglect may vary according to culture, microculture, or ethnicity (Singh & Clarke, 2006). The United States has its own culture, but within that culture there are limitless ethnic and microculture groupings, including Southern, African American, Hispanic, and Asian American groups. Additional groupings also exist within each of these, for example, small town versus city; and within each subgrouping are more microcultures, such as Jewish or Mormon and professional or laborer groups.

Research indicates correlations between some of the common cultural practices within groups and certain types of abuse and neglect. One example is found in Korean American families. Common cultural values for many Korean Americans (but not all) include an unquestioning obedience of children to family and authority, male domination within the family, and a cultural imperative for parents to teach and discipline their children. A common saying in Korean, "Sarang-Eei-Mae," means "the whip of love" and expresses the attitude of many. Several studies have noted a higher incidence of physical abuse in Korean families than in the general population (Chang, Rhee, & Weaver, 2006), which many feel is attributable to cultural attitudes.

Some commonalities and attitudes among ethnic groups can create happy and successful families, such as interest in children, importance of guidance, and emphasis on family involvement. But other commonalities may be at odds with the laws and attitudes of our society in regard to abuse and neglect. It is critical to remember that even if a child is from an ethnic group that promotes certain values, that does not mean the parents will be abusive or condone abusive behavior. Understanding attitudes of different ethnic groups can lead to greater understanding of general parental practices and decisions, and increase communication.

Often abuse occurs in immigrant populations because of misunderstandings about the practices in U.S. culture versus those in the culture they have left. Some children may be fed one meal a day because that was all the food available in the country the parents just left, and so the parents lack a concept of three meals a day. Holding an infant while riding in a car may seem more loving and humane than putting the child in a car seat, and it may have been common practice in the parents' previous country (DePanfilis, 2006). It is critical not only to learn about each child's ethnic background, but also to recognize that within each group differences exist.

Socioeconomic Status and Abuse

Adults from all socioeconomic levels abuse children; however, children living in poverty are 22 times more likely to suffer abuse than those who live with higher incomes (Children's Defense Fund [CDF], 2005). Neglect, in particular, is seen in greater numbers in lower socioeconomic levels. Many states differentiate between neglect that is the result of inability to provide food or shelter due to poverty and intentional neglect (DePanfilis, 2006). Several studies show that many families in poverty exhibit great resilience and that abuse factors in lower socioeconomic groups may be the result of a lack of family support, the family structure (single parents or other nonrelatives living in the home), and other variables (Herrenkohl & Herrenkohl, 2007; Weissman, Jogerst, & Dawson, 2003).

Sometimes child maltreatment in lower socioeconomic levels is a result of family stressors that create an environment where abuse and neglect is more likely, or an inability of parents to provide safe surroundings and adequate care due to poverty. The cause is not always clear. Maltreatment also can result from the same characteristics that have contributed to placing a parent in poverty, such as inability to delay gratification, few resources, and lack of relationship skills. Child maltreatment for families in poverty may be reported more often than that in other classes because of their increased involvement with public agencies (DePanfilis, 2006). Whatever the reasons, families in the lower socioeconomic strata benefit and show resilience when they have increased support and intervention (Juby & Rycraft, 2004).

Professionals can assist families in lower socioeconomic groups by:

- Providing information and access to community resources
- Being sensitive to families and their needs
- Examining biases and making sure that behavior the professional considers neglectful really is neglect, and not just a cultural interpretation of cleanliness and supervision

Religion and Child Maltreatment

Most Americans (81%) claim a religious affiliation, which is spread through more than 100 different religions (Kosmin, Mayer, & Keysar, 2001). Religion, for many, provides values, a sense of community, social and emotional support, and an explanation of roles and responsibilities. But some religious practices have led to controversy about what constitutes abuse and neglect. Some religious groups, for example, advocate the avoidance of medical care. Many states have religious exemption clauses within their child abuse and neglect laws for parents who deny medical care on the basis of religion. The American Academy of Pediatrics issued a policy statement in 1997 in which they called for the repeal of religious exemption statutes and stated that all children should have the right to medical care, but that physicians were to show "sensitivity and flexibility" in working with parents (Bioethics, 1997).

Religious communities can differ even within the same religion, giving different meaning to the roles of parent, husband, wife, woman, man, and child and to certain values and practices. Some religious groups teach democracy, shared love and roles, and peace. Others teach rigid role structures, often along age and gender lines, as well as patriarchal orders that allow for total domination by the male head of family (Hines & Morrison, 2005). There has been concern that this rigid structure may be a risk factor for child maltreatment. Many faiths have passages in their canonical laws that refer to disciplining children. Some speak of disciplining with love, while others imply that the use of the "rod," or physical punishment, is more appropriate. Some researchers see a strong correlation between corporal punishment and religious tradition, particularly with certain religious beliefs (Hamman, 2000; Xu, 2000).

The relationship between the degree of religiosity of a family and child physical abuse was examined in a survey which found that parents do distinguish between abuse and physical punishment. The survey also found that those with conservative religious affiliations are not more likely to abuse their children, and that risk of physical abuse was not related to how much a person believed or participated in a conservative faith (Dyslin & Thomsen, 2005). Religiosity, in and of itself, is not a risk factor for child maltreatment. In fact, many find that religion helps them to avoid the risk factors that increase the likelihood of child maltreatment. Individuals sometimes interpret religious dogma in their own way to support their illicit behavior.

Cultural Practices and Child Maltreatment

In discussing cultural and other influences on child maltreatment, we are not implying that being from a certain culture, religion, or socioeconomic group predisposes one toward abuse. Rather, it is a way to help professionals examine all aspects of children and their lives in order to better understand children and families. It is also a way to make professionals aware that some practices they may interpret as abuse may be something else. Recently, for example, a video on YouTube on the Internet demonstrated a toddler cussing and being verbally abusive while an adult's voice laughed, used the same language, and encouraged the behavior. Many people wrote comments on the website stating that they considered this child abuse, but others wrote that they found the exchange normal for the ghetto and did not consider it abusive.

Religion and Working with Families

1. When religious beliefs appear to be an important part of a child's life, try to find out more about these beliefs.
2. Do not assume that just because parents or caregivers have a certain religious belief, they are harsh or abusive in the guidance of their children.
3. When religion is given as a reason for harsh treatment of children, encourage the parents to seek out their religious leaders for further advice and counsel on this topic.
4. Never tell parents that their religious beliefs in spanking, discipline, and so on are incorrect. Rather, point out that by law certain types of physical punishment cannot be allowed, and provide information on alternative forms of discipline.

Minority populations are more likely to be economically disadvantaged, which increases the chances of child abuse and neglect. But prejudice and lack of cultural understanding on the part of teachers, doctors, police, caseworkers, and other professionals also may increase the number of reported cases in minority populations. Certain cultural practices and attitudes may contribute to increased abuse and neglect as defined by the larger culture in certain cultural groups. It is critical that teachers and other professionals who work with children and families understand cultural underpinnings. For example, a family from another culture may consider the role of the oldest child, even as young as five or six, as that of caregiver due to practices that are inherent in that culture, while the U.S. culture would probably consider a six-year-old child who is caring for younger siblings as being maltreated.

Certain cultural practices can seem inappropriate to a professional, but may not constitute child maltreatment. Asian American families, for example, are sometimes seen as coercive toward their children by some in our population, and they do generally use some physical punishment in the guidance of their children. Yet a large sample has indicated that this does not equal physical abuse in these families (Lau, Takeuchi, & Alegria, 2006).

Having a general knowledge of a culture, microculture, or ethnicity does not mean that a person understands an individual family. Many factors are at work in the attitudes, values, and practices of families. A family from Nigeria, for example, may have adopted the customs, practices, and attitudes common to those in the mountains of Georgia. Even within a generalized culture, differences exist; for instance, within Latino families, there are crucial differences between Guatemalan, Peruvian, and Puerto Rican families (DePanfilis, 2006). Singh and Clarke (2006) emphasized the care that must be taken when attributing certain characteristics to Irish families because significant differences exist due to religion, geographical location of the family, and the economic culture of the

---

Culture and Child Maltreatment: A Checklist

According to the U.S. Department of Health and Human Services, the following questions can help professionals make a culturally sensitive decision regarding a cultural practice and the issue of child maltreatment:

☐ Has the child been harmed or is there potential for harm?
☐ Is the child safe?
☐ What practice is in question?
☐ Is the practice legal?
☐ Does this practice interfere with meeting the child's basic needs?
  (DePanfilis, 2006)

family. Professionals must get to know each family with whom they work, and learning about their specific cultural practices can be helpful.

GENDER ISSUES IN CHILD MALTREATMENT

According to government statistics from reporting agencies, girls experience more abuse overall than boys; in 2005, of the children who were reported as abused, 50.7% were girls (USDHHS, 2007a). However, more boys (56%) than girls are dying as a result of child maltreatment. Numerous national and international studies have indicated that girls are two to three times more likely to be sexually abused (May-Chahal, 2006; Scher, Forde, McQuaid, & Stein, 2004).

Research supports variability in the type of abuse and gender. A study that surveyed 8,000 men and 8,000 women about their childhood experiences with abuse indicated that there were significantly more men than women who experienced violent behavior from adults who were parenting them (Thompson, Kingree, & Desai, 2004). A study that sampled almost 1,000 men and women about their childhood experiences found that of the men, 41.3% reported experiencing some form of abuse, while only 29.8% of the women reported abuse (Scher et al., 2004). These reports also indicated higher incidences of emotional abuse and neglect for women, and higher incidences of physical abuse and neglect for men.

What does this mean for professionals working with children? It may mean that professionals are not reporting abuse and neglect for boys as much as they are for girls. Often in a society where boys are expected to be "manly," they are given subtle cues not to speak out about emotions or pain; they may not report abusive behaviors, particularly if they are emotional in nature. The opening scenario of Justin is a good example. If Justin had been a girl, would his teacher, Amy, have been more likely to suspect a problem? Would she have told a female child to "be a big girl," or would she have comforted her and tried to find out why she cried about going home? Professionals who have rigid attitudes about how boys and girls should behave and what they should be able to handle may ignore signs of abuse in boys more readily than in girls.

As a professional, you should:

1. Examine your own attitudes about boys and girls. Is it okay for boys to cry? If they seem sad or unhappy, are you as comfortable talking about their feelings with them as you are with girls?

2. Do you encourage boys and girls equally to talk about their feelings, attitudes, and experiences?

Boys and girls need to be treated equally, and both need to learn about safety topics such as touching and strangers.

3. Do you teach boys as well as girls how to express emotions and how to tell someone if they are being mistreated?

4. Do you teach both girls and boys about good and bad touches and what to do if they are being touched inappropriately?

Perpetrators, Gender, and Abuse

More women (57.9%) than men abuse children, according to national statistics (USDHHS, 2008). However, in research reviews that have examined victimization on an international basis, the amount of physical violence perpetrated by men and women appears to be about equal (May-Chahal, 2006). Males are more likely than females to perpetrate sexual assault (May-Chahal, 2006); however, 25% of sexual abuse is committed by women (USDHHS, 2007a). Men culturally and physically are expected to dominate females in most societies, and females are sometimes seen as desiring or provoking sexual activity from a male even when they protest. In fact, in several studies that gave males and females scenarios in which a female child is sexually assaulted by a male adult, researchers found that men more than women tended to attribute some of the responsibility for the assault to the child (Graham, Rogers, & Davies, 2007). Males who are sexually assaulted are often too embarrassed to report the sexual abuse because of the cultural attitude that boys should be involved sexually and sexual behavior is part of manhood.

Women and men often have different reasoning and risk factors that make them more likely to commit abuse. For example, one study examined empathy in males and females in high-risk families. It indicated that men who are at high risk for child maltreatment have less ability to take a different perspective (such as the child's) when seeing behavior. This was not true with women who are at high risk for child maltreatment; however, high-risk women showed more personal distress than low-risk women or high-risk men (Perez-Albeniz & de Paul, 2004). When working with high-risk families it is important to be aware of personal distress in women and to assist men in "walking in the child's shoes" and seeing the child's perspective regarding behavior.

Professionals should be aware that abuse occurs from both males and females. But in working with families, it is important to recognize that males and females may have different views of what abuse is and may have different factors that affect whether or not they commit abuse.

AGES AND STAGES AND MALTREATMENT

Children of all ages are abused, but as pointed out in Chapter 2, younger children are more likely to be abused. They are more vulnerable, more dependent on adults, and less able to speak out when abuse is occurring. Children under the age of three are particularly vulnerable to neglect (USDHHS, 2008).

Children have basic needs that must be met, and often when they are not, development in other areas does not occur. It is not only the age of a child that makes him vulnerable but also the developmental stage. **Developmental stages** are identified by many theorists as specific time periods in a child's life when certain abilities are developed and specific types of development occur. Children at different ages and developmental stages interpret their world in different ways. According to Jean Piaget, an understanding of developmental stages is critical to the understanding of children's growth and development in all areas (Feldman, 2004). Violence, stress, and maltreatment can affect the behavior and long-term outcomes of children in different ways (Sternber, Lamb, Guterman, & Abbot, 2006). Each stage of development is impacted by child maltreatment, and the effects of child maltreatment are impacted by each stage of development. One example can be found in infancy. Infants have an age-specific crying pattern where the amount and intensity of crying increases and then peaks as the baby matures. There is an association between the peak period for the amount and intensity of crying in infants and shaken baby syndrome (Barr, Trent, & Cross, 2006). Developmental neglect is specific to the stages of a child's development (Miller-Perrin & Perrin, 2007). A child of two

— Fast Fact —
The most prevalent form of child abuse is neglect, and the highest percentage of neglected children are under three (USDHHS, 2008).

who is left alone while Mom runs to the store is neglected while a child of twelve is not. A child who is told to go find food in the kitchen is not neglected if the child is ten, but a one-year-old child is neglected in this situation, as she is unable to meet her physiological needs by following these instructions.

Children who are at different stages may exhibit certain behaviors and have needs that must be met appropriately in order for them to develop in healthy ways. Erik Erikson, a developmental psychologist, identified eight stages a child and adult go through and tasks they need to accomplish in order to function well socially (Erikson, 1963). Erikson's stages of **psychosocial development** are particularly important in understanding the effects of child maltreatment on children. Following are the childhood stages in Erickson's theory.

Trust versus Mistrust (0–1 year). This first stage involves a child's development of the ability to trust other people and develop healthy relationships. During this stage, a child learns to trust that his caregivers and environment will meet his needs. A child who has been neglected and abused during his first year may have difficulty forming attachments, having permanent relationships, and feeling hopeful. Some children who are neglected or abused during the first year become overly dependent and are afraid to explore and do new things.

Autonomy versus Shame and Doubt (1–3 years). During this stage, children learn to be independent and to think and act for themselves. A child who is abused and neglected may be told "no" and not allowed to do things for herself, or she may have to totally take care of herself and have too much independence. These situations can create in the child a sense of shame and doubt in her ability to do things, and may lead to the development of low self-esteem.

Initiative versus Guilt (3–6 years). Children at this stage want to try new things. They play and talk and learn about their world. A maltreated child may not have the freedom to learn new skills and try things, or may be told that he is not capable. Such a child feels guilty that he is not doing what he should or that he cannot do what other children do. The child may learn not to try things to avoid being punished or ridiculed, or may become reckless in his behavior.

Industry versus Inferiority (5–12 years). Children at this age begin to develop skills that they will use in the future, such as hobbies, work ethics, and academic abilities. The child who has been maltreated often does not have the ability to develop these skills or might be told she is not good enough and believe herself to be inferior. These children may give up, be unwilling to try new things, or act out to hide their feelings of inferiority.

Children experience growth physically, socially, and emotionally in a sequential set of steps. These steps are critical to the child's healthy development. Child maltreatment interferes with the healthy movement of a child from one developmental stage to another.

CHILDREN WITH SPECIAL NEEDS

In the vignette at the beginning of the chapter, Justin may or may not be a victim of abuse and neglect. But his disability puts him at greater risk. In fact, children with special needs are much more likely to suffer maltreatment than children without a disability (Hibbard & Desch, 2007). "The current national data indicates that compared to other children, children with disabilities are 1.6 times more likely to be physically abused; 2.2 times more likely to be sexually abused; 1.8 times more likely to be neglected; much more likely to be maltreated by a family member or someone they know; and, more likely to be abused if they have multiple disabilities versus one disability" (p. 1019).

It is often difficult to tell that children with special needs have been abused. The children may not be verbal and able to share. They may have a disability that masks the abuse, such as a condition that causes them to fall often. Such children may be verbal, but their particular disability might make their statements difficult to believe.

There are three generally recognized types of relationships between child maltreatment and special needs:

1. A disability can put a child at increased risk of maltreatment. A child who is ADHD and disruptive or aggressive may be at increased risk from a teacher who does not have the skills or understanding of how to handle such behavior appropriately, and parents may find that the discipline used with their other children does not work with the ADHD child. A child who does not understand the danger of going off with a strange person is at risk of being abducted.

2. A child's disability may have been caused by maltreatment. A child who is constantly in a state of fear and trauma can suffer brain changes that result in learning disabilities. Children who have suffered neglect may be smaller in stature, have delayed development, or experience coordination difficulties. A child who has been severely abused may have hearing or sight impairment, or brain damage.

3. The factors that increase a child's likelihood of having a disability also increase the likelihood of being maltreated. A child born to a heroin-addicted mother is likely to have disabilities and is at risk of being abused by her later because of her substance abuse (Sobsey, 2002). A child who is born to a mother living in severe poverty is likely to have disabilities related to the mother's inability to get proper nourishment during pregnancy, and is at greater risk of abuse or neglect if she is unable to provide for him physically later. A child who develops disabilities from living in a filthy home with vermin crawling around it is also at higher risk for abuse from her parents because of their inability to cope with daily life.

Parents and educators should observe children who have disabilities more carefully than other children for signs of abuse. There have been many reports of children with special needs being maltreated in educational and medical settings as well as at home (Ryan, Salenblatt, Schiappacasse, & Maly, 2001).

The Division for Early Childhood (DEC) of the Council for Exceptional Children (DEC, 2007) authored a position paper that is to be used along with a joint position paper written by the National Association for the Education of Young Children (NAEYC) and the National Association of Early Childhood Specialists in State Departments of Education (NAECS/SDE) in 2003. The DEC promotes policies and practices that encourage teachers, families, providers, and administrators to work collaboratively to include children with disabilities in all environments. All three of these national organizations are leaders in early childhood issues and set the standards for the child care industry, as well as the public and private school sectors. These national groups have collaborated and written recommendations to encourage the inclusion of all children, and they have provided codes of ethical conduct for professionals who work with children who have been maltreated.

Children with disabilities can be taught through role play and repetition safety measures such as what constitutes a good and bad touch (e.g., good touches are only on those areas not covered by your bathing suit), who are strangers and what to do if a stranger approaches, and how to tell someone if they experience abuse (Hughes, 2005). Such instruction must be done in a way that is developmentally appropriate for the physical and mental age of the child. Although a child's behavior does not cause abusive behavior by the perpetrator, certain factors can serve as triggers. Children with emotional disabilities seem to be at particular risk for maltreatment (Sobsey, 2002). A child with anger issues, bipolar disorder, or autism can have difficult behavior or mood swings that may serve as triggers for an adult who is herself not in control. The chronic care needed by a child with multiple physical disabilities may be exhausting to a mother who lacks family and other caregiver support and who feels angry and frustrated.

The needs of children with special needs may seem overwhelming, but research can help teachers make more informed decisions in working with

THEORY TO PRACTICE

1. Recognize a child first as a unique individual before considering the child's disability.
2. Be especially aware of bruises, changes in behavior, and other possible signs of abuse in children who cannot communicate.

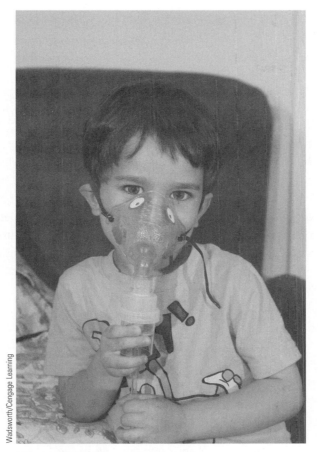

Wadsworth/Cengage Learning

When children have special needs, we must be even more aware and diligent in including and protecting them.

these children. Basic questions can be asked to identify whether a child has a disability. Identifying the type of disability and providing support to children and to the adults who care for them through educational resources, counseling, and family support services may protect such children from maltreatment. Children with special needs are at risk of maltreatment and do not always get the services they need. Professionals who work with children with special needs and child maltreatment need to be aware of these children's increased vulnerability.

RESILIENCY IN CHILDREN

Children who suffer maltreatment are at risk for many problems in the future. But, like Consuela in our opening case study, many children exhibit great resiliency and do well regardless of the depth of maltreatment. What is resiliency? **Resiliency** is the ability of a child to endure adversity, threat, or risk and to adapt positively in areas of functioning, even in the face of difficult circumstances (Friesen, 2007; Kim-Cohen, Moffitt, Caspi, & Taylor, 2004; Luthar, Cicchetti, & Becker, 2000). A resilient child can experience child maltreatment and still do well in life.

Resiliency research has indicated that children are usually resilient in one or more specific areas. For instance, they may be resilient academically, like Consuela, and do well in school despite their family situation (Kim-Cohen, Moffitt, Caspi, & Taylor, 2004). A child who is academically resilient receives continual positive feedback because of the resilience, and that positive feedback continues to protect and can expand his resilience into other areas. Resiliency is the result of an interplay of family, community, and personal characteristics and resources (Luthar, Cicchetti, & Becker, 2000). Figure 7.2 illustrates different factors that might contribute to resiliency of a child.

School and community supports found to promote resiliency include:

- Support of teachers, afterschool programs
- Extracurricular activities
- Religion and religious activities
- Nondelinquent peer groups
- Relationships with supportive adults such as coaches and other adults
- Physical and mental health community services
- Communities that experience less violence (Ward, Martin, Theron, & Distiller, 2007)

Family supports can include someone in the family (even extended family) the child can turn to for support and nurturing, high expectations, authoritative parenting, and warmth (Friesen, 2007). Internal characteristics that create resilience include intellectual ability, perserverance, internal locus of control (feeling that the child herself can be responsible for what happens in her life and that she is not controlled by luck or others), flexibility, resourcefulness, a sense of humor, and being an extrovert (Kim-Cohen, Moffitt, Caspi, & Taylor, 2004; Luthar, Cicchetti, & Becker, 2000).

Some researchers believe there may be a genetic contribution to a child's ability to adapt and be resilient that may protect some children in families where there is a higher genetic predisposition toward risk and maltreatment. Genes also may serve a protective function against a child's environment for some children. This might help explain why some maltreated children grow up to develop antisocial disorders while others do not (Cicchetti & Blender, 2004).

Resiliency influences are important to children who have been maltreated because resiliency allows them to withstand the traumas of their past and to

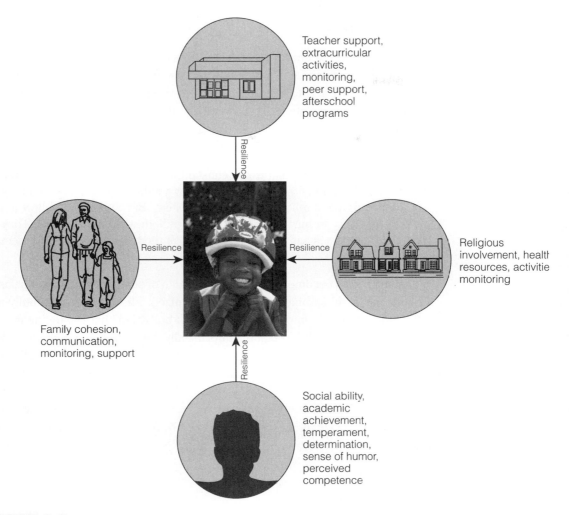

FIGURE 7.2

Factors that Contribute to Resiliency of a Child
A child's personal characteristics, family, community, school, and child care all send support to the child.

move beyond them. Children who have been traumatized can enhance their resiliency by:

- Developing hobbies or abilities, such as riding a bike, finishing puzzles, building and making things
- Being active in extracurricular activities
- Enrolling in afterschool programs
- Being encouraged in their academic work, or with younger children, being applauded and encouraged as they learn basic skills such as making the bed or taking out the trash
- Having mentors to support and encourage them

BULLYING

We have already defined bullying as "physical and/or verbal aggression, or withholding of friendship toward a child, usually by one or a group of other children, who are trying to gain power over the individual, take property from the individual or gain status in some way." Bullying can be frightening, and the trauma can last into adulthood. A college student from Africa recently related the story of her experiences as a young girl:

> There were two girls that would constantly threaten me. They would take my money and my food. When I told my mother and other adults they would laugh and tell me to stand up to them. But they would follow me home and try to hurt me if I did not give them what they wanted. They called me names and made me very sad all the time. I still think of them and feel fear.

Bullying has become a subject of hundreds of studies internationally, as the seriousness of this problem has been recognized. The prevalence of bullying is difficult to determine because the concept of bullying is hard to define in a way that is measurable. Children and adults usually define bullying in different ways (Naylor, Cowie, Cossin, Bettencourt, & Lemme, 2006). Yet, many studies have indicated that it is a problem that pervades every school and affects many children. Studies report high incidences of bullying among children and adolescents. A study looking at a representative sample of more than 15,000 students in the United States found that 29.9% reported either being bullied or bullying others (Nanse, Overpeck, Pilla, Ruan, Simons-Morton, & Scheidt, 2001).

Bullies

Bullying involves the use of power and requires that one child have some type of power, either physical or psychological, over another. Although most bullying is done by boys, girls commit almost as much bullying, but usually in the form of verbal or social aggression (Entenman, Murnen, & Hendricks, 2006).

A child who is physically more powerful will typically use physical threats and coercion and sometimes violence to achieve his goals. There is a relationship between some forms of bullying and later violence and delinquency or criminal behaviors (Smokowski & Kopasz, 2005). Researchers define four types of bullies (Beale, 2001), and here we add a fifth:

1. *Physical bullies,* usually boys, who often carry their violence into adulthood
2. *Verbal bullies,* who use words to shame, hurt, and attack
3. *Relational bullies,* who use a form of social bullying, which is often used by girls and includes social exclusion or isolation

4. *Reactive bullies,* who tend to taunt and coerce children to the point that they strike back

5. *School mobbing,* which is "ganging up on someone using the tactics of rumor, innuendo, discrediting, isolating, intimidating, and above all, making it look as if the targeted person were the guilty party or instigated the behavior" (Elliot, 2003, p. 5)

Bullies are often described as being insecure or having low self-esteem. Although that description may apply to some, research also shows that many bullies feel very secure about themselves. Bullies in middle school are often the less popular children, but in grade school they are often seen as the more popular ones. Common characteristics of bullies are that they use physical or verbal violence as a means to an end and they come from home environments that lack nurturance and support (Smokowski & Kopasz, 2005). In fact, school bullies commit crimes in adolescence and young adulthood at a rate four times higher than non-bullies (Parault, Davis, & Pellegrini, 2007).

Victims of Bullying

Children who experience bullying are victims. Bullying occurs for children of all ages, including preschoolers. Children who are bullied tend to be more compliant and submissive, quiet, cautious, smaller, and frailer than children

Relational bullying is often used by girls and can include social exclusion or isolation.

who bully (Smokowski & Kopasz, 2005). The damage from bullying to the victim can be physical, but even more devastating is the psychological toll that is taken. Victims of a bullying experience have many different problems. Health problems can include stomachaches, headaches, psychosomatic illnesses, anxiety, and depression (Fekkes, Pijpers, Fredriks, Vogels, & Verloove-Vanhorick, 2006). Children who are bullied often experience eating disorders, attention deficit disorder, chronic absenteeism, loneliness, isolation, nightmares, bruises, low self-esteem and lack of confidence, lower grades, cuts, torn clothing, and loss of property (Aluedse, 2006).

The effects on victims of bullying can last into adulthood and include problems in developing interpersonal relationships, sexual relationship problems, low self-esteem, low academic performance, and a tendency to overprotect their children, which may put their children at higher risk for being bullied themselves (Smokowski & Kopasz, 2005). Extreme responses to victimization have been recognized in some who have murdered or committed violent acts on those they perceive as having bullied them (Anderson et al., 2006). Children who are bullied may have characteristics that make them vulnerable to bullies, but the effects of bullying on these children can be lifelong and severe.

Ellen B. Senisi/Image Works

Bullying can have lifelong detrimental effects on children.

Cyber Bullying

A new form of bullying that has arisen is cyber bullying. **Cyber bullying** involves the use of technology, including the Internet (through e-mail, websites, blogs, and instant messaging), videos, and cell phones, to humiliate, tease, threaten, or in some way victimize (Hummell, 2007). While cyber bullying is predominantly seen in older children and adolescents, it also has occurred with children under eight. As more and more children are utilizing technological social networking at younger ages, cyber bullying becomes more of a possiblity. Even preschoolers are now accessing websites that allow them to interact with others. First- and second-graders are e-mailing other children during school to build literacy skills. These children continue these activities and other forms of online interaction at home.

Cyber bullying has become so prevalent that new terms have been developed to describe it. These terms have been identified by Willard (2007) as including:

Flaming: The use of vulgar and angry comments

Harassment: Messages sent continually that are mean, insulting, or threatening

Denigration: Sending information or posting comments that are rumors, gossip, or lies that can damage the victim's reputation

Impersonation: Pretending to be the victim for the purpose of damaging the victim's reputation or in some way using the person's identity for harmful purposes

Outing: Sharing the victim's secrets or personal information for the purpose of embarrassment or harm

Trickery: Tricking someone into sharing personal information and then sharing it with others electronically

Exclusion: Purposefully excluding someone from online groups, conversations, and social networking pages

Cyberstalking: Harassment and denigration repeatedly so that fear is created

Cyber bullying can have very harmful repercussions. Gossiping online, particularly on a social networking site such as MySpace, may allow hundreds or thousands to learn information about someone that may or may not be true. There have been many cases in elementary school of children creating websites where unkind and often untrue things were said about a child. Such sites are sometimes created while the children are at school, using school computers, and can be difficult to track and remove once posted. Victims often have been forced to leave school following harassment by other students who believed the things written on the site (Leishman, 2005).

Bullying: What Can Be Done?

Bullying can involve hitting, pushing, humiliation, name calling, social isolation from groups, stealing, teasing, manipulating friendship, exclusion, rumors, criticism, insults, theft of belongings, and physical attacks. It can be devastating not only to victims but also to those who victimize. Bullying is a form of maltreatment that often can be dealt with successfully within school programs, and many interventions have proven helpful in deterring it. Bullying can be curbed by teaching good communication skills, building empathy through teaching children to help and take on the perspective of others, and through immediate and firm intervention when it occurs.

SUMMARY

This chapter has dealt with the issues of gender, age, developmental stages, special needs, resilience, and bullying and their relationships to child maltreatment. Each issue requires special consideration as you work with children and families in order to protect children and resolve issues that relate to abuse and neglect. Children can build resilience so that they can overcome abusive experiences, but children who are young and those who have special needs are at particular risk and therefore need adults around them to be especially aware.

Application: When Working with Children

- Read storybooks that depict children in various places where they may be confronted by strangers, and include books dealing with abuse issues in the classroom library (e.g., stranger danger, friends, special needs, bullying, gender issues).
- Role-play situations that deal with bullying by a child, dealing with a child with a special need, what it means to be a friend. Talk about solutions to the role-playing situations with the students.
- Discuss "what do you do if" scenarios with children. Make the discussions age-appropriate.
- Avoid making toys gender-biased—allow boys to play with dolls and girls to play with trucks. Make sure you do not stereotype and expect certain behaviors from boys and not from girls, or vice versa.
- Find out more about the cultural practices of children in your classroom. Ask their parents to share with you and the class things from their culture.

Application: When Working with Families

- Provide all parents, and particularly those new to this country and those of lower socioeconomic status, with lists of agencies and organizations that can provide resources.
- Give parents of children with disabilities extra support and information on guidance and resources.
- At "Meet the Parents" night, discuss age-appropriate activities, behaviors, rules of the classroom, and documentation. Request that parents ask questions about their concerns.
- Provide information to parents on how to help their children deal with bullying and how to recognize bullying behaviors in their own children.
- At parent-teacher conferences, discuss milestones or ages and stages of children and the expectations of behavior at these times.

Projects/Activities

1. Observe a child with a disability and the adults who care for that child. How might the child's disability be difficult for adults to work with? Write a summary of your observations, and list five strategies for working with this child that could be used by the caregivers.

2. Develop a puppet show, video clip, or storybook on bullying and what a child can do if it happens. Review Erikson's stages of psychosocial development, and write strategies to help the child successfully complete her stage of development. Include your strategies in her portfolio.

3. Research the family practices of the culture of one child in the classroom. Write a report describing whether your research has provided you with more information and understanding about the child, and how it helps or does not help.

Questions to Consider

1. How do teachers address maltreatment issues with children from birth to age two? From ages two to five? From five to ten? From ten to twelve?

2. How do parents' behaviors affect their children's development?

3. Just because someone has a different culture, does it predispose that person toward child maltreatment?

4. What determines resiliency and a child's ability to overcome the effects of abuse?

5. Why do children bully, and at what age do we begin to see bullying?

6. How can educators, teachers, and families combat cyber bullying?

7. How do professionals differentiate between behavior caused because a child has special needs and behavior caused because a child has been maltreated?

Websites for More Information

For useful websites, visit www.cengage.com/education/hirschy

CHAPTER 8

Parents/Families and Child Maltreatment

WHAT YOU WILL LEARN

- The importance of parent-professional partnerships in preventing and treating abuse

- How to develop partnerships with parents

- How to help parents understand the issues around abuse and neglect

- Strategies for working with parents who are at-risk, abusive, angry

INTRODUCTION

Child abuse occurs for many reasons, as we have explored previously. Stress from a temporary situation or crisis, such as Joey's father experienced, can push a parent to lose control. Sometimes chronic conditions, such as lack of understanding of a child's development or social isolation, provide a background for abuse. Joey's father might have reacted differently if he had realized Joey was trying to get attention, and that children who are being ignored for long periods of time often prefer negative attention to no attention at all.

How can professionals such as teachers, administrators, child care providers, nurses, and caseworkers work more effectively with parents and families? It is critical that they first understand what makes families healthy, and then that they be able to handle crises and prevent abuse.

VIGNETTE

Joey, five, was brought by his parents to the pediatrician's office. The nurse asked about the reason for the visit. Joey's father began to cry and said, "I am so sorry. He was jumping on the sofa and yelling. All afternoon he had been getting into everything, and I had just had enough! I have been out of work for a long time, and I was on the phone with a possible employer. I couldn't even hear! I got off the phone and just lost it. I started spanking Joey, and I couldn't stop!" Joey's mother then lifted Joey's shirt to reveal dark bruises all over his back.

— Fast Fact —
Three-quarters (76%) of
parents of school-age children say it is a lot harder to
raise children today than it
was when they were grow-
ing up (Bostrom, 2003, p. 7).

"Research on problem families suggests that the absence of positive family processes can be as problematic for children as the presence of negative ones" (Moore, Chalk, Scarpa, & Vandivere, 2002, p. 2). Professionals who understand what makes families strong, who focus on the concept of family-centered care when dealing with an abused child, and who know how to form partnerships—even with abusive parents—find that they can better provide protection and treatment for young children. In this chapter, we recognize that children are influenced not just by parents, but also by siblings, stepparents, and others who may live in the home, and therefore we refer to working with parents and families.

UNDERSTANDING FAMILIES

Families come in all types and sizes. There is no one perfect type of family. Every family is influenced by the world around it. The culture, socioeconomic status, workplace of parents, laws, and the media all have a part in influencing how families function. Families function as part of a larger system. Many factors in a family can provide protection for children, such as parents nurturing children, having knowledge of how children grow and learn, and having family

Prevention of Child Abuse in Early Childhood Programs and the Responsibilities of Early Childhood Professionals to Prevent Child Abuse from NAEYC

The National Association for the Education of Young Children (NAEYC) has developed policies to promote close partnerships with families.

Ongoing program policies that strengthen partnerships with families can also help to minimize the likelihood of abuse in the program. . . . Close partnerships with families can also help to reduce the potential for child abuse by family members. Early childhood programs can provide information to parents and families regarding child development and effective strategies for responding to children's behavior. Teachers and caregivers should be knowledgeable about and alert to signs of family stress and provide support to families. Early childhood professionals can collaborate with state agencies, such as protective services, to promote understanding of child development, to support and empower families, and to advocate for children. Working with families in this way may help to break cycles of family violence and prevent children from becoming abusers themselves." (NAEYC, 1996) and community support (DePanfilis, 2006). The parent's work situation may provide protective factors, such as money for food and housing, but it can also provide risk factors, such as long work hours for parents and stress. Child abuse usually occurs within families. When it happens outside the home, the family must help the child cope and heal. Understanding family life is a critical component for professionals.

Characteristics of Healthy Families

What makes a healthy family? Much research has examined what factors in a family provide protection for children and strengthen families (Center for the Study, 2003; Covey, 1997; Moore, Chalk, Scarpa, & Vandivere, 2002; Stinnett & DeFrain, 1985; U.S. Department of Health and Human Services [USDHHS], 2007c). This research has shown many different characteristics of strong families. These characteristics can be divided into seven categories: (1) adult resilience; (2) involvement and supervision; (3) parent knowledge; (4) communication, appreciation, and guidance; (5) beliefs; (6) family affection, nurturance, and support; and (7) social support.

— **Fast Fact** —
Strong families know how to play together, which puts the family at ease and opens communication.

WORKING WITH FAMILIES

Professionals have a responsibility to protect children from abuse and to assist children who are abused in overcoming the emotional and physical aspects of abuse. Unless parental rights are terminated and the child is being adopted, this responsibility will necessitate working with the family. Even if rights are terminated, helping the child will still require working with adoptive or foster families to assist with the child's adjustment. Researchers focused on the medical field have recognized the critical importance of nurses, nurse practitioners, and doctors receiving training about working with families. It is critical that they provide parenting education and family support to prevent and treat child abuse (Chaney, 2000; Henry, Reiko, Shinjo, & Yoshikawa, 2003; Johnson, 2006). Social service workers and professionals who provide family support services also must form collaborative partnerships with all parents to

THEORY TO PRACTICE

1. Clearly define your expectations of family involvement.
2. Provide opportunities for all families to participate in the classroom by offering a variety of options.

Characteristics of Strong Families

1. **Adult Resilience.** This includes the positive mental health of the parents or caregivers, and their adaptability to crises, new situations, and differing personalities of children. Parental depression and substance abuse put children at risk for abuse (Berger, 2005). Parents who are emotionally healthy and free of addictions can support their children in positive ways.

2. **Involvement and Supervision.** Knowing where children are at all times, checking on children often, and being involved in the children's school, social, and home life all contribute to strengthening families. Families need to spend time together, play together, and eat together to be strong. Research has shown that teens who eat regular family meals with their parents do better in school and are less likely to be involved in drug and alcohol abuse (Court Appointed Special Advocates for Children [CASA], 2006). Parent involvement means parents spending time with children, and not involving them in too many organized sports and lessons that can create stress on the family. A lack of play in families also creates pressure and can put children at risk (Ginsberg, 2007).

3. **Parent Knowledge.** Knowing how children grow and develop, and what to expect at different ages and stages, helps parents and adult caregivers cope with stressful situations with children. Parenting knowledge requires study and practice. Yet most people's parenting knowledge comes from memories of what their parents did or observations of others. Few people can drive a car based on memory and observation.

4. **Communication, Appreciation, and Guidance.** Families where the different members spend time talking and showing appreciation for one another create protective factors from abuse and neglect. Strong families communicate both verbally and nonverbally in clear ways and ask for and give feedback about communication in the family. These families are more likely to use a variety of guidance strategies. They solve problems together as a family and share their feelings. Children are guided in the wise use of their time and are kept busy enough that they do not have time to get into trouble. Children who see and experience more aggression in their families tend to be more aggressive (Onyskiw, 2001).

5. **Beliefs.** Strong families have commitments to certain beliefs that the whole family supports. Many hold strong spiritual beliefs in a higher power. Others have strong values such as kindness and honesty and teach these to their children. They tend to find meaning behind difficulties in their life and maintain a positive outlook. They also have family traditions, often rooted in their culture, that they practice regularly.

6. **Family Affection, Nurturance, and Support.** Strong families believe in the importance of the family unit and work to support it. There are clear family roles and responsibilities. When roles must change, other family members problem-solve and help. Issues such as who does chores around the house, which spouse takes the children to school, and when homework is done and how it is supervised are worked out in a positive and defined way.

Children are nurtured and treated with affection, and attachment to parents and the family is encouraged and supported.

7. **Social Support.** Strong families have many resources. They create friendships and support with the people around them, and they have extended family that provides support. They are willing to use community resources when needed to help the family. They reach out when they have problems and accept assistance from others.

Ideas for Parents on Building Stronger Families

1. **Adult Resilience**
   - Take time for yourself. Do something that you enjoy doing. Read a book, take a walk, find joy in your life.
   - If you are feeling depressed, talk to someone or visit with your doctor.
   - When you feel overwhelmed by children, get help from a friend or family member, or pay for a babysitter.
   - If your family has a crisis, such as a financial one, talk about it together and problem-solve, without anger.

2. **Involvement and Supervision**
   - Have family mealtimes at least four times a week during which you all sit down with the TV off and keep the conversation pleasant. Ensure these times by looking at the calendar together.
   - Plan a weekly family time in which the family plays games, goes to the park, or takes walks. Try to keep the movies and TV off so that you can talk and visit. Allow each family member to take a turn at planning the time together. Plan a treat at the end!
   - Know where your children are, and insist that they call you regularly when they are away from home for long periods.

3. **Parent Knowledge**
   - Attend parenting classes. Check with teachers to find dates and times of classes in your community.
   - Read books about your children's ages or about topics that may concern you, such as potty training.
   - Talk to teachers and other parents about concerns with your children.

4. **Communication, Appreciation, and Guidance**
   - Listen to your children; don't always give advice.
   - Ask your children about their day; tell them about yours.
   - Tell your children daily that you love them
   - Have weekly family meetings to discuss problems and concerns in the family, and let the children contribute and help problem-solve.

(continued)

- Set some basic family rules, not too long, and post them. Allow all family members to contribute to the discussion. Use drawings for young children. Some examples for young children might be "walking feet" (for running in the house) or "quiet mouths" (for yelling).

5. **Beliefs**
   - Find a place of worship to attend as a family.
   - Talk about the things you value, such as honesty, and role-play with the children "What would you do if . . .?"
   - Read stories to children about famous people who made good choices and decisions.
   - Develop some family traditions. For instance, every Saturday you might make breakfast together, or each night you might read a story together before bedtime.

6. **Family Affection, Nurturance, and Support**
   - Spend time with your children talking and playing. Most children prefer positive time with parents to anything else!
   - Teach children to be polite to other family members and to show affection. Giving siblings a back rub or complimenting a brother or sister can go a long way toward creating good feelings in families.
   - Give lots of hugs and kisses.
   - Leave notes with hearts drawn on them on your children's pillows, or give them letters of appreciation.
   - Put a happy note in a lunchbox.
   - When your children tell you someone has hurt them or that they are afraid of someone, believe them and find out more.
   - Tell children often how much you appreciate them.
   - Praise and encourage children when they do well.

7. **Social Support**
   - Keep in contact with extended family, even if they live far away (use e-mail or the telephone).
   - Show your children family pictures.
   - Join organizations, churches, and clubs that provide you with people with common interests and concerns.
   - Get to know your neighbors—take them some cookies as a family, and introduce yourselves.
   - Find out about the kinds of community resources you have available for health needs, recreation, and so on.

effectively prevent and treat abuse (McCurdy & Daro, 2001; Sheppard, 2001; Turney & Tanner, 2001).

Educators, too, have responsibilities to meet parent needs and provide parent education and support. Education can take place only when children feel safe and are protected (Crosson-Tower, 2003). Teachers need to be aware of family situations to better provide support and education to a child. Often they need to provide parents with an understanding of how and why abuse and neglect can occur, and sometimes they must work with a family who is abusive. How can teachers and other professionals work most effectively with families? The concept of family-centered care has arisen from an ecological theory base to provide a better understanding and framework for family support.

Family-Centered Care and Services

Family-centered care is a term used in all professions that work with children and families (American Academy of Pediatrics [AAP], 2003; DePanfilis & Salus, 2003; Herman, Tucker, Ferdinand, Mirsu-Paun, Hasan, & Beato, 2007; Institute for Family Centered Care, 2007; National Child Care Information Center, 2007). The term is defined in the same general way in each profession. Family-centered care is providing services and care that focus not just on the child but also on the family and that empower the family to manage their own care. This concept recognizes that a child is best understood, treated, and educated in the context of the child's family.

Family-centered care provides professionals with the following set of principles:

1. Collaboration with families is key to working with the child. It is critical that families work together with professionals. Teachers need parents to work with children at home to teach them in order to provide the best education; doctors need parents to give children medications when they are sick to help them get well; caseworkers need parents to follow through with preventive measures to keep children safe. These professionals need the parents' efforts in order to do their own jobs. The family, in turn, needs the professionals to provide support. These partnerships must be cooperative and collaborative for the outcomes to be successful.

2. Each family has strengths that can be built upon. At-risk families and families that have been abusive still have some strengths that can allow them to be successful at supporting their children. The parents' knowledge of a child's fears, such as a fear of dogs, can be used by a teacher to support the child and help the parents feel that they do understand and can support their child. A caseworker can encourage a family that jokes a lot to develop positive ways to respond to a child's anger that will defuse the anger and keep the parents from becoming angry.

3. Parents or permanent caregivers are involved in decision making. If a child is having difficulty in school or child care, the parent and teacher problem-solve together and develop strategies they will both use to assist

the child. The doctor asks for the parents' opinions and listens when the parents explain that they will only be able to get the child to take medication once instead of twice a day. The caseworker presents the problems, such as lack of supervision for a child, and asks the parents for ideas on how the family can solve the problems, instead of telling them what should be done. Most of all, professionals listen to the parents.

4. Parents are provided with extra services that help their families. Many early childhood programs provide services such as meals that can be bought and taken home, shoe repair, dry cleaning, or a toy and book checkout program so that more time can be spent with the children than just time spent running errands. Other professionals provide child health screenings at shopping areas and health fairs, and opportunities to apply for food stamps at a place where children can receive immunizations. Coordination and integration of services is a critical element of family-centered practice that allows parents to receive the most services at the least cost of their time and resources.

5. Families are respected for their differences and uniqueness. A teacher may provide a translator at the parent-teacher conference, a nurse may give a parent a sheet with parenting tips in Spanish, or a caseworker may encourage a parent to share cultural guidance practices as strategies to show respect. Each family has its own unique family culture, but the family also may be part of several other cultural systems that all influence their child-rearing. A parent may be single, black, Jewish, and southern. Each one of these groups influences the parent. Professionals should ask if there are cultural traditions or ideas that the parent would like to share and should become familiar with pervasive cultural influences. For example, if a family has recently arrived from Cambodia, it would be appropriate to learn more about Cambodia's child-rearing practices.

6. Communication is critical. Sharing information with parents is a critical piece of assisting children. Communication is not one-way but is a shared system of listening, sharing, and then listening. Parents should not be told what they need to do, but rather asked for their opinions, listened to, and involved in the communication process.

Family-centered practice views the child as part of a system, and recognizes the importance of working with the system as an equal partner to effect change and promote protection. When professionals are family-centered in their approaches to children, the children receive better care and protection. Our beginning scenario with Joey is an example of where a family-centered health care provider could assist Joey's father in locating agencies that would help with employment, refer him to a parenting class, and encourage him to visit his own doctor for help with stress.

FORMING PARTNERSHIPS WITH PARENTS AND FAMILIES

How do you form such a partnership with parents? It can be hard. There are many barriers for both parents and professionals to creating partnerships. Partnerships should be collaborations, with parents and professionals as equal partners in working with the child. There is a difference between parent involvement, in which the professional provides activities or ideas for the parents, and parent participation, in which the parents are actively involved in decision making and working with the professional and the child (Herman et al., 2007). It is important that partnerships be based on mutual respect and the understanding that the professional, parents, family, and children all have rights and responsibilities in the partnership. Parents have the right to information about their child, but teachers also have the right to information about the child that may be impeding the child's learning ability. Parents have the right to communication from their health care provider, but the health care provider also has a right to learn from the parent about anything that may impact the provider's ability to treat the child.

Wadsworth/Cengage Learning

Good communication skills will ensure positive interactions with parents.

Parent Partnership Ideas for Teachers and Child Care Providers: Involving Families and Creating Partnerships

1. Invite family members to be a teacher's assistant or to plan get-togethers or meetings.
2. Establish a parent center where parents can go to find resources and share information.
3. Provide services such as dry cleaning, meals, or milk and bread.
4. Provide multi-age classrooms or opportunities for sibling visitation between classes.
5. Ask for assistance in putting on a fundraiser.
6. Ask a parent or family member to visit as a community helper or to discuss their occupation.
7. Ask family members to share their culture by teaching a song, making food, or sharing family traditions.
8. Request that parents cut and color classroom materials, repair equipment, or tutor.
9. Accommodate parents' work schedules when creating parent-involvement opportunities and setting up meetings.
10. Organize potluck breakfasts or family picnics, or ask parents to organize such activities for you.
11. Offer a parenting class, CPR class, or programs for parents, such as a talk by an expert on biting in a toddler class.
12. Visit homes or encourage a home visitor program for your school.
13. Set up a parent involvement team that meets to discuss how to involve parents.
14. Assign at-home projects for children that engage each child's family, such as a family interview about an adult's childhood, or a description of a parent's daily work.
15. Learn about the various ethnic, cultural, and socioeconomic backgrounds of the students and know how to communicate with diverse families.
16. Provide ideas on home-teaching techniques and educational games for parents of children who need extra help at home.
17. Develop a plan to promote teacher-parent partnerships at school.
18. Invite parents to serve in child care, school, or district committees and parent groups.
19. Ask parents to fill out a Family Information Form at the beginning of the school year.

Barriers to Partnerships

Caregivers, teachers, health care providers, caseworkers, and parents give many reasons for not forming effective partnerships. Teachers and other professionals working with families often feel that they are not respected, that there is not enough time to spend with each parent who has needs, or that they cannot speak the language of the parent and feel embarrassed when they try to

---

Parent Partnership Ideas for Medical and Family Support Personnel

- Ask or assist parents in filling out a Family Information Form.
- Have flexible hours when parents can contact you.
- Create a comfortable atmosphere for parents to wait.
- Provide multiple modes of contact, including e-mail, websites, and telephone.
- Listen to what parents say and ask questions.
- Speak to parent groups.
- Learn about the cultures of parents and families.
- Facilitate support and networking groups for parents.
- Provide information on community resources.
- Work with other agencies and programs to coordinate services for parents.
- Be willing to speak with other professionals on the parent's or child's behalf.

---

communicate. Parents often feel that they do not have enough time to talk to the teacher, that the school is overwhelming and they are intimidated, or that no one listens to them anyway. Cultural and language barriers often inhibit good communication, which can become a major barrier to forming partnerships. One strategy is to develop better communication skills. Another might be to have all parents fill out a Family Information Form (see Appendix I), and in it ask parents what they feel is a barrier for them in working with the professional. The Family Information Form can be translated into a variety of languages.

Professionals should examine the quality of each parent-professional partnership (Sheppard, 2001). Asking the following questions will provide effective evaluation. If the questions cannot be positively answered, a plan should be developed to improve the partnership.

1. Do the parents seem to communicate well with me? Are they unusually quiet? When I ask questions, do they respond? Do they ever ask me questions?

2. Do I involve the parents in decisions regarding their child? Do I ask for their input? When I offer ideas, do they just agree, or do they offer ideas of their own and discuss the ideas? Do I accept their ideas and incorporate them into plans?

3. Did I implement the plans we made together? Did the parents implement the ideas? Did I follow up to see if the plans were effective and change things if they were not?

4. Did I provide full information about the child and any decisions made? Did I feel the parent was providing full information to me?

EFFECTIVE COMMUNICATION WITH PARENTS

The most critical aspect of developing a good partnership is communication. Parents should receive both effective verbal and physical communication and written communication from professionals. Verbal and physical communication involves not just what is said, but also facial expressions, body stance, and even the way people hold their arms. Parents may say they agree with you and are willing to take their child every week for therapy, but their crossed arms, worried expressions, and turned-away bodies may indicate that there are problems and that they may not be as willing as they claim.

Communication is two-way, involving both speaking and listening. Effective speaking includes using a tone of voice that is clear, full of positive expression, and nonthreatening; using simple words that are not technical; and keeping your voice calm. Nonverbal language should include an open stance, where your arms are not crossed. Try not to put a person across a desk from you, as that can create a barrier. Sit at the side of your desk or facing the person in a chair.

Listening is often seen as a passive experience, but with such an approach you may find your mind wandering away from the conversation to thoughts about what you will do after work or the movie you saw the night before. Active listening is a technique that will help you to listen more carefully. When you listen actively, you will:

- Lean forward and act interested.
- Really listen and concentrate on the parent's words, instead of planning what you will say next.
- Meet the parent's eyes, but do not stare and do not continue eye contact if the person seems uncomfortable (note that some cultures consider eye contact rude).
- Assume an open posture with your arms and legs, and keep them relaxed and not crossed.
- Acknowledge what you hear often with short, simple sentences such as, "Uhmm, uh, uh. Oh, yes, I see."
- Rephrase what is said (e.g., "So you are saying . . .?") to ensure that you understand.

- Reflect feelings that you hear (e.g., "You seem to be very worried [sad, angry, etc.] about. . . ."

Another form of communication you will use is written communication. When you are writing to parents, be sure to consider the following:

- Use clear, simple language.
- Print your message on colored paper when possible, as it will be more likely to be read.
- Include a graphic, if appropriate—a picture often helps communication—but don't overdo this.
- Keep fonts simple and large enough to read easily.
- Translate messages into the parents' language.

There are many different forms of written communication that you can use. You can send notes to parents, write contracts with them, put up bulletin boards, and create simple sheets with parenting tips. Today most parents have access to video players, so you might want to put information on CDs or DVDs. Consider making a short video clip of yourself sharing information with parents!

Understanding Culture and Language

Communication may need to occur in a different way for some families of other cultures. Some aspects of active listening may be seen as intrusive or inappropriate in some cultural groups. Barrera, Coso, and Macpherson (2003) explain how to have positive conversations, understanding, and interactions with parents that can improve relationships with families regardless of culture. They refer to this method of communication as **skilled dialogue**.

Understanding of a family's culture results from both personal interactions and learning that others' behaviors make as much sense as your own. It is important to develop a new way of looking at others by adopting a mind-set that integrates diverse values, behaviors, and beliefs. Professionals can learn to communicate better with families by remembering the following principles.

THEORY TO PRACTICE

1. Remember the three Rs of communication: *respect, reciprocity,* and *responsiveness.*
2. Be aware of cultural diversity when speaking to families, including different meanings that might attach to body language and terminology.

1. ***Respect.*** Recognize the types of boundaries that family members may have that may differ from your own. Sometimes these may be physical, such as how close a person may stand to someone else. Boundaries also can be emotional, indicating which words or activities may be inappropriate or affectionate to different people, or they may be cognitive or spiritual. It is important to learn and honor the boundaries that other cultures promote. For example, some families may find making eye contact when talking to be very offensive, while others may expect it. Knowing cultural practices of the families you work with can allow you to demonstrate this respect.

2. ***Reciprocity.*** Balance power between the people in the conversation, and recognize that everyone has something of value to contribute. Make sure that even if you are in authority, such as at a teacher-parent conference, you give the parents power by asking for their opinions and making sure the conversation includes working together for the good of the child.

3. ***Responsiveness.*** Let go of preconceived ideas and judgments and allow room for flexibility in working with families. Just because a family is from a particular culture, do not automatically assume that they follow all of that culture's traditions. Recognize that when a parent chooses not to follow

Showing respect and being responsive to families from other cultures ensures a relationship where parents and children can feel safe.

Effective Communication Strategies

1. Listen to parents, rephrase their comments periodically, and reflect the feelings you perceive.
2. Use appropriate tone and body language to show you are concerned, interested, and calm.
3. Ask questions that indicate your interest.
4. Write down information for parents.
5. Periodically review information with parents, and have them repeat back what you have said.
6. Use clear, simple terminology.
7. Arrange for parents to have the support of other parents or a support group.
8. Schedule an appointment at least once or twice a year with parents.
9. During conflict, remain calm and be empathetic by putting yourself in the parents' place.

---

your recommendations or is resistant to working with you, there may be several reasons, and some may be very legitimate. If a parent is not sending a child to school appropriately clothed, it may mean a lack of clothing or lack of ability to wash clothing, or it may be the way the child was usually dressed in the country from which the family came. When you establish respect and reciprocity, and recognize that you may simply not understand, you can become responsive instead of being judgmental and build a relationship that will benefit you and the family.

Your ability to work with culturally diverse families will be enhanced when you:

- Learn to appreciate other beliefs and value systems.
- Stop making judgments of individuals and families based on biases and general ideas.
- Learn about the family's hopes, dreams, and plans for the future.
- Recognize differences between yourself and a family as complementary rather than contradictory.

Becoming aware of cultural diversity when interacting with parents and families is key to developing a successful relationship with the family and, therefore, with the child and to maximizing successful outcomes with the child.

PARENTS/FAMILIES AND FAMILY LIFE EDUCATION

A critical component of family-centered care is that parents and caregivers must have knowledge of good parenting practices and child development. **Parent education** is "programs, support services and resources offered to parents and caregivers that are designed to support them or increase their capacity and confidence in raising healthy children" (Pew Charitable Trust, 1996). *Family life education* provides families with information on various aspects of parenting and family life. While much of the previous research literature focused on parent education (Simpson, 1997), today there is an emphasis on family life education, which offers a broader perspective. According to the National Council on Family Relations (NCFR):

> Family life education includes knowledge about how families work; the inter-relationship of the family and society; human growth and development throughout the life span; both the physiological and psychological aspects of human sexuality; the impact of money and time management on daily life; the importance and value of education for parenting; the effects of policy and legislation on families; ethical considerations in professional conduct; and a solid understanding and knowledge of how to teach and/or develop curriculum for what are often sensitive and personal issues. (NCFR, 2007)

Parenting education and family life education are critical elements in the prevention of abuse and neglect and in the promotion of healthy families (Cooke, 2006; Hirschy, 2001; Hirschy & Jacobson, 2001). The National Council on Family Relations has recognized the importance of such education by developing a certification for family life educators, the Certified Family Life Educator, or CFLE.

Family life education is provided to parents in the form of books, pamphlets, newsletters, magazines, websites, television, videos, and more. There are hundreds of thousands of sources of information on parenting; however, parents need not only to receive information, but also to receive quality information based on appropriate standards of practice and from trained professionals (Cooke, 2006; Hirschy & Jacobson, 2001). Professionals should examine carefully the family life education forms that they provide to be sure that they convey what parents need and also what parents want. More information on how to implement family life education programs can be found in the next chapter.

DIFFICULT ISSUES WITH PARENTS

Many circumstances can make working with parents difficult. Parents who are identified as at-risk have special needs for support. Parents who are abusive need assistance, but may be hostile. Parents who are angry or uninvolved can create special challenges. How can you assist parents in these situations?

Working with At-Risk or Abusive Parents

Many circumstances create situations that put parents at risk for abusing or neglecting their children. In some families, the parents have already been identified as abusive. Often professionals are not aware of whether a family has been identified as abusive, but most of them can identify when a family seems to be at risk for abusive behavior. At-risk families may include those that have children with special needs, teen parents, parents who abuse substances, parents who are unemployed or families experiencing poverty, parents with physical or mental disabilities, and families in which there is a nonparent in the home.

When a family is seen to be at risk, a variety of supports should be provided. Parents who are teens can benefit from economic support, schools in which child care is provided onsite, older parents who provide mentoring and support, and from parenting education. Helping them identify babysitters and make plans for future schooling or training will prevent situations that can lead them toward abuse.

Stepparent situations and nonfamily members living in the home can create tension as different adults try to discipline children. Providing ideas on how to develop family rules and share household responsibilities can often keep situations from becoming volatile. When parents are in a crisis or in economic difficulty, professionals can provide community resources. If a child care provider is aware that a father has just lost his job, for example, she can let him know about programs that subsidize child care and medical needs for families. Families that have children with special needs can benefit from support groups with other parents, programs that provide respite care, and programs that help with medical needs. It is critical that professionals identify the basic needs of the family and then help them access resources for those needs they are unable to meet. Not all at-risk families will be willing to take advantage of these supports, but many will, and research shows that such supports reduce the incidence of abuse and neglect (Goldman & Salus, 2003).

The most effective method of assisting abusive and at-risk families is through the provision of integrated services, especially ones that are tailored to meet the individual needs of the parents and family (Marsh, Ryan, Choi, & Testa, 2005; Mertensmeyer & Fine, 2000). When professionals from many different agencies, including schools, social service agencies, and health care providers, meet as teams to provide support and services, there is the least likelihood of abuse and neglect (Goldman & Salus, 2003). At-risk families often do better when they are trained by therapists through coaching in how to interact with their children (Timmer, Urquiza, Zebell, & McGrath, 2005).

Dealing with Parents Whose Children Have Been Abused by Others. Children who have been abused by people outside of the family are very vulnerable. They often feel a sense of guilt, shame, and anger. Their behavior, academic achievement, and even friendships may be negatively impacted. Often they will react in anger to the person with whom they feel safest—the parent (Child Welfare Information Gateway, 1990). Children who have been abused often need to talk about their experiences. Parents can listen without judgment and reflect the child's feelings. "You are really angry that he did that" is one response to a child's comments. Therapy is usually an important component of helping the child get past the abuse. A mother whose child was sexually assaulted in a school bathroom found that by taking her son to a therapist, he not only expressed anger and fears and coped better but that she, the parent, did better as well. Children often re-experience the trauma as they enter new stages of development or as a family changes or crises develop. It is important to touch base with the child from time to time, and ask in a calm, subdued way if the child has thought about the abuse lately and if they have any concerns.

Dealing with Angry and Uninvolved Parents. Children in abusive and at-risk homes often have needs that require teachers and other professionals to meet with the parents. These parents can react to issues brought up about the child with indifference, frustration, fear, or anger. How can those emotions be dealt with in ways that do not put the professional at risk?

1. Identify what the parents' concerns are. Are the parents afraid that their child will be taken away? Are they frustrated because they cannot control their child's behavior? Do they seem angry that the teacher or professional is not teaching the child appropriately? Often when parents hear of a problem with their child, it becomes very personal. The parents feel that they are being accused of something, or that they are not taking care of their child properly. Some will withdraw and show even less concern about their child. Others will fight back and accuse the professional of causing problems. Decide why the parent is reacting this way, and then try to address it.

2. Use reflective and active listening, and remain calm. Listen to what the parent says, repeat or rephrase, and then name the emotions that are being expressed. "You are very upset because you think Johnny is not getting enough of my time." Use gestures and body language that indicate interest and willingness to work with the parents. Control your tone and pitch of voice so that it is low and neutral to convey calmness. Be aware of cultural differences in communication that may be important.

3. Diffuse the situation when parents are upset. Request that the child not be present. Tell the parents you will need to get your records to better discuss the situation, and give them about five minutes to calm down. If a parent is so angry that you feel threatened, do not meet with the parent alone. Ask a supervisor to join you, or tell the parent that the meeting must be postponed until things can be discussed more calmly.

4. Agree on ways to deal with the problem. Ask the parents what they would like you to do to help with the problem. Then ask them what they are willing to do. Write down what they are willing to do, and then set a date for getting it done.

5. Identify community resources if needed. Help the parents to find needed resources. Schools and agencies usually have a list of community resources that can help families. Local libraries and city and county websites also list resources that are available to help families.

6. Follow up with the parents. Check with the parents the next day and then a week later to see how they feel things went. Send home a summary of the meeting. Be sure to implement any steps that you said you would take.

A Word about Parents and Discipline

Many parents are unsure of how to effectively discipline their children. They often ask for advice from teachers, health care providers, and other professionals. Spanking is still used commonly in the United States, "with over 90% of parents of toddlers indicating that they have spanked their child at least once" (Grogan-Kaylor & Otis, 2007, p. 82). Parents use spanking for discipline for many reasons. Many parents are encouraged by family, culture, or religion to remember, "spare the rod and spoil the child." Yet there is great concern about the possibility of spanking and corporal punishment escalating to the point that abuse occurs (Walsh, 2002). Walsh found that parents are more likely to use spanking if they perceive that professionals recommend it. Therefore, professionals should be very clear that they do not endorse spanking. Parents often do not know how to use any other form of discipline. Schools can offer parenting classes, teachers can send out newsletters with articles on discipline strategies, health care providers can check out guidance videos to parents, and tip sheets on guidance strategies can be made available. Spanking and alternate forms of discipline will be addressed in more detail in the next chapter.

SUMMARY

Working with families and parents is critical to the healthy growth and development of children. All parents can learn to be more effective in their parenting. Teachers, health care providers, and social service professionals have a responsibility to learn methods of effectively communicating and teaching. Family-centered approaches to working with parents are based on a philosophy that involves the parents in decision making, as well as providing resources and service integration to meet their individual needs. Creating partnerships with parents is the key to providing the best possible outcomes for young children.

Application: When Working with Children

- Show interest and respect for children and their families.
- Ask children about fun things they do with their families.
- Encourage children to develop strong family relationships.
- Practice good communication skills by setting a good example and by teaching those skills.

Application: When Working with Families

- Provide families with information and training on children's ages and stages.
- Provide information and training on guidance and issues of concern to parents in rearing their children.
- Use multiple forms of communication with parents, including notes, e-mail, telephone calls, and other resources.
- Learn cultural practices in communication with parents of diverse cultures.

Projects/Activities

1. Interview three parents. Ask them what might keep them from forming a partnership with their child's doctor or teacher. What might help them to form such a partnership? What would they like their child's doctor or teacher to do more of to strengthen their partnership?

2. Role-play the following situations:
   a. A child has a horrible odor. His family has recently arrived in the United States, and the mother is at school for a conference. She speaks a little English, but not much.
   b. An angry parent confronts you about why his or her child is doing so poorly in class.
   c. You are a nurse speaking with a parent of a child with an infection that has not cleared up, and the parent says he or she keeps forgetting to give the child the medicine.
   d. A teen mother has come to your program to ask for child care at night so she can go out with her friends.
3. Develop a brochure for parents on discipline or child abuse.

Questions to Consider

1. What are the best forms of guidance and discipline for children?
2. How can I work more effectively with the parents of the children who are my responsibility?
3. How can I create more trust with the parents I know?

Websites for More Information

For useful websites, visit www.cengage.com/education/hirschy

CHAPTER 9

Prevention, Intervention, and Guidance: Families

WHAT YOU WILL LEARN

- The opinions and research on the use of corporal punishment as an effective guidance strategy

- What other guidance techniques work for families

- Effective methods of parent education

- What organizations provide services and resources for families

INTRODUCTION

What can parents do? They want what is best for their children. They want them to grow up to be good people. But how can that be best accomplished? The stress and anxiety of guiding young children is enormous. Guidance is such a difficult concept to master.

SPANKING

Spanking is a time-honored method of discipline in our society and around the world. **Corporal punishment** can be spanking, hitting, pinching, pulling an ear or nose, slapping, boxing ears, or anything else that is physical. But usually spanking refers to the use of a hand or an implement to hit a child, generally on the buttocks or legs, to change behavior. Parents who spank tend to be younger parents, mothers, and to have been spanked as children (Walsh, 2002). Parents who abuse their children tend to spank more often and more severely, which may indicate that spanking could be a trigger for abuse. Our case study is a good example of parents who, out of frustration, find themselves spanking more often and with more severity.

A review of existing research indicates that the practice of spanking is on the decrease, particularly with older children. Unfortunately, a large majority of parents still use spanking with toddlers (Straus, 2005), assuming that it is the best way to get them to change their behavior. Several studies have indicated that no matter what the discipline, including spanking, around 80% of toddlers will repeat misbehavior by the end of the day (Gershoff, 2002).

Children are not born understanding the rules of society and culture. They are developmentally incapable in the earliest years of absorbing and internalizing the values of our society unless they receive guidance from adults. The ultimate goal of guidance and discipline should be for children to internalize values and appropriate behavior and learn to eventually be self-disciplined. However, a meta-analysis of 88 studies indicated that while spanking and corporal punishment often leads to immediate compliance, it does not help children internalize the behavior and associated value (Gershoff, 2002). The studies overwhelmingly indicated a link between abuse and the use of corporal punishment. Corporal punishment is also linked to cognitive problems, aggression in children, later criminality, mental health problems, and abuse of children and spouses as adults (Barnett, Miller-Perin, & Perin, 2005).

Many people say, "I was spanked as a child, and so were most of the people I know, and we turned out fine." Although that is true for the majority of people, a significant minority exists for which that is not the case. How can you predict whether one particular child will be part of the majority or minority? If the goal is internalization of behavior, what does physical violence actually teach a child? It is critical that professionals speak out about spanking and other forms of corporal punishment and help parents learn other alternatives (Straus, 2005; Walsh, 2002).

Like the young couple in the scenario, many parents use spanking because they do not know what else to do. It is true that some researchers have not seen harmful effects of simple spanking in their research (Baumrind, Larzelere, & Cowan, 2002; Paolucci & Violato, 2004). But even Diana Baumrind, one of these researchers, has stated that they do not support spanking and believe there are better alternatives. As stated in an earlier chapter, the authors of this textbook believe that spanking has been correlated with enough questionable and harmful effects that it should be avoided.

DISCIPLINE ALTERNATIVES

There are other ways besides spanking to discipline children. We want children to grow up to be self-disciplined. The best way to meet that goal is appropriate guidance with children, rather than punishment. There are differences between guidance and punishment. Punishment typically:

- Does not allow children to make choices
- Is something done to the child by someone in authority
- Is increased if it does not work
- Is often used with humiliation, name-calling, or yelling
- Does not allow children opportunities to improve their behavior
- Causes children to become resentful, angry, and rebellious even if it does work

Guidance, however,

- Involves talking with children about behavior in a positive manner
- Presents alternatives to children
- Allows children choices
- Provides consequences that are related to the misbehavior
- Has children assume responsibility for their behavior and choices
- Redirects children in positive and appropriate ways

Guiding children effectively seems like an insurmountable task. The good news is that there is a lot of room for mistakes. Children are quite resilient and forgiving. The bad news is that it takes time to practice good guidance. But the time is worth the investment. If time is put into guiding them when children are very young, the benefits occur as soon as they begin to get older, and there are fewer discipline problems and increased internalization of values.

Parents often mistakenly feel that they must always be in control and demonstrate this to their children, that they have to be perfect parents, and that they need to have other adults' approval of their guidance techniques. However, parents can be flexible, and recognize that they will make mistakes and will not always be consistent. If they can develop a loving and nurturing relationship with their children, be as consistent as possible, and use positive guidance techniques, there will be positive outcomes.

The American Academy of Pediatrics (AAP) has recognized the benefits of good guidance techniques in this statement: "cultures with children with relatively few behavior problems have been characterized by clear role definitions, clear expectations for family constellations, and involvement of

THEORY TO PRACTICE

1. Use positive guidance techniques with children.
2. Redirect children from one activity to another when there is conflict.
3. Assist children in using their words by modeling for them.

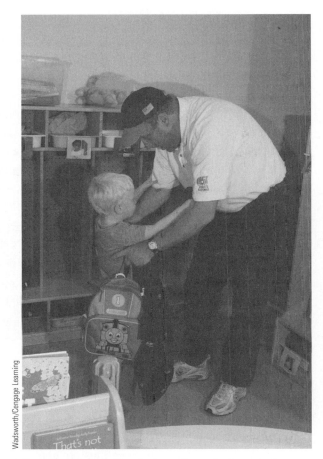

Parents who are firm but gentle and who set clear expectations for behavior find alternative discipline more effective than spanking.

other community members and child care and supervision" (AAP, 1998, p. 727). Parents can set clear rules and expectations and use community resources and family to assist in the stressful job of parenting.

Why Does Misbehavior Occur?

When misbehavior is occurring, it is important to try to identify why. Consider whether the misbehavior might be due to one of the following.

1. *The age or stage of development.* A two-year-old will look at you while you are saying "no" to his turning on the TV and continue doing the misbehavior. It is a normal response at a time when a child is developing independence. Such behavior might be handled by distracting the child. That behavior would be handled differently if the child were six, when the child

understands why and can communicate better. At six, a consequence such as losing TV privileges might be more appropriate.

2. *Lack of understanding.* Is the child frustrated or not understanding what is expected of her? Parents often assume a child knows what appropriate behavior is. However, children must learn what is appropriate—they are not born with that understanding. A child who does not close the door when she goes outside could live in a house where the doors are kept open. A child of three may not understand that a knife can hurt someone. A child of four often does not know what is socially appropriate to say in front of strangers and may relate an embarrassing fact about the family.

3. *The need for attention.* Children prefer negative attention to *no* attention. Sometimes children misbehave because they are being ignored. Many parents have noticed that the rate of a toddler's misbehavior will go up when the parents are on the telephone or watching their favorite TV show.

4. *Desire for control.* We all like to be in control of our lives. Children often misbehave in an effort to gain power and to control their lives and the lives of those around them. A lack of control or ability to reach a goal often results in frustration and leads to misbehavior.

5. *Anger.* Children often misbehave out of anger. This is usually a secondary emotion to something else—sadness, frustration, humiliation, powerlessness, or fear. It is helpful to figure out what is behind the anger.

6. *Changes in the child's life.* When something changes in a child's life, it causes the child to feel insecure, which can lead to anger, and to misbehavior. A child whose parents are getting a divorce will often begin to act out at school. A child who has moved to a new place may begin to show frustration and refuse to help around the house. A child whose pet dies may hit another child at school the next day. Parents need to consider whether there are any changes, such as moving, new people in the home, deaths, or other life changes, that may be affecting a child's behavior.

Ways to Guide Children

The boxed text entitled "How Do You Change Behavior?" lists some effective guidance techniques. Following are some other effective ways to guide children.

1. *Children can learn correct behavior through play with adults.* The simple process of playing with children can be an effective way to eliminate family stress, and prevent circumstances that lead to abuse. Playing with children more in the home instead of taking them to lessons and play dates can build communication, attachment, and positive feelings between parent and

child and lessen stress. In fact, the American Academy of Pediatrics strongly encourages parents to consider more play with their children (Ginsberg, 2007).

2. *Use choices liberally, as well as natural and logical consequences.* Rudolf Dreikurs (1991) proposed the use of natural and logical consequences. A natural consequence is one that will occur automatically as a result of behavior. If a child forgets his coat, he will be cold. If he touches a hot stove, he will get burned. Some natural consequences are dangerous, in which case it may be better to consider a logical consequence, one that would logically follow the behavior. A child who refuses to come when called for dinner because she is watching TV can lose her TV privileges. A child who does not pick up her toys can lose those toys for the rest of the day. Children can be given choices based on what is developmentally appropriate for them, for instance, a six-year-old may be told that he can either play blocks with his sister without arguing or choose to play with some other toy. Parents can let the children make the choice—but once it is made, the parents must consistently enforce it. Natural and logical consequences work best when parents discuss rules and expected behavior often with the children and, when possible, involve them in setting the rules and the consequences for breaking them.

Effective guidance can be very powerful. It lessens the stress and anxiety on parents and reduces the likelihood of abuse. It empowers children and teaches them self-discipline.

PARENT AND FAMILY LIFE EDUCATION

Why teach parents how to parent? Doesn't it come naturally? John and Ariana Cerillion, in the vignette at the beginning of this chapter, do not think so. They are very frustrated and do not know the right guidance techniques to use with their children. Our society requires people to take classes and tests before allowing them to have a license to drive a car or to cut hair, but anyone can become a parent. Good parenting is not instinctual. It comes only after much preparation.

Good parents read materials, attend classes, and talk to friends and family to get advice and ideas on child-rearing. Does it help? Several meta-analyses of studies have indicated that parent education has positive influences on parenting and is an effective means of reducing child abuse (Lundahl, Nimer, & Parsons, 2006; Lundahl, Risser, & Lovejoy, 2006; MacLeod & Nelson, 2000). The most effective parent education incoporates skill building, practice with feedback of skills, and modeling good parenting practices (Gershater-Molko, Lutzker, & Wesch, 2003).

How Do You Change Behavior?

- Think before you act. Discipline out of love and respect, not anger. Remember, if you impose a restriction out of anger, you may later regret it!
- Ask the child what happened, and then talk to him about his actions and why there is a problem.
- Be firm and gentle. Use a calm voice, and listen, but be consistent and stick to your decision. A soft voice really does turn away wrath.
- Teach a child what she is supposed to do; model the behavior you want, give examples, role-play, and get her to tell you what is appropriate.
- Give choices. Allow the child to choose between alternatives, but only between those that you are willing for him to choose. "Take out the trash or go to your room" may result in his going to his room and ignoring the trash!
- Redirect misbehavior. A young child who is beginning a tantrum or is throwing something can often be redirected to a different activity.
- Set up rules with your children, and consequences for not following them. Remember to include some rewards when they are followed, such as an outing with Mom or playing a game with Dad!
- Plan for mistakes, for both you and your child. Do not expect either one of you to be perfect. A sloppily made bed is still one that was made!
- Provide a quiet space for your child or for you to go so you have time to think about the behavior before you act on it or speak about it with your child.
- Take time to practice the behaviors periodically that you are expecting. Young children have very short memories and attention spans and often forget what is expected of them.
- Choose your battles. While consistency is critical, occasionally ignoring misbehavior, especially if it is done to get attention, may stop the behavior better than putting too much focus on it. For example, young children who use a bad word often find it rewarding to repeat it after a parent has a strong reaction to it—even when they have no idea what it means!

There are three types of parent education: individual, group, and self-directed (Lundahl, Risser, & Lovejoy, 2006). **Individual parent education** involves working one-on-one with the family. Home visitation programs fall into this category and have been very effective in building parenting skills and reducing abuse. Individual parent education has been the most effective form of parent education, particularly when combined with group parent education (Lundahl, Nimer, & Parsons, 2006). **Group parent education** usually occurs in a school or office setting in which parents gather for one or a series of classes aimed at improving parenting skills. Some of these programs target skill building, while others focus on attitude and more general perceptual skills, such as teaching children to be good citizens, or being a more positive parent. Many judges and Child Protective Service workers now routinely require group parent education for parents who abuse and neglect their children. **Self-directed parent education** occurs when a parent reads materials or watches audiovisual information on their own in an effort to improve their parenting.

Parent Education Programs

There has been increasing demand for parent educators who are trained in parent education and programs that utilize assessment and core knowledge as part of their ongoing development and presentation (DeBord & Matta, 2002). Parent educators are now found in schools, community settings, social service agencies, courts, and medical offices. A certification for family life educators, the Certified Family Life Educator, has been developed by the National Council on Family Relations. Some states and private organizations have also developed parenting certifications, and many states have developed professional organizations for parent educators, such as the Texas Association of Parent Educators (TAPE) and the North Carolina Parenting Education Network.

Individual Parent Education

Individual programs that work one-on-one with the family and use home visitation seem particularly effective in preventing abuse (Gershater-Molko, Lutzker, & Wesch, 2003). The programs often use people in the community who are trained as parent visitors. They go into the home and model guidance and play, as well as teach lessons and discuss with the parent different parenting

Designing Parent Education Programs

The following guidelines are helpful when designing parent education programs.

1. Identify what parents want and need. The survey in Appendix J will assist you.
2. Provide written materials that are short and easily read, with illustrations if possible.
3. Adapt programs and materials for the different cultures and languages of your parents.
4. Provide transportation, child care, and incentives (food, gift certificates) for parents to attend programs.
5. Involve parents in planning and design of programs.

Family life education is a critical component of child abuse and neglect prevention, but it can only be effective if parents are willing to utilize these resources.

Individual Parent Education

For direct, up-to-date links to these sites and more, please visit our website at www.cengage.com/ education/hirschy.

Parents as Teachers	Parents as Teachers (PAT) was founded in 1981 and implemented by the Missouri Board of Education. It was so successful that it was expanded to all the school districts in Missouri, and now can be found all over the United States and internationally. The basic components of PAT include a curriculum that is taught to parents in their homes by professionals who have attended a required five-day training (now also online), group meetings, provision of resources, and developmental screening of children. PAT professionals usually have at least a bachelor's degree.
HIPPY	The Home Instruction for Parents of Preschool Youngsters program helps parents learn how to teach their preschool children. HIPPY began in Israel in 1969 and has become very strong in the United States. Home visitors, usually community members, role-play the use of activity materials and packets with parents who then use them with their children. The program offers a combination of home visits by a trained community member and group meetings.
AVANCE	This nonprofit organization, established in 1973, works with Latino families on aspects of child development, nutrition, literacy, and brain development. (The name is a Spanish word meaning "to progress" or "to advance.") This nine-month program supports parents of children who are newborn to 3 years old. AVANCE provides home visitation, and parent education classes for parents while children attend educational programs.
Even Start	Even Start Family Literacy Programs promote partnerships between parents and professionals to assist in the development of literacy for children who are newborn to 7 years old. The programs integrate services for early childhood, adult literacy, and adult education and provide parent education. There are programs in all 50 states that are funded by the federal government. A national organization to support local Even Start programs provides professional support and a listing of programs.
Visiting Nurse Associations	Visiting Nurse Associations (VNAs) began in 1983 as nonprofit organizations that support community-based home health care. They advocate for best health practices for families by being involved on community, state, and national levels.
Healthy Families America	Healthy Families America was developed by Prevent Child Abuse America and Ronald McDonald Charities to prevent child abuse by providing home visitation and services to parents of newborns. The services, which often continue for three to five years, include home visits, parenting information, and health services. The programs are located in more than 450 communities.

techniques. Some well-known programs include those shown in the table entitled "Individual Parent Education."

Group Parent Education

Group parent education involves bringing together two or more parents in a teaching setting. One or two people lead the group and provide information and

Group Parent Education Programs

For direct, up-to-date links to these sites and more, please visit our website at www.cengage.com/education/hirschy.

STEP	Based on the work of Alfred Adler and Rudolf Dreikurs, STEP is a parenting program using books and videos to discuss the reasons for misbehavior and the use of consequences. Leader guides and workshops are available, but training is not required to lead these programs. STEP offers a series of programs targeting different ages of children.
Nurturing Program	This program was specifically developed for the prevention and treatment of child abuse. It uses video, parent materials, and trainer guides for many different audiences, including several ethnicities, teen parents, military families, and other targeted groups. It can be used in group, individual, and self-directed parent education. The program is developed to be taught with both the parents and the children. Assessment and evaluation tools are provided. Training is offered but not required. The program materials can be purchased separately or together.
Practical Parent Education	Practical Parent Education has a unique approach by requiring an organization or parent educator to subscribe to the program and attend a training of two and a half days to receive initial materials. They offer a variety of parenting education, including programs for parents who are incarcerated, divorced, or dealing with ADHD. Materials for additional programs can be bought after initial subscription.
Ready for Life	Parenting programs developed by KERA Public Television provide parenting workbooks, trainer guides, and children's materials as well as a website with video clips, resources, and parenting programs on temperament, attachment, literacy, and nutrition and fitness. Training is not required to receive the materials. Some materials have a small cost, but the online resources are free.
Love and Logic	Love and Logic is a parenting and teacher program that focuses on teaching communication and guidance skills using consequences. No training is required to buy the materials.
Active Parenting	Founded in 1980, this was the first video-based program for parent education. It offers a variety of programs, including some on self-esteem and parenting teens. No training is required to obtain the materials.
Parent Effectiveness Training	One of the earliest parenting programs, P.E.T. was founded in 1962. It was the first program to discuss active listening and the use of I-messages. The program can be used in group or self-directed parent education and offers video, workbooks, and other materials.
Without Spanking or Spoiling	This is a popular parenting program focusing on guidance and discipline based on a book by the same name. A leader's guide is available.
Parents Anonymous	PA is a self-help organization founded in 1969 that offers parenting programs for those who need family support. The primary goal is the prevention and treatment of abuse and neglect. The weekly sessions are led by parents and professionals together. There is no cost, and the program is supported by government and private resources. The program provides sessions for parents and children. Chapters are available in all states and internationally. Anyone can start a group by contacting the local network and receiving their free training.

instruction. Most group education is done by parent educators, social workers, counselors, ministers, and teachers. However, some group meetings are conducted by parents who create a sharing support system. While most group parent education has specific goals and is organized around a specific topic, some programs allow parents to decide on topics and allow time for discussion. Most group parent education uses curricula that have been designed for the particular topic and audience. Group parent education may be limited to a one-time, one-hour session, or may be several weeks or even months in length.

Many parenting programs have been developed that offer curricula and materials. Some are research-based while others are not. When choosing a parent education curriculum, it is wise to ask:

- Is it research-based?
- Has it been adapted to meet the needs of specific audiences, for instance, teen parents?
- Are there trainer materials? Videos? PowerPoint presentations? Activities or workbooks for parents?
- Are the parenting materials easy to read and understand?
- How expensive is the program?
- Can it be easily adapted to meet differing needs for length and environment?

One excellent resource to better understand how to choose a good-quality parent education curriculum is the National Extension Parenting Education Model Framework developed by the National Extension Service. The model, which is available online, provides information on what constitutes appropriate parent education and how to develop it. For a direct, up-to-date link to this site and more, please visit our website at www.cengage.com/education/hirschy.

Self-Directed Parent Education

Self-directed parent education is parent education that parents can access, review, and learn on their own. There are videos, books, magazines, radio and television shows, websites and other resources that provide tons of information on parenting. There are so many different forms of individual parent education that it can be overwhelming, and parents often find contradictory information. Professionals should carefully consider what parent education materials they recommend to parents. Parents should carefully consider the following before choosing the information on which they rely.

1. Does it sound appropriate for the age and stage of the child?
2. Is it rigid, teaching only one way to do things?
3. Does it take into account the individual needs of the child?

THEORY TO PRACTICE

1. Be familiar with the types of parenting programs in your area.
2. Keep a resource list available for parents.

4. Is the information research-based?
5. Does it come from a reputable organization?
6. Is it simple to read and understand?

Determining Appropriate Parent Education

Parent education in all its forms is invaluable in the prevention of child abuse. How do you decide what is the best type of parent education and what programs should be offered? First, perform a needs assessment of your audience. A sample is included online. Determine what the parents you are working with want to know—that will increase the likelihood of a successful program. Second, ask what the preferred delivery method is. Would they prefer a parenting class, several classes, videos to take home, or materials to read? Would they prefer classes at a school or church? How long would they like the course to be? Do they want to buy materials or would they prefer to download them from the Internet? Planning is critical to successful parent education. The family in the vignette at the beginning of this chapter, for instance, might benefit most from a group program where the parents can socialize with other young parents. But they would also need child care services, and the program would need to be at night after work.

Also remember that parents of other cultures may have some hesitation about being a part of parent education. They may not speak English, or may understand it only in a limited way, and may be concerned about being embarrassed. They may have cultural traditions that are different from the skills discussed in a parenting program. It is critical to be empathetic to possible needs and concerns of diverse parents. Translators may be provided, and some things may need to be reworded to make them more appropriate to the culture.

ORGANIZATIONS THAT WORK WITH ABUSE AND NEGLECT

Many organizations work to help parents find alternatives to child abuse, and many of these are oriented toward **global prevention**. The focus is on funding and services to prevent child abuse on a broader scope. Some programs are concerned with **primary prevention**, working directly with parents who are at risk for abuse. Parents Anonymous, which was mentioned as an example of group parent education, offers a variety of services and support for parents at risk for abuse and neglect. Others have a more **secondary prevention** strategy, providing resources and support to all families with child abuse prevention as a secondary goal. Many group parenting programs fall into this category.

Conducting a Needs Assessment

Plan ahead. You may think the parents in your program need training in literacy skills, while they are actually more worried about toilet training. Providing the training they want first will make the programs more effective, as the parents will feel you are responsive to *their* needs. Use the following checklist:

- Develop a questionnaire. It can be a yes-or-no, Likert scale, or open-ended questionnaire. Find out the type of program the parents want, what services (such as transportation or child care) they will need to be able to attend, and when and where they would like the program.
- Get parents to fill out the questionnaire. It is best to have parents fill it out while they are with you. You will get the most information that way. If you send it home, put it in a take-home folder and give the next day as the due date. Some programs offer incentives, such as coupons or entering names in a drawing, for return of the questionnaire.
- Do a formal tally of responses, and create a table to show the number of responses for each question. This can be helpful not only now, but also later when you apply for funding or fill out reports when the program is over.
- Develop your program based on the responses, making sure you meet *their* needs, and not just what you think are their needs. Such programs are the most effective ones!

Global Prevention

Global prevention programs are international, national, or state organizations that fund or provide resources for local programs, not direct services. One example of a global prevention program is the Children's Trust Funds (CTF), a fund established by legislation in each state. The CTF began due to the efforts of Dr. Ray E. Helfer, who envisioned a fund in each state set aside for the prevention of abuse and neglect. The first trust fund was established in 1980 in Kansas, and soon all 50 states had passed legislation setting aside money. Most of the funding comes from licenses, such as marriage licenses. Other funding comes in the form of corporate contributions and taxes on certain items (CTF, 2005). According to the website of the National Alliance of Children's Trust and Prevention Funds, $100 million is given yearly for prevention programs with services to more than 2 million children. The funding is used to develop parenting programs, community outreach, resources, and materials aimed at the prevention of abuse and neglect. Many private foundations, such as the National Exchange Club Foundation and the Annie E. Casey Foundation, also have abuse prevention as the only area, or one of the major areas, that they fund.

Primary Prevention

Primary prevention programs are usually local in nature. They may be developed from a national pilot or model program, but they are administered locally with a plan to prevent abuse and neglect by direct services to families. Child Protective Services in each state performs this function, but many other programs—such as shelters, food and shelter programs, individual and group parent education programs, and Head Start and other child care programs—state the prevention of abuse and neglect as their main goal, or one of their major goals. Many churches also offer primary prevention programs through counseling, parent education, and support services.

Secondary Prevention

Secondary prevention programs are those that benefit families in more general ways. They do not have the prevention of abuse and neglect as one of their main goals, but their services assist families in that process. One example is the Parent Teacher Association (PTA). The PTA was founded in 1897 to promote not only education but also the general welfare of children (PTA, 2007). The PTA is a national organization with local affiliates in many schools across the United States. Although most chapters are in schools, some communities form their own PTA programs. The PTA provides advocacy on legislative issues that affect children, local support for schools through local funding and volunteering in schools, and parent education materials and resources.

Another secondary prevention program is the USDA Cooperative State Research, Education, and Extension Service. The Extension Service has as one of its goals the welfare of children and families. They fund local programs for children and parenting programs, and provide other resources to assist families. Most counties in the United States have Extension Service Offices that offer free or low-cost parent education, and other services for the well-being of families.

Many excellent programs provide services to families, including county health departments, local ministries, schools, community service organizations, shelters, and others. Each of these plays a critical role in the prevention of abuse and neglect by providing support and resources to all families.

SUMMARY

Information on a variety of parenting issues has been discussed in this chapter. Parenting skills involve the roles and responsibilities expected by society. In every community, there are families who are potentially abusive or neglectful. All families need to learn basic skills and need information about the development of children, developing relationships and communicating with children, how to nurture and show love to children, and how to guide them appropriately. Parent education programs and materials can provide such assistance to high-risk as well as all other parents. A communitywide commitment must be made to these programs in order to make a significant impact on the problem of abuse and neglect, and ensure the safety of children.

Application: When Working with Children

- When working with children, encourage them to communicate about the activities that go on at home without judging the family.
- When an incident takes place in the classroom, assist children in developing skills to work out the problem and to find a solution. Encourage children to "use their words" with one another. Allow children to set the "rules of the classroom" by discussing them, writing them down, and posting them in the room.

Application: When Working with Families

- Conduct parent-teacher conferences, emphasizing the positive aspects of the child, and ask questions about what goes on at home.
- Conduct a parent survey to assist you in getting to know the parents and families, including their expectations for their children and for you as the teacher, and let them know what you expect of the parents in your classroom.
- Provide parents with articles and information on alternatives to spanking. Ask parents what kind of parenting information they want and need.

Projects/Activities

1. Research a parenting organization that assists parents in learning how to work positively with their children. Present this information by way of a PowerPoint presentation with important highlights of the program you chose.

2. Conduct a debate on the pros and cons of spanking children. Set up a mock courtroom in your classroom and allow students time to research the issue of spanking. Divide students into three groups: for spanking, against spanking, and judge and jury.

3. Invite a guest speaker from a community program, agency, or organization to come to the classroom and share information with the students about how the community can help to publicize the program.

4. Students pair up as couples and care for an egg or a sack of flour. The egg or flour represents their baby, who must be given proper care. They must carry it with them at all times or get babysitters, write down feeding times, and describe how they play and interact with the baby. Provide consequences for those who do not take appropriate care of or damage their egg or flour. Role-play parent-teacher conferences, incidents between children on the playground or in the classroom, and telephone conversations to parents about those incidents.

Questions to Consider

1. What are some prevention methods that can be used to assist parents in parenting their children?

2. What are some ways that families can be involved in prevention?

3. Why are some parents hesitant to become involved with parenting programs?

4. How can professionals become involved in prevention efforts?

5. What if parents do not think their treatment of their child is a problem?

6. What may be some of the cultural challenges for parents in parenting education programs?

Websites for More Information

For useful websites, visit www.cengage.com/education/hirschy

CHAPTER **10**

Teacher Styles/ Ethics and Child Maltreatment

Ellen is a teacher of four-year-olds in a child care program. She and a co-teacher, Mary, teach a group of 20 children. Ellen has been a teacher for 8 years. This morning Joey came in crying because his family was running late and he didn't get to finish his cereal. His mother dropped him off quickly and left. Ellen, from across the room, yelled, "Hang up your bag and stop that crying or I'm putting you in time out!" Joey sat down on the floor and began to cry louder. Ellen stomped over to him, angrily grabbed his arm, yanked him up, and said, "I said, hang up your bag. You never do what you're told. Everyone else comes in okay. What's wrong with you?" Joey crumpled to the floor again, and Ellen walked away, saying to all the other children, "Look at Joey. Isn't he a big baby?" Mary, a new co-teacher, observed all of this quietly.

WHAT YOU WILL LEARN

- Teacher styles and stages
- The importance of communication skills and relationships
- Relationship building
- Cultural issues in the classroom
- Temperament and maltreated children in the classroom
- Teachers and emotional abuse
- Teachers and physical and sexual abuse
- Teacher roles and responsibilities
- Teachers and ethics

INTRODUCTION

Most teachers recognize their responsibility to help children avoid abuse and neglect, to work with children who have been maltreated, and to avoid abusing children themselves. Yet most teachers do not report abuse and neglect, primarily because they do not feel adequately trained to recognize symptoms (Kenny, 2001). Teachers of young children are often unsure of how to help the child who has been maltreated, and many times they are unsure of how to deal with difficult children's behavior. These teachers tend to be understaffed, undertrained, and underpaid. Such factors can lead a teacher to resort to inappropriate behaviors in the classroom, which can lead to abuse or neglect of some children. They also limit a teacher's ability to help a child in the classroom who has been maltreated.

Most children (60–70%) are in some form of early childhood program (Committee on Early Childhood, Adoption, and Dependent Care, 2005). According to the Department of Labor, child care teachers will earn a median income of under $17,000 a year. Preschool teachers with degrees who teach in public and private schools may earn between $23,000 and $36,000, with most falling in the lower categories. While public school early childhood programs require a bachelor's degree, most private child care and private programs do not. In fact, in most states child care workers are required to have only a GED or high school diploma, or even less. Preservice requirements for teaching may be as little as 10 hours or less of training, and most of that is in the procedures of the center. Yet, these teachers often are with the children more of their waking hours than the parents. Long hours are also a common hallmark of teaching young children. The turnover rate of child care providers is more than 30% according to federal statistics. The National Center on Educational Statistics reports that 20–30% of public school teachers leave in the first year, and as many as one-half leave during the first five years.

Why are low salaries and high turnover rates critical to child maltreatment? Children who have been maltreated need consistency in their lives. Maltreated children also need teachers who have been trained in working with behavioral issues and learning barriers. Teachers who are untrained and underpaid and who are unhappy in their work will not only be less likely to provide the quality environment and guidance that a child needs, but also will exhibit higher levels of stress and fewer coping skills, which could put some of them at risk to become perpetrators of abuse.

— **Fast Fact** —
Teachers who use positive guidance and empathy in the classroom have fewer behavioral problems.

TEACHER DEVELOPMENT AND CHILD ABUSE AND NEGLECT

Educators play a vital role in the prevention of abuse as well as the identification of its victims. Because schools and child care are in the business of nurturing and teaching children, it is important to recognize how teachers develop in their profession. What kind of training have they received? Is all training equal? Do all teachers understand, observe, and have the same knowledge base of working with children, and particularly, with children who are maltreated? *What factors contribute to their professional growth and abilities to work with children?*

Most teachers want nothing but the best for their students. These teachers are driven by the heart and are not afraid to accommodate the needs of each and every student (Wolk, 2002). They wish to foster an environment in which every child feels valued and motivated to learn. High expectations and positive interactions are the focus of these teacher's thoughts. Unfortunately, not all educators have the same goals. Some lose sight of what brought them to the field in the first place. These teachers are negative in their interactions with students and make them feel dissatisfied. They show no concern for how students view the teacher's behavior or their classroom.

It is beneficial for teachers to discover how children view their classroom environment in an effort to better motivate them to learn. As much as we want to believe that teacher interactions are positive, motivating, and respectful, teacher displays of frustration, anger, and disrespect do exist in the classroom (Tschannen-Moran, Woolfolk Hoy, & Hoy, 1998). The first time a teacher enters the classroom, children have ideas about the teacher based on what they have experienced and what they have been told. The image children have is then altered and fine-tuned by what the students perceive during the following days (Neill, 1991). A progressive, cumulative process leads to a more stable perception of the relationship between teacher and children.

Research on teacher behavior from an interpersonal perspective has shown that the perceptions a class has of its teacher are strongly related to the children's learning outcomes (Brok, Brekelmans, & Wubbels, 2004). These perceptions influence the interactions and climate within that specific class.

Teacher Behavior

A significant amount of behavioral research has consistently proven that a teacher's approval or disapproval is a strong influence on children (Beamen, 2000). Teachers who are positive use praise and empathy in the classroom. The teacher's facial expressions and body language strongly influence children's ability to learn and feel comfortable in the classroom (Glaser, 2001). Praise and encouragement can often motivate children to learn when used appropriately, and children prefer and feel safe in a classroom where they feel appreciated and nurtured (Burnett, 2002).

Unfortunately, many teachers use negative guidance. Extreme and excessive negative guidance techniques that include reprimanding and using disapproving remarks can be abusive and can create additional trauma for children who have been maltreated. **Reprimanding** is verbal or nonverbal behaviors toward a child that are hostile or negative and critical (Beamen, 2000). Children who have been maltreated may fight back or may dissociate and retreat in these situations. These teacher behaviors rarely lead to improved behavior in children. Glaser (2001) points out that reprimanding diminishes self-confidence, and emphasizes that it is inappropriate teacher behavior.

Nevertheless, teachers, especially inexperienced teachers, often use inappropriate guidance techniques in classrooms. New teachers may use guidance strategies that can lead to either abusive behavior or lack of support for children who have experienced maltreatment. Inexperienced teachers, as we discussed in previous chapters, may feel less confident in the identification of possible abuse and neglect as well. The teacher's stage of development in teaching can influence the teacher's actions in the classroom, and understanding this can guide a teacher's reflection about what has occurred (Steffy & Wolfe, 2001). This chapter outlines the stages of development in teachers.

Teacher Training

Training of all teachers should include a general knowledge of child abuse. Many states require a minimum amount (in some, one hour) of training in child abuse and neglect. This training usually focuses on identification and reporting. Much more training should be provided that focuses on the teacher's knowledge of symptoms of abuse, the teacher's personal attitudes toward abuse (particularly sexual abuse), and the legal and ethical obligations of teachers (Hazzard, 2004).

The value of training for teachers has been shown in several studies. Teachers are at many different stages in their careers. Ellen in our opening scenario is an experienced teacher, while Mary, like many teachers, is new to the profession. Just as children develop their intellect and knowledge in stages, so do teachers (Feixas, 2001). Improved understanding of the stages of teachers' growth suggests ways of guiding that growth and therefore strengthening the teacher's performance in the classroom.

The term *teacher development* can mean activities such as workshops and graduate classes. It can also involve reading for self-improvement, and coursework meant to develop teachers' professional abilities. Teacher development is a process that occurs with time, experience, and training. All teachers should be concerned about furthering their development, and seek ways to promote their own positive growth. This is especially important in developing new and better guidance strategies and in working with children who have special needs as a result of trauma.

— **Fast Fact** —
Teachers learn in developmental stages in a similar way to how children grow and learn in developmental stages.

TEACHER DEVELOPMENTAL STAGES

Teachers are at many stages in their careers. Researchers, such as Burden (1990) and Gregorc (1973), have pointed out that teachers, like children, go through developmental stages. Can a teacher's stage of development affect a teacher's behavior toward children in the classroom? Is the likelihood that a teacher will abuse and neglect a child or report abusive behavior toward a child impacted by her stage of teacher development? Let's examine four stages of

THEORY TO PRACTICE

1. Determine the stage of development you are in as a teacher and consider your impact on the children in your classroom.
2. Look at each child and his stage of development to plan age-appropriate activities.

teacher development identified by Lillian Katz (1972): *survival, consolidation, renewal,* and *maturity.*

Survival

During the first year of a teacher's career, the survival stage, the new teacher wonders if she will be able to cope and get through each day. The teacher's focus is often on herself and her own needs. Teachers at this stage have less understanding of children and their needs, and are often overwhelmed by the new rules, regulations, and requirements. A teacher who is feeling overwhelmed by her first year of teaching can blame the children for her own inexperience and lack of planning. It is easy to choose one or two children who tend to be disruptive and make them the scapegoats for everything that goes wrong in the classroom. Teachers in this stage often feel that situations are beyond their control, and they feel helpless. A teacher who has not developed a variety of tools for guidance can easily resort to yelling, ridicule, pushing, yanking, and even hitting in an attempt to control the children and the classroom. They often lack the experience and skills to assist children whose behavior and learning is hampered by previous or current trauma.

New teachers are also at risk for not reporting instances of abuse and neglect that they observe in children. The fear that because they are new, what they are seeing might not really be an abusive situation, often causes new teachers to ignore, overlook, or simply "drag their feet" instead of immediately reporting an instance of abuse or neglect.

Consolidation

The second to the third or fourth year of teaching is one of consolidation, where teachers begin to focus more on instruction and the needs of individual children. Lesson planning is better understood, and teachers have usually developed some rules and routines for children that help them feel more in control. Usually the needs of the average child are more easily met, although children who have special needs can still cause the teacher to struggle.

The teacher at this stage is feeling more in control of her classroom. Sometimes this means that the teacher becomes too controlling. Some teachers at this stage begin to use methods like humiliation, ridicule, and manipulation as guidance strategies. These teachers may also be more aware of the children who are not conforming and may try to exert more control over such children, which can result in abusive behavior.

The teacher may also feel that he can handle an abusive situation himself and may be reluctant to report or talk to administrators who can help determine whether an abusive situation has occurred. Teachers at this stage can feel the need to work with the family themselves, as opposed to making a report.

Renewal

In the third or fourth year of teaching, many teachers become more competent in teaching children. The activities and schedules of the previous years can become routine and boring as teachers have become comfortable with their routines and methods. Teachers at this stage become interested in trying new ideas and new activities. They become interested in professional development.

The danger for teachers at this stage is that if they have developed management strategies in the classroom earlier that utilize yelling, ridicule, jerking children, or even hitting, these strategies can become used on a broader scope. The new teacher may occasionally use such methods with one or two children. As the more experienced teacher relies on old routines and habits, punitive strategies may become more prevalent and implemented with more children.

Maturity

Most teachers who reach this stage begin to look more at their philosophies and perceptions about teaching. They look for ways to mentor or bring about change in programs and children's lives. But some teachers feel trapped when administrators or programs are rigid and not open to change. Some mature teachers also feel that they are unable to change or progress, and may be more rigid in their interactions with children. This rigidity can contribute to abusive and neglectful behavior. Mature teachers may also become apathetic toward the issues of abuse and neglect, especially if they are in a school with many at-risk children. They may feel that reporting serves little purpose and, therefore, may ignore possible abuse.

Each stage of development for teachers brings with it new insights and new challenges. Abusive behavior toward children can begin at any one of the stages if teachers do not understand appropriate guidance strategies and feel the need

Wadsworth/Cengage Learning

Teachers at the renewal stage are interested in trying new ideas and activities in their classroom.

to exert power over children in order to control their classroom, or if they do not learn and practice new skills and guidance strategies. Each stage may provide reasoning that impedes the reporting of possible abuse and neglect.

TEACHERS AND CULTURAL ISSUES

Teachers must be trained to work with children in appropriate ways. It is also critical that they receive training and preparation in working with children of different cultures in order to minimize the impact of child maltreatment. Children who are suffering from maltreatment may have additional risk factors for intellectual, emotional, and social problems if they are also dealing with a lack of cultural understanding from teachers. Teachers who have had multicultural teacher education are less likely to see children of different cultures from a demeaning or deficit viewpoint (Irvine, 2003). These teachers can learn to adapt their teaching and interventions with children to their specific cultures, which will provide important benefits (Fontes, 2002).

Understanding your own and other cultures helps to clarify why people behave in certain ways, how reality is perceived, and what is seen as good and desirable. Avoiding ethnocentric explanations of children's behavior, that is, not interpreting a child's behavior from your own culturally biased viewpoint, requires awareness of your own cultural expectations. You may have been raised

---

Avoiding Abusive Behavior Checklist

Survival Stage

☐ Watch experienced teachers for ideas on dealing with difficult behavior.

☐ Read and watch videos on guidance strategies for the classroom.

☐ When you are overwhelmed and feel out of control, take a few deep breaths, and sit down for a minute. Read to one or two children, sing, or get out the modeling clay and play yourself—it actually helps to calm you!

☐ If you feel you are going to strike out or yell, call your director and tell her you need a 10-minute break. Take a walk alone or go to a quiet place, close your eyes, and think only positive thoughts. Do not think about what you should have done, about your anger with a child, or about any of the children!

Consolidation, Renewal, and Maturity Stages

☐ Examine your guidance techniques: What are your goals? Do you want to control behavior or teach the children to guide themselves? Are your techniques meeting those goals? What could you do to make guidance more positive in your classroom?

☐ Attend workshops and read books on new guidance strategies. Try at least one new strategy a month, and give it time to work.

☐ Have someone come and observe you in your classroom or videotape yourself and critique your current strategies. How can you change them?

☐ Examine your learning environment and your lesson plans. Are there ways to improve them that will increase learning and positive interactions in the classroom?

---

to face adults and smile, but some cultures see children facing teachers and smiling as a sign of disrespect. There are some benefits when the child and teacher have similar cultural backgrounds, especially when dealing with such sensitive topics as abuse and neglect (Horton & Cruise, 2001), but developing an understanding of your attitudes and learning more about cultures can provide greater sensitivity and increased ability to form connection with children.

TEACHER GUIDANCE

Gallup polls on education continue to find discipline as the public's primary educational concern (Rose & Gallup, 2006). Teachers have been reported to view lack of school discipline as a serious problem, often blaming the problem first on lack of discipline at home, and second on lack of educational resources. This lack of discipline on the part of children can be seen in all ages from preschool through high school. The National Prekindergarten study done by Yale University examined more than 4,000 prekindergarten classrooms. The researchers found that one out of ten teachers had expelled a preschooler from their classroom over the past year. Nationally, 6.67 preschoolers were expelled for every 1,000 enrolled. Children of color were more likely to be expelled.

What do these statistics have to do with maltreated children (Gilliam, 2005)? Children who are abused and neglected often find a safe haven and protection from harm by their attendance in child care and school. Children who have suffered abuse and neglect are also much more likely to have behaviors that are difficult for teachers, and therefore, they are at higher risk for being expelled as well as receiving harsher treatment from frustrated teachers. If expelled, some are sent home to endure greater maltreatment because of increased time with abusive parents who may continue to punish the child because of the expulsion. Teachers who learn and practice appropriate guidance techniques provide protection and skills for these children that can help them and can minimize the effects of abuse and neglect. The next chapter provides practical ideas for guiding maltreated children.

Children who are dealing with stress and anger create particular issues in guidance. Teachers may ignore angry behavior because they are afraid the child's anger will become worse (Boynton & Boynton, 2005). But consistently ignoring extremely angry behavior does not help children deal with underlying issues and improve their actions. Children who have been maltreated may exhibit extreme behavior due to stress, and it is critical that teachers use appropriate guidance techniques in working with them.

There are critical differences between guidance and discipline. Adults often consider discipline to be the same as punishment (Fields & Boesser, 2002), but we use the word *discipline* in a very broad sense to be synonymous with *guidance.* We want children to be able to discipline themselves—to learn responsible behavior and to know the difference between right and wrong themselves. Guidance, therefore, requires setting up appropriate guidelines in a classroom that will transfer to other settings outside of the school and child care environment.

Teachers often conclude that behavior of children should be managed by consequences and rewards. This follows a teacher-directed classroom style that perceives the teacher as all-knowing and totally in charge of learning. This model is at odds with research that shows that children benefit from and develop appropriate behavior in classrooms where they are active participants and have some control over learning (Larrivee, 2005). Moving away from teacher-directed to interactive and cooperative learning strategies will provide

THEORY TO PRACTICE

1. Give choices to children to empower them and give them self-confidence.
2. Do not continually ignore angry behavior; visit with children about strategies they can use in working appropriately with their anger.

children, particularly those who have been maltreated, with a sense of control over their environment that can assist them in developing their coping skills.

Teachers need to be able to identify specific behavioral problems and how to work with them. Many children who have been maltreated have multiple behavioral problems (Goldstein, 2007). Teachers can use the following strategies in working with challenging and traumatized children:

1. Identify problems by keeping a record of specific examples, including times and descriptions of how the child acted.

2. Define and prioritize these behaviors according to those that are most injurious to the child or the teaching environment.

3. Decide exactly how much change in the behavior is required. Although you might like for a child who has been kicking and hitting to learn to verbalize and discuss her feelings instead, you may need to settle first for getting her to walk away and yell at an inanimate object rather than at a person.

4. Develop specific interventions you will use to help the child change his behavior.

5. Discuss the need to change the behavior with the child when possible, and decide on consequences, both positive and negative.

6. Keep a record of the types of interventions you try, when you use them, and how effective they are.

Communication with Children

No teacher would deliberately encourage negative behavior, yet it is possible to send messages unconsciously that are better not sent. Nonverbal communication is especially likely to reveal inner feelings. Body language, tone of voice, and intensity are often "heard" more than what is said (Gordon & Browne, 1996). If you are convinced that children want to work and play constructively, your whole manner of relating to them communicates that expectation.

However, if you believe that they want to get away with whatever they can and have no interest in learning, this expectation, too, will be communicated by your tone of voice as you speak to the children and by the amount of freedom you give them. You can certainly expect children to meet whatever expectations you have of them.

When teachers are working with children who have been maltreated, it is critical that they be aware of body and facial language. Maltreated children are often hypervigilant to what they see and may misinterpret frowns, negative body language, or a harsh voice to be directed negatively toward them and to be a danger sign. Teachers should be aware that the way they talk, stand, and interact with children can communicate negative attitudes to the children.

When working with traumatized children, you should:

- Use a calm, soothing tone of voice when the child is upset.
- Keep your arms at your side and your body relaxed, not tense, when facing the child.
- Be careful when openly facing the child not to look confrontational.
- Smile or maintain a pleasant or concerned look, not an angry one.
- Listen carefully to the child and respond to his feelings.
- Reassure the child that you have confidence that she can make good choices.

Teachers teach children about mutual respect by showing respect for them. How we talk to children demonstrates how much we respect them. Too often adults speak to children in ways they would never consider speaking to an adult. Respecting children also involves accepting them for who they are instead of trying to make them into what teachers want.

Another critical area of communication that is key to reducing child abuse is to improve parent-teacher communication. Establishing relationships with parents often encourages a parent to reach out for help and protects at-risk children. Teachers can:

- Send home notes that are positive and encouraging about the child.
- Call or e-mail parents to touch base and share something positive, such as "Thank you for helping Ellie with her homework last night. It really helped her to do better today."
- Send home newsletters with short articles offering strategies for guidance.
- Send home articles to all parents on issues related to their child's age.

Teachers should send friendly notes home that address children's overall performance in school. They should also make sure that they address problem behaviors in face-to-face or phone conferences with at-risk parents as much as possible. This provides an opportunity to also emphasize positive aspects about

Wadsworth/Cengage Learning

Remember how important body language and tone of voice are when guiding children.

the child and can provide protection against harsh punishment. A communication with parents that is negative may precipitate undue punishment. Teachers need to initiate parent contact in a positive manner by emphasizing the accomplishments and abilities of the child at the beginning and at the end of the conversation when a problem is discussed.

Relationship Building

Building relationships is an important activity for classroom teachers. Children who feel their teacher does not support them have more behavioral problems and fewer positive behaviors (Goldstein, 2007). Teachers who get to know the children they teach and their families, who show interest in the children's lives, and who work at developing a relationship with each child make an important contribution to the healthy development of the children, and particularly any who are maltreated.

So, how do you build a relationship with a child who demonstrates challenging behavior? How easy or difficult is it for a teacher to accept these children for who they are and care about them no matter how they behave?

Relationship building with children who are challenging involves first getting to know the child. Ask about his interests; talk to him when he is calm. Provide activities in the classroom that he enjoys, and ask for his input when you are planning activities. Be sure that you find times when you can laugh with him and play with him.

When problems occur, make sure to sit down with the child after she is calm and discuss what happened. Help her identify other ways to handle problems, and offer encouraging words when you see her use those strategies.

It can be very difficult for teachers to accept a child who has difficult behavior. It can help to make a list of the positive characteristics of the child and to examine it when you have had a particularly challenging day. You can "reframe" the child's behavior by thinking of positive ways to look at it. The child who constantly wants to talk and ask questions can be seen as very social and inquisitive instead of annoying. This behavior can be a plus for the child if it is directed. The child might benefit from more activities involving science and the use of questioning, as well as the use of a tape recorder to record ideas.

Showing care and concern for all children in the classroom equally can be hard when a child is challenging, but it is possible. It can help if the teacher focuses on saying each child's name in a positive way and on thinking positively about each child on a daily basis.

TEACHER STRESS AND ANGER

Teachers become stressed due to life experiences. Lack of training and concerns over low pay and high teacher-child ratios can culminate in extreme stress and frustration for teachers. Personal experiences, including family, physical and emotional health, and relationships, can also create stress in teachers, which comes through in the classroom. Stress can be a factor in lack of preparation for classes, less creativity, higher absence rates, anger management, and use of inappropriate guidance techniques. Studies have revealed that while 70% of teachers and parents believed that yelling and swearing at children is harmful to them, most teachers and parents admit to having insulted or sworn at a child (Fields & Boesser, 2002).

Sometimes the stresses of life push people beyond their limits, and adults' behavior does not live up to their personal expectations. If this is a frequent occurrence, intervention is needed. If it is a rare occurrence, it is best to forgive yourself, speak to the child, and try to redeem the situation. In our case study, Ellen displayed anger and inappropriate behavior toward Joey. Is this a frequent or rare occurrence? We don't know. But Mary, as a new teacher observing this behavior, was put in a predicament. How does she need to deal with this situation? Were there extenuating circumstances that we don't know about? Are such circumstances usual in the classroom environment, or did Ellen get pushed beyond her limits? Knowing the importance of being in control of oneself to effectively deal with discipline issues is important.

EMOTIONAL ABUSE BY TEACHERS

Teachers sometimes inappropriately reprimand children, and sometimes they go beyond this and commit emotional abuse. Many researchers believe that while physical and sexual abuse occurring in child care and educational settings is harmful, emotional maltreatment is the most overwhelming to children (McEachern, Aluede, & Kenny, 2008).

The authors of this text have taught preservice teachers for many years, and we have often asked students to share why they want to become a teacher. Many share stories of wonderful teachers and their examples. But some share darker, more frightening tales of teachers who told students they were not worthwhile and would never be able to do things. Some speak of teachers who were harsh and punitive, and who emotionally assaulted them. These students often speak of wanting to be teachers to protect other children from the abuse they suffered. "Teachers, particularly in the early school years, can either provide feelings of security or intensify insecurity. Elementary students often use the phrase 'teacher says' to cap a family argument. Teacher approval is so important that the potential for emotional abuse is nothing less than alarming" (Nesbit & Philpott, 2002, p. 33).

Research on emotional abuse in the classroom has been small, but international in its scope. Researchers in Israel, Botswana, Zimbabwe, and the United States as well as other countries have explored this phenomenon (Benbenishty, Ziera, Astor, & Khoury-Kassabri, 2002; Nesbit & Philpott, 2002; Osei-Hwedie & Hobona, 2001; Shumba, 2002). Yet there seems to be a reluctance to focus too strongly on this topic. Many stereotypes of teachers in the past portrayed them as unyielding and stern, ready with a paddle, ruler, or dunce cap to force the children into line. There still seems to be some prevailing attitudes that a good teacher must be stern or harsh in order to get children to listen and learn. This is incorrect, and much research has shown that children who are treated harshly find it difficult to learn (McEacher, Aluede, & Kenny, 2008).

What types of behaviors constitute emotional abuse in the classroom? "Emotional abuse usually describes an ongoing pattern of interaction" (Nesbit & Philpott, 2002, p. 32). Although isolated incidences can occur, emotional abuse usually takes place as the result of behaviors that are inflicted on a child on a regular basis over a prolonged period of time. A teacher may become angry and raise her voice or speak harshly to a child once, followed by an apology and a redirecting of behavior and emotion. This would probably not be considered emotional abuse. But a teacher who regularly gets angry and yells at a child might be emotionally abusive. Other behaviors that may be seen include verbal abuse, harsh criticism, lack of nurturing behavior, not allowing the child to explore and develop independent thoughts and ideas, discriminatory and prejudicial comments and attitudes, demeaning children, controlling, humiliating, labeling, belittling, threatening, name calling, sarcasm, and intimidation (McEachern et al., 2008).

Nesbit and Philpott (2002) created a Scale of Subtle Emotional Abuse (SSEA) that teachers can use to rate their behaviors to determine if they are abusive. A checklist for teachers to guide them in thinking about their behavior with children and determine if they are emotionally abusive ("Am I at Risk to

Avoiding Emotional Abuse in the Classroom

As a teacher, you can avoid emotional abuse of children in your classroom by using the following techniques:

1. Put away personal problems when you walk into the classroom. Mentally bundle away your problems and place them in a "basket" until your break.
2. Identify the different temperaments in your classroom and your own. Consider whether the children you react to most negatively are those with temperaments that are different from your own or more difficult. Then develop a plan for being more positive with those children.
3. Attend guidance workshops, read books, watch videos, and talk to colleagues about your guidance techniques. Remember that the more strategies you have to guide children, the less likely you are to resort to emotionally abusive behaviors.
4. Get to know each child in your classroom on a personal basis. Learn what they like, their hobbies, their fears and joys. Become each child's friend and mentor—they need you and look up to you.
5. Be loving and kind.
6. When you are feeling overwhelmed by a child, take a deep breath, ask for someone to come in and relieve you for 10 minutes, and take a walk—or send the child to another teacher on an errand. A child who is often challenging may need to be given opportunities to go to other classrooms or to help with activities—not to be punished, but to give you a break!

Emotionally Abuse a Child? A Checklist for Teachers") can be found in Appendix E. Teachers are often stressed and frustrated from their jobs or personal lives. Teachers today experience overwhelming paperwork and pressure for accountability and test scores, even in preschool and child care settings. Children sometimes have temperaments that make them more difficult for some teachers to deal with. Research indicates that teachers view more negatively children who have difficult temperaments and who are more resistant to learning (Oren, 2006). Teachers also are more negative when children have very different temperaments than the teacher. Information on the impact of temperament on maltreatment and children can be found in an earlier chapter.

Teachers are a critical part of children's lives. Children will learn self-confidence or feelings of inferiority from their interactions with teachers. This is why it is so important that teachers be positive, nurturing, and help children to feel they can do anything.

PHYSICAL AND SEXUAL ABUSE BY TEACHERS

According to a set of school rules for students in 1860, children in classrooms were to "sit straight at all times" and not "squirm," "fidget," or "whine," among other things. Infractions were met with severe punishment. Children who wrote with their left hand in 1860 received a rap on the knuckles with a ruler; talking in class meant a whack with a rod. Historically, spanking, rapping on the knuckles, whacks with a paddle, pulling of ears, and other forms of physical punishment were typical in the classroom. Sometimes these punishments culminated in physical abuse.

Today, almost half of the states in the United States condone spanking in the schools. However, most school districts have very strict policies about how this can be done. Most require another adult to be present, parents to be notified, and are specific about how the physical punishment can be given. Child care programs in most states are prohibited by state licensing regulations from administering any form of physical punishment to children. Yet, physical abuse can occur in child care and schools. Child care situations where children are too young to talk about the experience and unlicensed family child care homes are particularly of concern. It is critical that teachers learn appropriate guidance techniques and avoid physical punishment as a form of discipline. Not only can it get out of hand, but also the risk of personal liability and lawsuits or legal action from parents and schools is significant.

Sexual abuse by educators is a frightening and terrible violation of a child's trust. The incidences of child sexual abuse by teachers are difficult to assess. The American Association of University Women (2001) surveyed more than

THEORY TO PRACTICE

1. Involve families in the classroom by sending notes and newsletters, and inviting them in for conferences or to observe.
2. Avoid any form of physical punishment.

1,500 public school students and found that 38% of the students reported being aware of sexual harassment by teachers or school personnel, and 7% reported having been sexually harassed. Although sexual harassment may include behaviors that may or may not be quantified as sexual abuse, no type of sexual harassment or abuse should be tolerated from teachers. Sexual abuse committed by teachers and administrators in child care settings is difficult to determine and probably underreported, as many of the victims may be too young to verbalize the problem. Most sexual abuse in child care settings occurs from males, but female teachers also sexually abuse young children (Moulden, Firestone, & Wexler, 2007).

Many teachers today are concerned about inaccurate reporting of sexual abuse, and fear touching and showing affection to children because they are afraid of being accused of abusive behavior. Teachers can demonstrate appropriate affection and nurturing behavior to young children without fear of being accused of sexual abuse. The next chapter provides ideas for teachers on how to show affection that is appropriate.

Sexual abuse and harassment of young children should never be tolerated. Teachers should seek help from counselors and others when they have children who have been sexually abused in their classroom in order to provide appropriate support for them. Young children who have been sexually abused often exhibit sexualized behaviors and want inappropriate physical contact with teachers and other children. Teachers need to inform the administration immediately if a child exhibits any unexplained or unusual sexualized behavior toward them or other children, document what has happened and the teacher's response, and ask for further guidance.

TEACHER AND FAMILY INTERACTIONS

Teachers must also work with the families of abused children. Sometimes they must report parents to authorities, even parents with whom they may have developed a good relationship. Teachers can help parents see positive behaviors and improvements in children's behavior, which may help avoid stressful and punitive situations. When parents are more understanding of their children's developmental levels and have information on their abilities or disabilities, they can be more patient and positive (Goldman, 2005).

The National Association for the Education of Young Children ([NAEYC], 2006) identified some things to think about when working with families of children who are challenging:

1. Welcome new children and families. Get to know them, and help the parents feel comfortable with you. Be warm and caring.

2. Contact the parents frequently by phone, e-mail, and letter to let them know what is happening in the classroom, particularly positive things.

3. Offer compliment sandwiches. When you need to tell parents something negative, begin by telling them something positive about the child, then discuss the challenging issue, and end with another positive.

4. Keep discussions with parents private and respectful.

5. Build your own support system by talking with mentors, reading, and using supervisors to help you in dealing with the parents and family.

6. Engage others in using a comprehensive approach. Be willing to talk with caseworkers, medical personnel, and counselors, and encourage parents to involve you with these professionals to build the best possible interventions for a child.

It is important to build strong relationships with families before problems occur so that a foundation of mutual trust and respect is established when problems arise. It is critical that the procedures for dealing with suspected child abuse be in the school policies and that parents be made aware of them. Teachers can also inform families of how to identify and report abuse.

ETHICAL CONSIDERATIONS FOR TEACHERS AND OTHERS WORKING WITH CHILDREN

— Fast Fact —
Teachers are mandatory reporters and can be prosecuted if it is found that they knew about the abuse and did not report it to the authorities.

The National Association for the Education of Young Children (NAEYC, 2005) has identified ethical guidelines for those who work with children. The National Education Association (NEA) has also identified ethical standards for teachers. What are ethical standards?

Beyond legal requirements, most school professionals have as a part of their profession ethical codes that state how teachers should act to provide appropriate experiences and interactions with children. These ethical codes include following legal mandates. Thus, to suspect but not to report abuse would be in violation of professional ethics. Those who do not report abuse not only risk legal proceedings but also risk losing licensure or certification (Horton & Cruise, 2001).

Some professionals feel unsure of whether or how to report. Mental health professional codes consistently mention confidentiality as critical, and sometimes reporting may be a violation of this code. Once confidentiality is violated, many families leave treatment programs. Teachers who have been trying to help the family of a child may feel they are betraying them by reporting. Distrust and a sense of betrayal can develop, and families may move away from the school or cancel their children's participation in any counseling or supportive relationships. Horton and Cruise (2001) remind us that in order to act in a way that is consistent with not just the letter of the law, but also the spirit of the ethical codes, teachers should ask: "This child has placed his/her trust in me. How can I act in his/her best interests? I have the power of privileged information. How will I use it for good? Given all that I understand may be happening in this child's life, what is the caring thing for me to do?" (p. 56).

Once professionals have considered these ethical principles, they can move toward the next rationale for reporting, the moral considerations. Without someone willing to make a report, children are denied the protection they need —at times, from severe abuse and imminent harm. Reports can protect children from severe physical injury or even death. Psychological suffering may be lessened and dysfunctional patterns interrupted. Families may get needed services. It takes courage to acknowledge and report the abuse while weighing the dilemma of what happens if the abuse is not reported. Some professionals do not report abuse, and they must live with their decision.

Teachers have ethical issues not only in terms of dealing with abuse, but also in their interactions with children and families. Confidentiality, following state standards on care and education of children, and providing appropriate guidance all fall under ethics. The NAEYC ethical standards are included in Appendix C of this book, and the NEA ethical code for teachers can be found online.

Teacher Roles and Responsibilities

Role models are most effective when they are people whom children look up to: important, powerful, nurturing people (Eisenberg, 1992). This puts a lot of pressure on teachers who work with children of all ages. Teachers need to seize the opportunity to make a difference in children's lives because as children get older, they increasingly look less to adults for their models, and turn more to their peers.

If parents do not shield their children from harmful influences, schools must try to counteract the effects. It is the responsibility of adults who work with children to help them think about and analyze the positive and negative modes they are sure to encounter both in real life and on television. Children will learn negative behavior patterns from models as easily as they learn from positive ones. Teachers and parents must work together to ensure that the negative does not overwhelm the positive.

How a teacher as a role model deals with her own feelings and those of others will affect how children handle their feelings. Demonstrations of caring, kindness, and compassion will make a lasting impression on young children. A willingness to take risks in learning new skills and trying out new ideas will help students more bravely try out their emerging skills and ideas. When a teacher sets an example of being responsible and of following good safety habits, children are more apt to pay attention than when she lectures about those issues. As an adult role model, teachers have a powerful influence on young children.

SUMMARY

Teachers are very important in the lives of all children, but particularly those who have been maltreated. Teacher styles, guidance strategies, and communication critically impact children's lives, especially the lives of children with families that are unstable (Kaiser & Rasminsky, 2003). Significant increases across all categories of child maltreatment have been noted (Aldridge & Goldman, 2002). Teachers have a unique opportunity to help alleviate both the occurrence and effects of child abuse and neglect. Teachers are sometimes at risk for emotional abuse of children, and they must be vigilant to avoid those behaviors. A teacher has an important opportunity to truly make a positive difference in the life of a child who has been maltreated.

Application: When Working with Children

- Do not become involved in gossip about children and their behavior. Remember your ethical obligations to the child.
- Remain calm and relaxed when working with children, especially children who are at risk.
- Consider the stages of teacher development that you are experiencing. How does this influence your behavior with the children you work with in the classroom? Write down your answers, and explain where you are and where you need to go.
- Examine your attitudes and behaviors toward children in the classroom. Are they appropriate? Are there children you tend to "pick on"? How can you change your behavior to be more supportive?

Application: When Working with Families

- Make parents aware of your efforts to improve your teaching.
- Send home classroom rules so that parents can reinforce them with children.

- Communicate often with parents about positive behaviors.
- Build relationships with the adults in your students' lives.

Projects/Activities

1. Choose a local agency that works with abused children. Prepare a PowerPoint presentation on the philosophy, description, contact information, and objectives of the agency or organization.

2. Schedule a family activity at your facility that allows parents to get to know you as the teacher and allows them to get to know one another, or write a plan for a family activity a school could do. What would this activity look like?

3. Read three articles on working with difficult children in the classroom, and write a plan for helping one child with her inappropriate behavior.

Questions to Consider

1. What is your view or philosophy of guidance when working with children?
2. Is there a difference between guidance and discipline?
3. What rules would you implement in your classroom, and how would you decide which ones are most important?
4. How can you avoid being emotionally abusive?

Websites for More Information

For useful websites, visit www.cengage.com/education/hirschy

Wadsworth/Cengage Learning

CHAPTER 11

Prevention, Intervention, and Guidance: Teachers

WHAT YOU WILL LEARN

- How the teaching environment can protect children from the effects of abuse

- In what ways the teaching environment can promote prevention

- How policies and procedures of child care and educational institutions can prevent abuse

- How to teach children who have been victims of abuse

- Types of curricula that are available to teach young children about abuse and neglect

INTRODUCTION

Children who are living in homes where abuse and neglect has occurred or who are at risk for such behavior have unique needs in the classroom. Their ability to do well in school, pay attention, act appropriately, and do well with classmates is negatively impacted. How can these children function well in a classroom environment when stress, fear, and anger govern their lives? How can teachers, caregivers, and professionals respond? What about prevention? Can teachers implement curricula that can provide protection and teach children how to avoid abuse and what to do if it occurs?

VIGNETTE

Michael was a teacher of four-year-olds. His classroom was a busy, happy place. But Michael worried about some of the children in his class. They lived in high-risk neighborhoods that were filled with violence and abuse. He knew that Child Protective Services was working with a couple of children in his classroom. He had talked to the children and read them some books on avoiding strangers and wanted to help them understand how to avoid abuse and how to tell someone if they were abused. But how could he introduce this information in the classroom? Michael also knew there had been times when his classroom was very chaotic, and he got angry with the children for not following the rules and yelled at them. Was he teaching and modeling peace and coping skills in his classroom? How could he help the children in his classroom who had already been victims of abuse and neglect?

PREVENTION, INTERVENTION, AND GUIDANCE: POLICIES AND PROCEDURES

Schools and child care settings have an obligation to establish practices that support children at risk for abuse, their families, and those that teach these children. According to the National Association for the Education of Young Children (NAEYC) position statement on child abuse, prevention programs should "adopt policies and practices that promote close partnerships with families" (NAEYC, 2004). Appropriate classroom practices can assist teachers in identifying child maltreatment and avoiding child maltreatment themselves, and teach children skills that can provide protection and resilience, and support children who have been maltreated. Such collaborations can reduce child maltreatment in families (NAEYC, 2004). NAEYC recommends the following policies.

1. *Ratios: Provide enough adults to children in the classroom.* Classroom **ratios** are critical to healthy functioning in a classroom. Many studies have indicated that overcrowded classrooms interfere with learning, lead to aggressive behaviors, and impair the teacher's ability to appropriately supervise children (Finn, Gerber, & Boyd-Zaharias, 2005). The National Education Association (NEA) recommends that children, particularly those in the earliest grades, be in classrooms where the ratios in the classroom are one teacher for every 15 children (NEA, 2006). The NAEYC has also identified the optimal ratios for children and teachers in child care and education according to age levels. They recommend for infants no more than a 1:4 ratio; for toddlers, a maximum of 1:4 or 1:6, depending on the toddler's age; a maximum of 1:10 for preschoolers; and 1:12 for kindergartners (NAEYC, 2005). It is also important that not too many children be in one room even if the ratio is right. When there are 30 preschoolers in the same room, even if there are three teachers, it is difficult for teachers to supervise, and the chaotic environment can cause aggression, emotionality, and frustration in young children.

2. *Schools and child care programs must set up policies regarding appropriate hiring practices.* Screening of teachers and all personnel involved with children should include a background check, fingerprint check, checked references, and interviews. Teachers should be trained before hiring and routinely after hiring in issues regarding abuse and neglect, including identification and reporting, guidance strategies, and methods of preventing abuse (NAEYC, 1996).

3. *Programs must establish reporting practices for teachers and personnel and provide information on these policies to teachers and parents* (Dombrowski &

Gischlar, 2006). Many school programs set up a Child Protection Team (Crosson-Tower, 2003) within their program. The team consists of several members of the program who are trained in identification and intervention in abuse and neglect. Teachers can go to the team with questions and help in deciding if a case of abuse and neglect exists, reporting, and interventions with the child.

4. *Teachers and staff should be adequately supervised and trained.* There should be safeguards to protect children that include supervision of staff. Although no teacher needs or wants to be observed every minute, it is critical that administrators occasionally walk halls and listen to what is going on in classrooms, make unannounced visits into classrooms, and in other ways observe the behavior of teachers with the children. Teachers should not be alone with one child for periods of time, and there should not be areas in the classroom that cannot be observed easily. Many programs have implemented video surveillance in classrooms that allow the program administrators and sometimes parents to observe the children and teacher on a website at any time of the day. Teachers should receive ongoing training in dealing with abuse and neglect.

5. *Allow touching.* Many programs discourage teachers from touching or hugging children out of concern that it may be misinterpreted as abuse. However, this practice can be detrimental to all young children who need to be touched in order to have optimal intellectual, emotional, and social development and who may feel disliked and unloved if the teacher refuses to touch and hug them. Children and adults experience a physiological response to touching that often allows them to feel more relaxed and happy and to learn better.

6. *Provide secure environments for children.* Programs should restrict access to children by outsiders. Fencing around playground areas, limited and monitored access to classrooms and hallways, and careful screening of people picking up children after programs are critical. Most child care programs provide a secure system of signing in the child when a child arrives. Allowing only those on a list provided by the parent to pick up the child, checking identification on those people, and having the adult sign the child out of the program restricts the access of outsiders and also ensures that no child is left in the program unsupervised. Careful checks of rooms at the end of the day and of buses and cars after field trips will ensure that no child is left alone.

Elementary schools should make sure that no young child walks home alone from school and that adults picking up children are known to the teacher. Having teachers walk their children out to meet parents at the end of the day,

Children need to be comforted and held at times.

and ensuring that at least an older child approved by the parent walks the child home, will create a safer environment (NAEYC, 1996).

PREVENTION, INTERVENTION, AND GUIDANCE: CLASSROOMS

The teacher, caregiver, and classroom can have a powerful effect on children who have been abused and in preventing abuse. Many children spend the majority of the time they are awake in a child care or school setting. Even when abuse may be occurring in the home, the classroom can provide a protective environment and the teacher a stable, positive adult who can build resilience in the child. Good classroom environments for prevention and intervention of child maltreatment require the following components: *appropriate environments,* and *policies and procedures that promote consistency.*

Appropriate Touching for Teachers

- Touch children on the hand or arm when talking to them to show interest and concern, but only when you know a child is comfortable being touched.
- Pat and rub children's backs by being careful to keep all patting above the waistline and using a soft, rhythmic pat rather than sensual rubbing.
- Elementary-aged children benefit most from "one-arm" hugs, pats on the arm or shoulders, and shaking or touching hands.
- Hug children when they hug you first by putting your arm around their shoulders and giving a pat or a soft squeeze. Avoid hugs where you are face-to-face with the child with a full, prolonged embrace.
- Kissing should be avoided.
- Allow the child to initiate physical affection and stop when the child stops.
- Infants and young toddlers need lots of hugs and affection for good development; full hugs, embraces, rocking, holding, and touching for them is appropriate and necessary.

Appropriate Environments

Classroom environments for young children that are warm, inviting, and comforting can provide a child who comes from a stressed home situation with a blanket of protection. Michael, in our scenario at the beginning of the chapter, would find that by setting up a better environment, the children in his classroom would be less likely to be aggressive or fearful and more likely to trust and feel protected. The following principles will assist a teacher in setting up a classroom that can protect children.

1. Room arrangements should create open and quiet spaces. Children should be able to find quiet areas, such as a book area with pillows or a large box with the top off in which they can sit. Quiet areas where children can be alone or in small groups can provide rest and peace to children who receive little of each. However, there should not be any area of the classroom that is not easily seen or that cannot be supervised from anywhere in the room. A child who has been a victim should not be placed in a situation where she can become a victim in the classroom unseen by the teacher.

   Room arrangements should also provide for an appropriate placement of activities. The book center should not be next to very noisy, active areas such as the blocks. Quieter activities should be grouped on the same side of the room, and more active areas should be placed separately. Art and science materials should be placed on noncarpeted areas next to sinks to prevent frustration from spills.

2. Sounds in the room should be kept at a calming level most of the time. The sound of happy, busy children is a wonderful one. But classrooms where children are continually loud, where loud music is often heard, or where teachers are yelling contribute to discipline problems and aggravate aggressive feelings in children who have been traumatized as well as those who have not. A classroom should have noise, but most of the time it should involve normal tones of voice in the children, soothing or no music, and walls that minimize outside or other classroom noise.

3. Visuals in the classroom should be at eye level, and should not be overwhelming. Many teachers feel it is important to put all the children's artwork on the walls, hang mobiles from the ceiling, put up colorful posters, and otherwise flood the room with color, shapes, and things! Sensory overload is common in these classrooms, and discipline problems usually escalate. Overstimulation from the classroom environment can lead to out-of-control behavior for some children. The traumatized child will experience sensory overload and be less able to concentrate and learn in such an environment. A good classroom will display some of children's artwork and a few posters or pieces of art, but not too many. Minimal or no materials will be hung from the ceiling, and none that would obstruct the teacher's view of the classroom. Wall colors may be primary colors, but the use of red should be diminished; muted pastels, especially in blues and greens or earth tones, are usually preferred for a more calming influence.

Policies and Procedures That Promote Consistency

All classroom teachers establish **policies**, **routines and schedules**, and **rules** for their class. The more consistent these are and the more predictable the environment, the more all children will feel safe and protected, and the easier it will be for traumatized children to learn to feel safe.

Policies. Policies in classrooms should cover issues such as how parents pick up and drop off children; what happens when parents are late, to protect children from experiencing feelings of abandonment; how children come into the classroom late, which can cause feelings of insecurity, anxiety, and isolation; when a sick child should and should not be at school; how child abuse is handled; who supervises the children in class and when and how that supervision occurs; when and how the playground is used and supervised; and the types of food that can be brought into the classroom, as some snacks can cause allergic reactions and others seem to contribute to negative behaviors in the classroom.

Field trip policies should be in place to govern who is allowed to accompany or meet the class on trips, how supervision will occur during field trips (e.g., buddy systems, who is in charge of whom), ratios of children to adults, expected behaviors and consequences for children and adults, and what will happen if a child becomes out of control on the trip. If you know a child has the potential for outbursts or uncontrolled behavior, a specific behavioral plan should be developed for this child and extra supervision may be necessary. However, leaving such children out of field trips is not a positive option, as it singles them out and contributes to their feelings of low self-esteem and anger.

Holidays are another area where policies are important. Which holidays do you celebrate? Children of different faiths may be unable to participate in certain religious holidays, such as Christmas, and may feel uncomfortable. Holidays are also a time when parents are more likely to bring food and other treats that may be inappropriate. Parties often create a chaotic environment where children who are stressed feel overwhelmed and may act out in inappropriate ways. A classroom party should have structure and take a minimum amount of time, and the number of adults should be limited if possible.

Visitation policies in the classroom can create dilemmas. Although it is important for all parents to feel they can come to visit and an open-door policy is good, children who have been traumatized may fear strangers and can be overwhelmed by large numbers of adults in the classroom. It is best if adults schedule visits ahead of time, and the visits occur at times when the children are less tense and excitable.

Routines and Schedules. In our vignette, Michael noticed the chaos in his classroom. One problem he found was that he did not always follow routines. He would set up a schedule, but would not always follow it. Children would line up for the bathroom single-file on Tuesday, but then all walk together in a cluster on Wednesday. He would have outdoor time before lunch one day and after lunch on another.

Routines are critical in classroom prevention and intervention. Children need routine in their lives. Children who have been traumatized often fear sudden changes and possible violence. Routines provide stability and create a calming atmosphere where children know what to do and what to expect. Classroom routines should be established for all the major activities in a classroom, such as how the class will leave and arrive, how they will get ready for lunch, how they will act when a visitor enters the classroom, what to do and say when they need help, and so on.

Schedules should be established for classrooms that are flexible but consistent. Young children do not know exact time, but they do know what is supposed to happen before or after something. Most days should follow the same sequence of activities, for example, first centers or small-group work, then large-group or class instruction, then outdoor time, and so on. If the schedule needs to be different for a special visitor, field trip, or other activity, children should be prepared ahead whenever possible, and told the sequence of activities and how the schedule will be different for the day.

Schedules should also allow for a mix of active and quiet play. Quiet activities such as rest time should not follow extremely active play, such as outdoor time. If these are scheduled back-to-back, then a transition activity, such as reading a book or a quiet game, should be used to smooth the transition and prepare the children.

Rules. Knowing the rules in any situation creates structure and safety. Rules should be established for every classroom. When the children assist in making the rules, they are more likely to follow and enforce them. The children and teacher should also talk about consequences, and everyone should agree on them.

Rules for classes of young children should be short and general. Rules such as "calm feet," "caring hearts," and "quiet hands" can be discussed in the context of specific situations so children understand that these phrases mean to walk, not run; stay on the floor, not climb; be kind, not hit; show concern; be giving, and not take things from others. Teachers can question children using these phrases when they see a specific behavior, such as, "Are you showing a caring heart when you do this?" Consequences for breaking rules should be established and should be as logical as possible. When a child knocks down blocks, he is unable to play in the block center for a time. When a child hits a friend, she is unable to play with that friend for a period of time. There should be time limits set on consequences, and they should not be long ones.

When new things or procedures are introduced into the classroom, children should be given instruction both verbally and visually. Remember that all children, but particularly maltreated children, often need repeated reminders and explanations before they understand.

APPROPRIATE GUIDANCE FROM TEACHERS

What does it mean to guide children? **Guidance** is providing children with direction and support. *Guidance* is a much better term than *discipline,* which has a connotation of correction and punishment. Guidance provides positive assistance to the child in learning to self-regulate. **Self-regulation** is the ability of a child to control his emotions and responses, and to react to situations in the context of expected behaviors.

How can teachers guide children appropriately? Good guidance strategies work for all children, although children who have been traumatized by abuse or other events may need additional, more specific guidance strategies. We will discuss these strategies later in this chapter. Teachers can provide appropriate guidance for all children through the following basic guidance strategies: *being consistent, communicating clearly and calmly, listening appropriately, understanding why misbehavior occurs,* and *guiding choices and providing consequences for behavior.*

Being Consistent

Consistency is critical to all children. If a rule is developed, the teacher must always enforce the rule and do it equally for all children. If a teacher says "no" to something the children want to do, she should not allow children to routinely change her mind. Does that mean the teacher should be rigid? No, it means that most of the time the teacher should follow what she has stated, but that at times, with good reason and lots of explanation as to why, a change can happen. The more consistent rules, schedules, and teacher behaviors are, the more the children will feel safe and protected, and the less likely it is that the teacher will experience problems in the classroom.

Communicating Clearly and Calmly

Speaking clearly and calmly allows children to understand expectations in a positive manner. Teachers should tell children the rules in a positive manner and clearly, so that they are understood. "Johnny, you need to walk" instead of "Stop running!" tells a child what he should do rather than what he should not do. This lets the child know what the expectations are at school and sets up a predictable situation for the child. Children who have been maltreated tend to behave more appropriately when they understand and can predict what the consequences are for their actions. Getting at the child's eye level to speak to a child tells her that you respect her and that she has your attention. A calm, quiet voice usually requires the child to listen more closely, and often helps an agitated child feel soothed and calmer.

Remember that conversations with children should not be you telling them what to do, but should be a two-way communication. When adults care enough to ask children about what they are doing, how their day is, or what they did last night, that tells the children they are important and that what they think is worthwhile. Children should hear their teacher say positive things to them daily as individuals. Each child should hear her name used in a positive way every day. Too many children hear their names from their teachers only when they are doing something wrong!

Good teachers spend time talking and listening to all the children in their class.

Listening Appropriately

Michael, the teacher in our scenario, has a bad habit. When Julie, one of the children in his room, comes over to talk to him, Michael rolls his eyes. Julie comes from an abusive home and always wants to be right next to her teacher. She will tell Michael long stories about things that never seem to end. Michael usually pretends to listen while doing something else, occasionally saying, "hmmm," and finally just turns away and goes to help another child. Julie sadly watches him go, puts her head down, and quietly moves to the book corner where she sits on a pillow and stares at the covers of the books on display.

Michael, like many teachers, does not understand that listening to children creates trust and increases self-esteem for them. It also models a behavior that most teachers want to see in the children they teach. Good listening involves:

- Leaning close and looking at the child (but don't necessarily expect the child to look back at you).

- Really hearing what he is saying by concentrating on the moment and not on what you will eat when you get home or the movie you saw yesterday.

- Getting down on the child's level by sitting down, kneeling, or bending, and reflecting back what you hear.

- Reflecting feelings and occasionally repeating or summarizing words, which is an important skill to model. If a child says that John took her truck, you can say, "You seem pretty upset. You are angry that John took your truck," and give her a chance to respond. The child will learn to recognize and label her feelings appropriately and will learn to respond to situations verbally instead of physically.

- Letting the child know appropriate ways to get your attention. If, like Michael, you have a child who talks constantly, you can respond by listening for awhile and then saying, "You seem to be very concerned (happy, sad, etc.) about this! I want to hear about it, but right now I am _____. Why don't you come and tell me more about it when we are outside and I will have more time to listen?" If this child is always wanting to talk, you may develop a secret signal, such as a finger to the side of your head, that tells the child when it is time to stop; or you can say, "When the hand on the clock gets to 8, I will need to help the other children, and you will need to pick a center and go to it." But always let children know that they can come back to talk to you. Stay friendly and approachable.

Understanding Why Misbehavior Occurs

Children act for reasons. Misbehavior is purposeful. A child may want attention, recognition, or power. The child may feel angry, confused, inadequate, powerless, or sad. A child's misbehavior is aimed at meeting an unmet need. If the child is angry because his father left home, he may hit other children in an effort to release his anger and to feel that vicariously he is getting back at his father. If a child is neglected, she may demand all your attention in an effort to have someone recognize her as a person.

Before responding to misbehavior, it is important to take a moment and ask yourself, "Why would Jenny do this?" Understanding why misbehavior occurs allows you the opportunity, in helping the child correct the behavior, to also meet her needs. It is critical to remember that you do not want to correct the behavior yourself, but rather help the child correct her own behavior, so that she can learn to self-regulate.

Guiding Choices and Providing Consequences

Children continually make choices. Even choosing not to do something is a choice. You can guide those choices and provide structure through appropriate consequences. Behavioral consequences should be related to the behavior. When Joey throws paint on the floor, he would need to clean it up and maybe not use the art center for the rest of the day. When using choices and consequences follow these guidelines:

1. Set up your rules ahead of time whenever possible, with the children's agreement on consequences. Make sure the consequences are not too punitive or too long.

2. Give children a choice. "Juan, you can pick up those blocks and put them in the container, or you can go and pick up the puzzles. You choose." Allowing them choices lessens the power struggle. Make the choices between two good things whenever possible. Avoid "Juan, pick up the puzzles or go to time out." Sometimes children need time to make their choice. If they are upset or angry, allow them time to calm down before insisting on choices.

3. Maintain consistency and a positive attitude. The same behavior should require similar consequences for other children. When a child misbehaves, do not get angry. Respond to the child positively or neutrally. Keep your response quiet and peaceful when a child hits or kicks or screams at you. This will model an appropriate reaction for the child.

4. Discuss behavior during a calmer time and problem-solve. When a child has hit, thrown, kicked, yelled, refused to do something, or in other ways acted inappropriately, revisit the situation at a time when the child is calm. Ask the child what he could do differently next time so the situation does not happen again. Role-play appropriate responses, with you taking the child's role, using puppets, or involving other children in a light, playful experience. Guided play will provide a child with the opportunity to develop new coping skills and to learn appropriate behavior.

INTERVENTION: WORKING WITH STRESSED AND TRAUMATIZED CHILDREN

Children who have been abused or in some other way traumatized may need more specialized guidance than other children. Following are common behaviors and characteristics of these children and ways in which you can effectively guide them.

1. Children may pull themselves away from the current situation by daydreaming or not responding when you speak or ask them to do things. This is a survival skill that many children develop to protect themselves. They simply stop thinking and listening, and take themselves somewhere else in their minds. If this has been their coping strategy, it will continue in the classroom and may be misinterpreted as disinterest, defiance, or not paying attention.

2. A child may exhibit sudden anger, fear, or sadness that seems unrelated to the situation. These children often experience post–traumatic stress disorder, in which they have a delayed response to trauma. They may be fine one minute, but a book that reminds them of their parent, a story a child tells about his home, or a smell, sound, or picture may suddenly

bring back their feelings of trauma. They cannot always verbalize why they act, so do not expect them to be able to explain their behavior; just offer them other methods of expression. Providing stress balls and materials with a variety of textures as well as opportunities for running and large-motor movement give good alternatives. Provide a place where such a child can calm down, such as a grouping of pillows, a three-sided box to sit behind, or even a couple of manila folders stapled together and put on a desk in front of the child to allow her privacy. This should not be a place used as punishment, but rather a place of retreat and sanctuary.

3. These children will often be oppositional, resist the teacher's efforts to involve them in play, and feel frustration. Unfortunately, when this occurs, some teachers respond by "upping the ante" and telling them that their punishment will be worse if they continue the behavior. That just sets up a cycle for the child of misbehavior, confrontation, and more misbehavior. Talk ahead of time with these children about what they can do if they are upset. Give them a signal they can use when they need to go to the established method of retreat for a period of time before complying or discussing their frustration.

4. They do not know how to calm down and self-soothe. Traumatized children must be taught skills to develop self-regulation. When you tell the traumatized child he needs to find another activity to do and he does not want to, he cannot calm himself. Other children may use self-talk and in their mind say, "I will come back and do this tomorrow" or "It doesn't matter, I was finished anyway." But traumatized children often lack the skill of self-talk that allows a child to soothe herself. These children can learn this skill when the teacher verbalizes these things and says things such as, "When I am told I can't do something, I tell myself that I will be able to do it later." Teachers can help the children figure out what is soothing for them, such as going to a quiet corner with a book, playing in water or modeling clay, or putting their hands in sand.

5. They often want to hang on and hug anyone who comes into the room. Many of these children have attachment problems. They will run to new people, give them hugs, and hang on them. They may never want to leave the teacher's side. Sometimes children who have been sexually abused will react sexually to others and will exhibit provocative behavior or attempt to act out sexual behavior in play. When this occurs, the teacher should not become emotional and upset, but stay calm and explain that the behavior is not something we do at school. This type of behavior should be reported to the parent if appropriate or to the counselor, caseworker, or therapist.

Other times these children may not want to be touched or may be very antagonistic.

When faced with extreme misbehavior by a child, teachers often react rather than act. Yet many children who have been abused react with extreme behavior. Their anger, hitting, and screaming may be survival behaviors to protect themselves. What can a teacher do? According to Bruce Perry (2001), an expert on trauma in children and others, a teacher working with traumatized children should:

- Be sure to understand their behavior. Learn as much as you can about the child's previous experiences and how he has reacted in the past. If you know that the sight of a bathtub makes the child hysterical, avoid exposing the child to one or prepare him ahead of time for what he will see, what will happen, and how he can handle it. Do not surprise traumatized children! New experiences such as parties, field trips, and visitors to the classroom can be very difficult. Prepare these children ahead of time, tell them what will happen, show pictures of what is coming, discuss how they need to act, and provide them with a way to let you know if it is too much for them and a safe, quiet retreat if needed.

- Treat them according to their developmental age. Traumatized children are often delayed physically, socially, and emotionally. Do not expect a five-year-old who has been traumatized to behave like a five-year-old. She may respond to stress with tantrums and two-year-old behaviors. Rather than telling her that big girls don't act that way, respond as you would to a two-year-old with distraction, ignoring, and soothing afterward. *The Boy Who Was Raised as a Dog* (Perry & Szalavitz, 2006) gives the example of a foster mother who helped a severely traumatized seven-year-old, as well as other traumatized children, by providing rocking and holding that the child had not received as an infant. Teachers can provide sensory materials that can help a child to calm herself and be flexible in allowing the child to be her developmental age.

- Help them learn appropriate behaviors and responses. Do not allow misbehavior just because the children have been traumatized, but redirect and teach them appropriate behaviors. Be sure to stay calm, smile, and use a calming and soothing voice as you explain what is appropriate. These children are often unable to react appropriately in social situations and when they are emotional. Role-play often how to act in different situations. Give them practice. Let them see you model appropriate behavior and bring it to their attention, such as "Naliah, next time you are upset about losing your pen, you can do what I did, and throw your hands up in the air and say, 'Oh well!'" When the children do show appropriate responses, you can call this to their attention, such as "I noticed when Eugene took your truck, you just went and found another truck. That was a good decision!" If children are having trouble relating to peers, you can ask them how other children probably feel about situations to help them develop empathy and perspective. Role-play and practice how to ask to join a group, how to play appropriately with another child, and how to carry on a conversation. Use pictures of different situations, and ask the children how they should act if this happened to them, or if someone said ____.

- Help them develop emotional intelligence. Say positive things to them, such as "You are a real help to me in the classroom" or "You really know how to stay with something and finish it." Help them learn to express their feelings verbally by role playing and giving them appropriate words to use, such as "You are really angry with John right now. You can say to him, 'I am really angry that you took my car.'" Children can also express their feelings through the use of sensory materials, or you can have pictures showing different emotions that they can play with and talk about. Give them approval and make positive comments whenever possible. Help these children feel that they are part of the class. Be sure they have their own space, and display their work as well as the works of others in the classroom. (See Figure 11.1.)

- Keep the classroom calm, and provide soothing activities such as water and sensory play.

- Teach children how to calm themselves with breathing and other techniques, and practice what to do if they become stressed (counting, breathing, closing eyes, turning away from a situation).

- Learn the cues that may set off a traumatized child. When you see situations in which a child may be stressed, watch for signs of stress such as clenched hands or teeth; rapid breathing or tightened, narrowed eyes; or unnatural calmness or activity. Go to the child to assist her in calming down, or distract the child.

CURRICULA AND PROGRAMS FOR INTERVENTION AND PREVENTION

Teachers can impact children's behavior through the curricula that they teach. Setting up centers and activities where children can find appropriate outlets for aggressive and anxious feelings, soothing and calming materials that allow a child to de-stress, and activities that help children know what to do if they are being bullied or in danger of harm from an adult can provide the tools and information for children to protect themselves and develop self-regulation. While most teachers worry about strangers and children being taken, most abuse and neglect occurs from people the child knows. Helping the child learn assertiveness skills, social skills, who to go to when maltreatment occurs, and good and bad touches are critical for children's protection. "Curricular Activities for Teachers" on the website contains some examples of activities for teachers

Disobedient, willful, destructive, aggressive, out of control

Positive, calm, quiet, on child's level, responsive, protects child and other children by separating child from group if needed, holds child carefully to avoid hurting self or child but only when necessary

Child begins to calm and gain control, responds to teacher

States child's feelings, that they are okay, talks about fears and concerns of child, gives choices

Child is calm and responsive to teacher

Discusses alternative behaviors, role play, reassures child that teacher still cares; discusses consequences of behavior and child's feelings

FIGURE 11.1

Working with Behavioral Issues

to use. Some general guidelines are shown in the table entitled "Curricular Resources for Teachers."

Art and Music

Art and music are powerful resources for teachers to use in preventing and intervening in abuse. Children can learn to express fears appropriately through their art. Soothing music can calm children who are anxious. Songs that encourage children to go to teachers or the police for help, that teach emotional expression, and that identify community helpers can help in prevention. Teachers should be watchful for children whose art shows extremes of monsters, anger, aggressive behavior, or depicts the child as always small and helpless. Sometimes these can be clues that something in the child's life is not right. If the art depicts sexual acts or the child being attacked by a parent, further discussion with the child through open-ended questions such as "Tell

Curricular Resources for Teachers

For direct, up-to-date links to these sites and more, please visit our website at www.cengage.com/education/hirschy

General Curricular Resources

I Care Positive parenting and mentoring curricula for teachers, parents, and children that promotes discussion and the teaching of positive character traits. It is based on more than 30 years of parenting research and follows best parenting and teaching practices.

Stop Bullying Now Best practices in bullying prevention and helping children change aggressive behavior. Autonomy, belonging, and cause-and-effect thinking are the basic components of the program. Children are given training; and a sense of strong student-teacher relationships and a stop bullying now committee strengthen this program.

Second Step A violence protection curriculum program based on 20 years of research. Children from preschool to eighth grade learn the skills of anger management, cooperation, problem solving, and respect through teacher and parent curricula.

Talking About Touching A program that empowers children to talk about touch, the difference between good touch and bad touch, and encourages children to tell someone. There is collaboration between children, parents, and teachers.

Steps to Respect A prevent-bullying program with three major components. It is important for the entire school to be actively involved in the program. Staff, teachers, parents, and children are trained to recognize the signs of bullying, to refuse to play a part in it, and to report it to someone who can do something about it.

Teaching Tolerance Ideas for teachers on helping children develop understanding of others, and avoiding violence.

Center on the Emotional and Social Foundations of Early Learning Website provides information, video clips, and research briefs and curricula on guiding young children in classrooms and helping them develop emotional and social skills.

The Alert Program Defines steps for building and teaching self-regulation awareness in children. Children, teachers, parents, and therapists are taught ways to choose appropriate strategies to change or maintain stages of alertness.

TARGET (Trauma Affect Regulation: Guide for Education and Therapy) Helps victims of trauma begin to understand their response to what happened to them and how to handle any future trauma.

We Help Ourselves Offers curricula for all ages from kindergarten through high school on how children can protect themselves from victimization. The program, developed and used over the past 20 years, provides training and curricular materials to teachers and adults who work with children.

National Crime Prevention Council Offers a variety of curricular guides, videos, and activities for children on child safety, bullying, strangers, and so on.

Stranger and Touching Resources

Safety Kids Addresses issues of personal safety for children, including abduction, abuse, violence, drugs, and more.

Safe Child Resources On how to teach about strangers.

A to Z Offers lesson plans for teachers on bullying, strangers, and so on.

(*Continued*)

Curriculum Sites on Bullying (Continued)

Stop Bullying Now! The U.S. government site on bullying includes animated webisodes, activities, and curricula.

Kids Against Bullying A website for children and adults to help them avoid bullying—particularly children with disabilities.

No Bully! A New Zealand site with ideas and resources about bullying.

Peacemakers Provides curriculum and activities to help children learn to be peacemakers.

Kidscape A British site for the prevention of bullying with curricula and activity ideas.

---

me about this picture. What does it mean?" will help you know if the art is a cry for help, something a child saw on television, or an expression about something that has happened and needs to be addressed. If the art is an expression of significant problems, Child Protective Services or counseling services should be contacted.

Dramatic Play

Dramatic play offers children the opportunity to act out their feelings and fears in a safe environment and to practice protection skills. A dramatic play center with puppets and dolls of family members, police, doctors, nurses, and teachers can provide forms of expression. Children can be encouraged to read a book about a child who was lost and then talk about what they would do. Then puppets from the story can be provided. Children, especially older ones, can role-play situations about strangers, what to do in a dangerous situation, and how to be assertive to protect themselves.

Social Studies, Science, and Math

Social studies, science, and math are all subjects in which child abuse prevention can play a part, and in which children who have been exposed to violence can learn things to help them heal.

Social Studies. Children exposed to violence may have difficulty expressing a positive worldview. Include activities in the classroom that allow the children to focus on positive interactions within their family, their community, and their world. Trips to a police station or doctor's office may prevent much anxiety for children who have been exposed to abuse. Those we see as community helpers may appear to be community adversaries to children whose fathers or mothers have been taken away from them by the police. Help children learn that the role of police in the community is to help maintain safety, rather than cause trauma, by having law enforcement officers visit the classroom, and providing books and other materials that are positive. Communicating and interacting within their environment with community helpers may assist in establishing children's ability to feel more positively about their world and to see the people in it as positive influences rather than negative ones.

Learning social skills is also an important part of social studies. Children need to learn negotiation, problem-solving, and conflict resolution skills by working together on group projects, books, dramatic play, and other activities. Modeling is probably the most critical form of curriculum for children. Learning that their behaviors cause things to happen and that they can control the way they relate to others is critical for children who have grown up not being allowed any control in their life.

Science. Children can learn a lot about their bodies and what constitutes appropriate and inappropriate touching through science activities. Children exposed to maltreatment, sexual abuse, or violence often experience anxiety when studying science. Whether the curriculum involves learning about the senses, body awareness, or doing some experiments, an uncomfortable sense or feeling may be invoked in children who have been abused. It is important for the teacher to be sensitive and engaging to such children, equipping them with words to communicate while, at the same time, being cognizant that these children may or may not ask questions to reduce the anxiety they are feeling. The teacher needs to anticipate that children may be uncomfortable and that open-ended questions will need to be asked and sensitive responses given so as not to further alarm children who have been the recipients of abuse.

Math. Children who have been exposed to violence often have difficulty with cooperative interactions and reciprocity in relationships. Math is about relationships and can take place in the block center, at the manipulative table, and in cooking activities, as well as in structured activities in classrooms. Activities need to allow children to engage in cooperative activities with peers. Puzzles can be done together so that children who are placed side-by-side can see what can be made when two pieces are put together.

Literacy. Literature provides children with the knowledge that others may have experienced similar situations, gives strategies for handling problems, and opens avenues for discussion. There are books for all ages on all topics related to child maltreatment and to developing coping skills. Children who have experienced maltreatment often find therapeutic assistance through the use of **bibliotherapies**, or using books to examine and work through issues and problems (Prater, Johnston, Dyches, & Johnstun, 2006). There are many books dealing with specific issues such as abuse, foster care, adoption, bullying, and many other topics related to child maltreatment that are targeted for ages from preschool through adolescence. Children can find in books information, release of emotions, modeling, and a host of other helps. Teachers can make books more valuable by asking questions about what happened, asking the child what he would do in the situation, or having the child develop a picture, create a sculpture or collage about their feelings on the book, or act out the book. When a teacher is concerned about a particular behavior in the classroom, such as a child being ostracized or treated harshly by several children in the classroom, a book can provide a forum for discussion of the behaviors and alternatives. Teachers often find that a favorite book in the classroom can be used to discuss loneliness, fear, support, and other topics that can assist children who have been traumatized or are at risk.

SUMMARY

Schools and child care programs have a responsibility to protect children from abuse and neglect. Developing appropriate policies and guidelines, such as careful hiring and supervision of staff and keeping ratios of children to adults low, will ensure this protection. Teachers are powerful in their ability to help children who have been maltreated and traumatized. Room environments that are supportive—providing routines, following schedules, and using appropriate guidance strategies—will help children self-regulate and learn the skills to avoid and overcome abuse. The curricula provides a method of teaching children in all areas about how to be assertive, what is appropriate and inappropriate behavior toward children, and what to do if they are in an abusive situation. The school and child care program is often the one place a child can find protection, comfort, and support.

Application: When Working with Children

- Create safety in the classroom by having calming and centering activities that encourage problem solving, explore cause and effect, and foster community and relationship building.
- Have consistent expectations of children, especially those who have been traumatized.
- Create predictable situations and predictable consequences for children to provide a safe environment.
- Be sensitive, encouraging, and positive with all children about their feelings, language, and thoughts.
- Reframe thoughts and feelings about the "difficult" children in a classroom. Instead of thinking, "How can I get rid of this child?" think

in terms of "Why is this child having this problem? What can I do to assist her?"

- Emphasize what the child can do, not what he cannot do.
- Children who have been traumatized have difficulty reading facial cues; teachers need to verbalize to children and let them know what happens to children if they act out.

Application: When Working with Families

- Allow families time to speak about the challenges with their child, and ask questions or make comments.
- Speak about the positive attributes of the child, even while emphasizing the child's difficulties, for example, with generalizing and thinking in terms of cause and effect.
- Be hypervigilant about safety. Explain to families whose child has difficulty recognizing that time has passed that their child's mind might be somewhere else. Let parents know that it is important to gently remind children about completing a task or calming down before overreacting.
- Remind parents about the importance of remaining calm and focused while speaking to their child so their child can match their calmness and focused emotional state.

Projects/Activities

1. Draw a diagram of your classroom that will ensure a cooperative, safe environment for children. Label all areas of the classroom—doorways, windows, furniture, and so on. Write a description of the classroom and the strategies you used for placing the items in particular places in the classroom.

2. Find a center or school that has a mentor program and become involved with a child who is in need of one-on-one attention. Plan a day and time each week or every two weeks to spend with this child. Keep a journal of your experiences with the child, and focus on the child's emotional and social development during the time you are together in order to track the development of your relationship. Write a reflection paper at the end of your experience, charting your progress—particularly in the areas of self-regulation, interpersonal interactions, intrapersonal interactions, curriculum, and in general regarding your relationship to the child.

3. Observe a caregiver or teacher for one hour. Write the guidance strategies that you see the person use. Do you notice any changes in the behavior of the children based on the guidance strategies used? Are there rules in the

classroom? What are they? Are the children aware of them? How is the children's behavior influenced by the teacher's behavior? What would you do differently from what you have observed? What would you do the same?

4. Explain what this means to you: "If he places high value on himself, there have been key persons in his life who have treated him with concern and respect; if he holds himself lowly, significant others have treated him as an inferior object" (cited in Nesbit & Philpott, 2002, p. 32).

Questions to Consider

1. How is the environment important in creating a peaceful, cooperative, and safe classroom for children?

2. What must teachers know about themselves before they can begin to work with children who have been abused and neglected?

3. Which guidance strategies promote self-regulation in children?

4. What resources are available for teachers to utilize when working with children who have been traumatized?

5. Which personnel in your center or school will support your ability to work with children who have been abused or neglected?

Websites for More Information

For useful websites, visit www.cengage.com/education/hirschy

APPENDIX **A**

Should I Leave My Child Alone? A Checklist for Parents

Know your state law regarding when a child should be left alone and then ask yourself . . .
Does my child . . .

- ☐ Know his/her name?
- ☐ Know my name?
- ☐ Know my place of work?
- ☐ Know his/her own phone number?
- ☐ Know his/her address?
- ☐ Know how to dial 911?
- ☐ Know who to call for emergencies?
- ☐ Know how to use the phone?
- ☐ Feel confidant and comfortable staying alone at home?
- ☐ Want to be alone at home?
- ☐ Stay calm generally in emergencies and react well in difficult circumstances?
- ☐ Usually tell me the truth?
- ☐ Know how to say no to an adult or another child when the situation is unsafe or unsure?

- ☐ Come to me with problems or try to hide things often?
- ☐ Understand basic safety procedures around the home?
- ☐ Know what to do if a stranger comes to the door?
- ☐ Know what to do if someone calls and asks if the parents are home?
- ☐ Know our neighbors and feel comfortable with them?
- ☐ Know what to do in case of fire or various home accidents that could occur?
- ☐ Know that if something is broken or happens at home, he/she can tell me without fear?
- ☐ Make snacks and food on his/her own and know how to clean up after him/herself?
- ☐ Know where first aid supplies are kept and how to use them for basic first aid?

APPENDIX **B**

Identifying Child Abuse Checklists

Child Abuse Checklists: Check all that apply or might apply. Any one of these indicators could either be normal behavior for the individual child or due to other problems such as illness. This is a guide when trying to determine if abuse has occurred. If you see several indicators or one indicator that is life threatening, you should consider making a report.

Indicators of Child Physical Abuse

Physical Indicators

☐ Tenderness of abdomen, vomiting

☐ Headache, disorientation, dilated pupils, blackouts, or other manifestations of head injury

☐ Complaints of pain without obvious cause

☐ Swelling

☐ Bruises in various stages of healing

☐ Scarring and bruising around the mouth

☐ Multiple bite marks

☐ Burns that have specific shapes, patterns, or occur often

☐ Difficulty seeing or hearing or pain in eyes and ears

Emotional/Social Indicators

☐ Withdrawn or very passive behavior

☐ Aggressive behavior in play or difficulty getting along with other children

☐ Fear when with a particular adult, parent, or sibling or of going home

☐ Fear of being touched or loud voices

☐ Cringes when someone moves quickly as if afraid of being hit

☐ Suicidal behavior or discussion

☐ Problems in school work, concentration, learning difficulties

☐ Explanations for injury that are inconsistent or unbelievable

☐ Wearing long sleeves or pants when very warm

☐ Unwillingness to undress or remove clothing in front of other children or adults

---

☐ Avoids physical contact
☐ Complaints of pain without obvious cause
☐ Learning problems, poor academic performance, short attention span, language delayed

Parent Indicators
☐ Parent talks of child being out of control, or as bad or evil
☐ Parent very rough and threatening when talking to child

Child Abuse Checklists: Check all that apply or might apply. Any one of these indicators could either be normal behavior for the individual child or due to other problems such as illness. This is a guide when trying to determine if abuse has occurred. If you see several indicators or one indicator that is life threatening, you should consider making a report.

Indicators of Child Emotional Abuse

Physical Indicators
- ☐ Speech difficulties, such as stuttering
- ☐ Developmental delays
- ☐ Toileting problems—pants wetting or soiling that is not age-appropriate, or excessive interest or behavior in regard to toileting
- ☐ Head banging, rocking behavior
- ☐ Listless, lacking energy
- ☐ Failure to thrive
- ☐ Self-destructive behaviors

Emotional/Social Indicators
- ☐ Cheating and stealing
- ☐ Aggressive behavior
- ☐ Extremes in disposition—very happy, then very sad
- ☐ Overly compliant or clingy
- ☐ Destructive behavior including fire setting
- ☐ Anxious, insecure
- ☐ Avoids other children
- ☐ Extremely immature or overly mature behavior
- ☐ Poor peer relationships
- ☐ Unable to react emotionally to things
- ☐ Does not form emotional bonds to people
- ☐ Obsessive behaviors, such as hand washing

Parent Indicators
- ☐ Fear or no reaction to parents, especially lack of interest in parents in young toddlers
- ☐ Parent constantly speaks of child as "bad" and a "monster," or belittles child and sees no good
- ☐ Parent always blames child for own and family's problems

Child Abuse Checklists: Check all that apply or might apply. Any one of these indicators could either be normal behavior for the individual child or due to other problems such as illness. This is a guide when trying to determine if abuse has occurred. If you see several indicators or one indicator that is life threatening, you should consider making a report.

Indicators of Child Sexual Abuse

Physical Indicators

- ☐ Torn or stained underclothing
- ☐ Pain, odor, or bleeding in anal or genital area
- ☐ Difficulty sitting and walking
- ☐ Fear of being alone with an adult
- ☐ Promiscuous behavior
- ☐ Loss of appetite, trouble swallowing or eating
- ☐ Complaints of painful urination or bowel movements

Emotional/Social Indicators

- ☐ Secrecy
- ☐ Fear of men or women
- ☐ Low self-esteem
- ☐ Withdrawn or overly aggressive
- ☐ Fear of being touched
- ☐ Knowledge of sex beyond what is age-appropriate
- ☐ Suggestive sexual behavior
- ☐ Extreme fear of bathrooms
- ☐ Sudden change in behavior or performance in school
- ☐ Sexual behavior or words used in play with peers or dolls (beyond playing doctor or normal exploration)
- ☐ Describes sexual encounters
- ☐ Unusually focused in play or artwork on sexual parts
- ☐ Fear of medical exam or of others seeing child naked
- ☐ Child describes being photographed without clothing
- ☐ Nightmares, fear of the dark, trouble sleeping
- ☐ Unreasonable fear of "monsters"
- ☐ Child acting much younger than age, wanting to be taken care of at level inappropriate for developmental stage
- ☐ Talking about new adult in life a lot or about a stranger child has met

Parent Indicators

- ☐ Using new terms for sexual behavior or body parts that have not been part of their vocabulary or seem out of character
- ☐ Parent seems overly attentive to child in a more sexual way

Child Abuse Checklists: Check all that apply or might apply. Any one of these indicators could either be normal behavior for the individual child or due to other problems such as illness. This is a guide when trying to determine if abuse has occurred. If you see several indicators or one indicator that is life threatening, you should consider making a report.

Indicators of Child Neglect

Physical Indicators

☐ Poor hygiene
☐ Dental decay or poor dental care
☐ Inadequate, oversized, undersized, torn, or dirty clothing
☐ Chronic impetigo, sores, diaper rash, or lice
☐ Begging, hoarding, or stealing food
☐ Chronic tiredness
☐ Height and weight significantly above or below age level
☐ Lack of immunizations
☐ Undernourished or signs of malnourishment (swollen or distended stomach, etc.)
☐ Chronic insect bites, sunburn, or respiratory illness that seems to indicate overexposure to the elements
☐ Lack of medical treatment for illness or injury

Social/Emotional Indicators

☐ Overdressed or underdressed
☐ Missing a lot of school
☐ Lack of supervision for a child
☐ Child continually complains of having no bed, or sleeping in cars or different locations
☐ Child describes drugs or dangerous elements in the home
☐ Has little energy

Parent Indicators

☐ States there is no one at home when child is there
☐ Parent seems unconcerned about child
☐ Parent avoids appointments or coming to school

Child Abuse Checklists: Check all that apply or might apply. Any one of these indicators could either be normal behavior for the individual child or due to other problems such as illness. This is a guide when trying to determine if abuse has occurred. If you see several indicators or one indicator that is life threatening, you should consider making a report.

Indicators of Child Exploitation

- ☐ Child exhibits any symptoms of other forms of abuse
- ☐ Child is overly tired, withdrawn
- ☐ Child shows signs of working
- ☐ Child talks about work
- ☐ Child seems older than other children
- ☐ Child cares for other siblings when too young or for long periods of time
- ☐ Child describes being photographed inappropriately
- ☐ Child discusses illegal activities
- ☐ Child describes and is familiar with drugs, paraphernalia, and drug terminology
- ☐ Chronic back, hearing, cardiovascular, or respiratory problems as a result of sweatshops or work situations
- ☐ Unwilling to make friends, avoids other children

NAEYC: Code of Ethical Conduct and Statement of Commitment

A position statement of the National Association for the Education of Young Children*

PREAMBLE

NAEYC recognizes that those who work with young children face many daily decisions that have moral and ethical implications. The NAEYC Code of Ethical Conduct offers guidelines for responsible behavior and sets forth a common basis for resolving the principal ethical dilemmas encountered in early childhood care and education. The Statement of Commitment is not part of the Code but is a personal acknowledgment of an individual's willingness to embrace the distinctive values and moral obligations of the field of early childhood care and education.

The primary focus of the Code is on daily practice with children and their families in programs for children from birth through 8 years of age, such as infant/toddler programs, preschool and prekindergarten programs, child care centers, hospital and child life settings, family child care homes, kindergartens, and primary classrooms. When the issues involve young children, then these provisions also apply to specialists who do not work directly with children, including program administrators, parent educators, early childhood adult educators, and officials with responsibility for program monitoring and licensing. (Note: See also the "Code of Ethical Conduct: Supplement for Early Childhood Adult Educators," online at www.naeyc.org/about/positions/pdf/ethics04.pdf.)

Core values

Standards of ethical behavior in early childhood care and education are based on commitment to the following core values that are deeply rooted in the history of the field of early childhood care and education. We have made a commitment to

- Appreciate childhood as a unique and valuable stage of the human life cycle
- Base our work on knowledge of how children develop and learn
- Appreciate and support the bond between the child and family

---

- Recognize that children are best understood and supported in the context of family, culture,** community, and society
- Respect the dignity, worth, and uniqueness of each individual (child, family member, and colleague)
- Respect diversity in children, families, and colleagues
- Recognize that children and adults achieve their full potential in the context of relationships that are based on trust and respect

NAEYC: WHERE WE STAND ON CHILD ABUSE PREVENTION*

As the nation's largest organization of early childhood professionals and others dedicated to improving the quality of early childhood programs, the National Association for the Education of Young Childhood (NAEYC) is committed to safeguarding the well-being of all children. NAEYC recognizes that early childhood professionals and programs play an important role in preventing—not just reporting—child abuse and neglect.

NAEYC's position statements "Prevention of Child Abuse in Early Childhood Programs and the Responsibilities of Early Childhood Professionals to Prevent Child Abuse" (1996) and "Code of Ethical Conduct and Statement of Commitment" (1997) and other NAEYC publications clearly outline that early childhood programs and professionals should

1. Adopt policies and practices that promote close partnerships with families

---

** The term *culture* includes ethnicity, racial identity, economic level, family structure, language, and religious and political beliefs, which profoundly influence each child's development and relationship to the world.

SCOPE OF THE PROBLEM

- In 2000, there were nearly three million reports concerning suspected abuse of five million children, and about one million children were confirmed as victims of abuse or neglect.
- Boys and girls are equally likely to experience neglect and physical abuse. Girls are four times more likely to experience sexual abuse.
- Children of all races and ethnicities experience child abuse.
- Children of all ages experience abuse, but the youngest children are most vulnerable.
- Most abuse happens within families.
  (DHHS 2003)

---

2. Promote standards of excellence for early childhood programs
3. Provide families a variety of supportive services
4. Advocate for children, families, and teachers in community and society
5. Collaborate with other professionals in the community
6. Understand their legal and ethical obligation to recognize and report suspicions of abuse

1. Adopt Policies and Practices that Promote Close Partnerships with Families Close partnerships with families can reduce the potential for child abuse by family members. Early childhood programs can provide information and support to families regarding child development and effective strategies for responding to children's challenging behavior (NAEYC 1996, 2003). Communicating with families, especially about difficult topics, is crucial if educators are to provide support to families. This kind of communication is much easier when a supportive, reciprocal relationship already exists. Early childhood professionals should also

- acknowledge and build upon family strengths and competencies;
- respect the dignity of each family and its culture, language, customs, and beliefs;
- help families understand and appreciate each child's progress within a developmental perspective;
- help family members enhance their parenting skills; and
- build support networks for families by providing opportunities for interaction with program staff, other families, community resources, and professional services (NAEYC 1997).

2. Promote Standards of Excellence for Early Childhood Programs
High-quality care and education helps to strengthen families and promote healthy social and emotional development, as well as preparing children for later school success. Programs should use developmentally appropriate practices and pursue NAEYC Accreditation, which requires a rigorous self-study process and an independent external assessment to determine whether high standards are met. Early childhood professionals should also inform the public about the need for and benefits of high-quality early childhood programs (NAEYC 1996).

3. Provide a Variety of Supportive Services to Families
In addition to knowing the signs of abuse and neglect, early childhood

This publication is part of Supporting Teachers, Strengthening Families, an initiative to expand NAEYC's efforts to help early childhood professionals and families prevent child abuse and neglect and achieve the best possible social and emotional outcomes for all children. The Doris Duke Charitable Foundation generously supports Supporting Teachers, Strengthening Families. Other products of this initiative include a national survey of early childhood professionals, the report *Early Childhood Educators and Child Abuse Prevention: NAEYC's Perspective, Research Findings, and Future Actions*, a brochure, and more. Download these and other resources and obtain more information about Supporting Teachers, Strengthening Families at www.naeyc.org/ece/supporting.asp.

professionals should be able to recognize situations that may place children at risk. When working with families who are in those situations, professionals should provide appropriate information and referrals to community services, and follow up to ensure that services have been provided (NAEYC 1996, 1997). Families' access to health care, housing, income support, and other social services may help protect children from abuse and neglect.

4. Advocate for Children, Families, and Teachers in Community and Society
Early childhood educators, as individuals and as a profession, should participate in the policy-making process by

- advocating for well-designed, sufficiently funded, and effectively implemented public regulations, programs, and community support services that meet the individual needs of children and families and promote their well-being;

- cooperating with other individuals and groups in advocacy efforts; and
- opposing policies that impair child and family well-being (NAEYC 1997).

5. Collaborate with other professionals in the community

The early childhood community should work with other professionals concerned with the welfare of young children and families (NAEYC 1997). Collaboration with other agencies and disciplines promotes understanding of child development, supports and empowers families, and strengthens advocacy efforts (NAEYC 1996).

6. Understand their legal and ethical obligation to recognize and report suspicions of abuse

Early childhood professionals should

- be familiar with the symptoms of child abuse and neglect, including physical, sexual, verbal, and emotional abuse;
- know and follow state laws and community procedures that protect children against abuse and neglect; and

- report suspected child abuse or neglect to the appropriate community agency and follow up to ensure that appropriate action has been taken. When appropriate, educators should inform parents or guardians that a referral has been made (NAEYC 1997).

References

DHHS (U.S. Department of Health and Human Services, Administration on Children, Youth and Families). 2003. *Child maltreatment 2001.* Washington, DC: U.S. Government Printing Office.

NAEYC. 1996. Position Statement. Prevention of child abuse in early childhood programs and the responsibilities of early childhood professionals to prevent child abuse. Online: www.naeyc.org/about/positions/pdf/pschab98.pdf.

NAEYC. 1997. *Code of ethical conduct and statement of commitment.* Rev. ed. Brochure. Washington, DC: Author. Online: www.naeyc.org/about/positions/pdf/pseth98.pdf.

NAEYC. 2003. *Early childhood educators and child abuse prevention: NAEYC's perspective, research findings, and future actions.* Washington, DC: Author.

APPENDIX D

Health and Well-Being Assessment

Date: _____

Your Name: _____ Child's Name: _____

Place an X or line through the appropriate symbol.

		Health and Well-Being Assessment
☺	☹	Appearance: Child appears healthy and happy
☺	☹	Hygiene: Clothing and body appear clean
☺	☹	Skin: Skin is not pale or sallow; feels cool to touch; is not cold or clammy; no serious rashes, bites, scrapes, or bruises
☺	☹	Eyes: Eyes are bright and clear; no evidence of redness, oozing, or problems
☺	☹	Nose: No discharge, or if some, clear only
☺	☹	Ears: Child responds to questions or sounds and appears to hear; no discharge
☺	☹	Mouth: Child has no sores around mouth; breath smells clean and not bad
☺	☹	Speech: Child's speech is normal and not slurred
☺	☹	Scalp and hair: Scalp is clean and without sores, nits; hair is clean and not dull and severely broken
☺	☹	Behavior: Child's behavior is normal for child; not overly withdrawn, shy, outgoing, or aggressive
☺	☹	Extremities: Hands, arms, legs, and feet appear normal; no evidence of severe bruising or cuts; child does not wince at touch or use of extremity
Concerns:		

APPENDIX **E**

Am I at Risk to Emotionally Abuse a Child? A Checklist for Teachers

Am I aware of my own temperament?

Am I aware of the temperaments of the children I teach, especially those who are particularly difficult?

How do I react when I am angry or frustrated with a child?

Do I view certain children as "troublemakers," "difficult," "mean," "dumb," or "not likeable"?

Are there certain children whom I always find in trouble?

When something in the classroom happens, do I automatically assume it is a certain child or group?

When I discipline a child would the discipline be different if it was one of my easier, more favorite children?

Are all the children in my classroom given second chances, and opportunities for rewards and for improving behavior?

When something happens, do I react in ways that I regret later?

Do my reactions to a child lower the child's self-esteem or make the child feel like a failure?

Consider your answers to these questions, and then write an action plan below for improving your guidance and behavior with the children you teach:

Glossary

A

abdominal and internal injury trauma—type of trauma found more often with younger children; has a higher death rate than other types of trauma

abrasions, cuts, bites, and burns—types of injuries inflicted purposefully on a child; can be caused by a body part such as a hand or foot, or an instrument such as a knife, curling iron, hot pan, and so on

absenteeism—not attending school for a period of time

Adam Walsh Child Protection and Safety Act of 2006—a law enacted by Congress to establish a national registry of individuals who have substantiated child abuse cases

adjudication—determination of abuse, and how confirmed cases will be processed and handled

adjudication and disposition—the court system may go through several types of hearings to determine the outcome of a petition; hearings may be held to review evidence, to hear testimony, to issue orders, to place a child in temporary or permanent custody, to sever parental rights, and to make a disposition of the case

adoption—the legal permanent placement of a child with someone other than the biological parent

adult resilience—includes the positive mental health of the parents or caregivers, and their adaptability to

crises, new situations, and differing personalities of children

age of onset—when maltreatment first began

appropriate environments—classroom environments for young children that are warm, inviting, and comforting can provide a child who comes from a stressed home situation with a blanket of protection

assignment and investigation—the assignment of a suspected child abuse case to the appropriate government agency for the purposes of determining whether child maltreatment has occurred.

at-risk—social, psychological, physiological, and educational factors that may cause difficulties

attachment—the bonding of a child to a significant caregiver

attachment theory—states that, during the first year of life, infants must form a secure attachment to a caregiver

authoritarian parenting—often requires absolute obedience from the child without discussion

authoritative parenting—involves guiding the child through setting rules and standards, and through the use of discussion, persuasion, consequences for behavior, and consistency

B

baby trafficking—the illegal sale of infants

battered child syndrome—Dr. Henry C. Kempe coined the phrase after seeing so many unexplained internal injuries that were identified as "accidents" by parents

behavioral theories—focus on how stimulus in the environment creates a response from the individual receiving the stimulus

beliefs—strong families have commitments to certain beliefs that the whole family supports

bias—to have or display partiality or favoritism and influence to a certain individual or group of people

bibliotherapies—using books to examine and work through issues and problems

bio-ecological systems theory—developed by Urie Broffenbrenner (1979) to explain the impact of the child's environment and biology on his growth and development

bruising—the physical injury seen most often in abuse, which is dependent on several factors; when it is the result of abuse, it is usually found in places on the child's body that would not typically show marks

bullying—physical and/or verbal aggression, or withholding of friendship toward a child, usually by one or a group of other children, who are trying to gain power over the individual, take property from the individual, or gain status in some way

C

CASA (Court Appointed Special Advocate) program—a program in which volunteers serve as advocates for children involved in abuse and neglect

child abuse—any act or failure to act that endangers a child's physical or emotional health and development

Child Abuse Prevention and Treatment Act or CAPTA (Public Law 93-247)—the first comprehensive federal legislation on child abuse; provided money to states for identification, investigation, prosecution, and treatment of child abuse and neglect, and established a minimal definition of child abuse and neglect

child advocacy centers—promote coordination of agencies in their work with child maltreatment under one roof

child exploitation—the use of a child by an adult to achieve some tangible benefit; occurs when a child is used for labor in hazardous work or in work that is beyond her abilities, or when her labor is used for the parent's gain

child labor—the economic exploitation of children through the performance of any work that is likely to be hazardous, be harmful to the child's health, interfere with the child's education, or hamper the child's physical, emotional, mental/intellectual, moral, or social development

child maltreatment—the umbrella term for the multiple forms of abuse and neglect, and their characteristics

child pornography—using children in the creation of sexual materials usually for the purpose of sale, although it is also used to initiate children into sexual activity

child prostitution—the use of children sexually for profit

Child Protective Services (CPS)—identifies services that will prevent or alleviate abuse and neglect in the family, assists the family in getting needed services, and monitors the family situation

children and warfare—children are killed or maimed as a result of war, and children in war zones are often psychologically and economically affected

Children's Aid Societies—organizations established and supported by private and public funds to protect urban children who are considered neglected

child trafficking—according to UNICEF, the recruitment, transportation, transfer, harboring, or receipt of a child for the purpose of exploitation, which includes, at a minimum, the exploitation of the prostitution of others or other forms of sexual exploitation, forced labor or services, slavery or practices similar to slavery, servitude, or the removal of organs

chronicity—the duration and repeated instances of a child's maltreatment experience

chronosystem—the impact of time, the child's growth, or the historical setting on the child

civil courts—proceedings involving a judge but not a jury; can include family court, probate court, juvenile court, and other types as well

collaboration—families work together with professionals

communication, appreciation, and guidance—a shared system of listening, sharing, and then listening; families where the different members spend time talking and showing appreciation for one another create protective factors from abuse and neglect

community resources—places and/or people whom families can call upon for assistance

criminal courts—courts of law in which criminal cases are tried and determined; a judge and jury are involved in the proceedings

cross-cultural—combining two or more cultures or groups

cultural practices—pertaining to certain practices, customs, and attitudes common to a specific group of people

culture—the geographic location, values, attitudes, beliefs, characteristics, language, rules, traditions, rituals, artifacts, and ideas that one group of people hold in common

custody—legal responsibility for a child; can also denote who has physical charge over a child

cyber bullying—involves the use of technology, including the Internet (through e-mail, websites, blogs, and instant messaging), videos, and cell phones, to humiliate, tease, threaten, or in some way victimize someone

cyberstalking—harassment and denigration repeatedly so that fear is created

D

denigration—sending information or posting comments that are rumors, gossip, or lies that can damage the victim's reputation

developmental stages—identified by many theorists as specific time periods in a child's life when certain abilities are developed and specific types of development occur

discipline—the process of teaching children to follow certain rules and principles and the enforcement of the behaviors an adult feels are appropriate.

dissociation—a psychological response to abuse and trauma that can include disengagement, distancing the mind from the trauma or from others, numbness, separation from emotion and even amnesia.

diversity—a variety of something; may be used in regard to gender, ethnicity, opinion, color, or style

documentation—a record of concerns, including dates, times, behaviors, appearance, and any conversations that are suspicious

drug exposure—abuse of children that occurs through ingestion of chemicals used in drug production or accidents in drug labs, or through exposure to parents or other adults who use drugs prenatally or after birth, who may abuse or neglect the children

E

educational neglect—not ensuring that children receive an appropriate education

ego—the central force that balances the id and super-ego and integrates these into the personality according to Freud

emotional abuse—behavior toward a child that is not physical but harms the child's psychological capacity and/or ability as evidenced by changes in the child's emotions, abilities, or behaviors now or over time

emotional development—characterized by significant developmental sequences of emotions

emotional neglect—the lack of provision of a nurturing emotional environment or emotional deprivation that results in changes in the child's emotions, abilities, or behaviors now or over time

enmeshed—describes family members who are overly involved with each other, where they have limited communication with those outside the family and are totally self-involved

ethics—principles or values that govern a particular culture or group; rules of conduct followed by an individual

ethnicity—includes many elements of culture, but usually involves a group of people with commonalities over time and often who have a geographic commonality or heritage either currently or from ancestry

ethologist—an individual who works with animals; ethologists have demonstrated that some infant animals and birds have a critical period during which they must form an attachment with their mother in order to develop appropriately

exclusion—purposefully excluding someone from online groups, conversations, and social networking pages

exosystem—those things that influence society, and therefore the child and family generally, such as laws, government, media, and culture

externalizing behaviors—to exhibit patterns of maladjustment such as aggressive, noncompliant, and disruptive behaviors

F

failure to thrive (FTT)—a condition in which an infant or child fails to gain weight or loses weight in a significant manner and usually not corresponding to height gain

family affection, nurturance, and support—strong families believe in the importance of the family unit and work to support it

family-centered care—providing care that focuses not just on the child but also on the family, and which empowers the family to manage their own care

family-centered services—services that focus on building the strengths of the family so that they can provide a healthy and safe environment for the children; they provide the family, not the individual child, with the ability to function well

family life education—provides families with information on various aspects of parenting and family life

family preservation services—given to families who have been identified as being abusive or neglectful but who are felt to be able with the services to keep the child in the home

family support services—preventative services, aimed at strengthening the family

family systems theory—developed from a general theory that examined types of systems that exist in nature

female circumcision—the surgical removal of the clitoris or sewing up of the vaginal opening; often done with very crude instruments and little or no anesthetic

fetal alcohol spectrum disorders—developmental problems caused by the mother drinking alcohol

fetal alcohol syndrome—a group of physical, emotional, and intellectual characteristics that are often seen as the result of a mother drinking alcohol during pregnancy

fight or flight syndrome—an aggressive or withdrawal reaction

flaming—the use of vulgar and angry comments to hurt someone

forensic interviewer—a person who is specially trained to ask nonleading and appropriate questions of children

foster care—temporary placement of a child outside the home, usually with a relative, a foster home, a group home, therapeutic home, or special institution for children

foundling—(orphan) homes that provided care for abandoned infants

fractures and skeletal injuries—usually breaks in bone that occur as a result of severe trauma to a child from an instrument, a body part (such as a hand or foot), or from being thrown against an object or the ground

frequency—the number of reports and the duration of maltreatment

G

global prevention—focusing on funding and services to prevent child abuse on a broader scope

goodness of fit—the ability of the parent and child to adapt their different temperaments to meet one another's needs

grooming—a process where the perpetrator develops a relationship with the child to create comfort and trust and gradually moves along a continuum before initiating sexual activity with the child

group and institutional care—provides an option for those children who do not fit into a home situation

group parent education—occurs usually in a school or office setting in which parents gather for one or a series of classes aimed at improving parenting skills

guardian ad litem (GAL)—a person appointed by the court to serve as a special advocate just for the child; the GAL does not represent parents or agencies involved, but only the child; the GAL will get to know the child, do an independent investigation of the case, and make sure that courts and social service agencies are meeting the child's best interests and that the case is resolved as quickly and painlessly as possible

guidance—methods of providing children with direction, structure and support that will encourage the development of self-discipline and positive emotional and social development.

H

harassment—messages sent to a child continually that are mean, insulting, or threatening

health and well-being appraisal—enables teachers to detect early signs and symptoms of many illnesses, health impairments, and changes in appearance and behavior

hearing—held as soon as possible to determine if a child is to be placed in substitute care, to appoint counsel for the parents (if they do not have one) and an attorney or guardian ad litem for the child, to order assessments and services for families and children, and to explain expectations for the parents and what needs to happen next

homeostasis—families strive to maintain a balance in the family and to keep things the same

hyperarousal—a coping mechanism in which the child, instead of dissociating, becomes hyperactive

I

id—according to Freud, the part of the unconscious that deals with instinctive drives such as hunger and sexual needs

impersonation—pretending to be the victim for the purpose of damaging the victim's reputation or in some way using the person's identity for harmful purposes

incest—sexual maltreatment among families' members

indicated case—where child maltreatment cannot be substantiated but there is still reason to suspect, and a case is opened

individual parent education—involves working one-on-one with the family

infanticide—the intentional killing of infants through violence or neglect

informal assessments—routine health and well-being appraisals that are performed on children

intake—the initial processing of an original allegation

intergenerational transmission of abuse—people abusing because they were abused; abuse based on other generations of individuals being abused

internalizing behaviors—exhibiting depression, anxiety, and social withdrawal behaviors

internal locus of control—feeling that the child himself can be responsible for what happens in his life and is not controlled by luck or others

intervention—occurs when a child is at risk for or has been abused or neglected, and needs more specialized guidance

involvement and supervision—knowing where children are at all times, checking on children often, and being involved in the child's school, social, and home life all contribute to strengthening families

J

jurisdiction—authority

L

Likert scale—measures level of agreement to a statement that describes something

logical consequence—one that would logically follow a behavior; a child who does not pick up her toys, for example, might lose those toys for the rest of the day

M

macrosystems—systems that influence the child indirectly by impacting teachers, parents, or others who directly affect the child, for example, the parent's workplace, the community and its resources, or religion

mandatory reporting—the responsibility of every professional, teacher, caseworker, nurse, and anyone who works with children to report abuse and neglect that they *suspect*, not just that which they know is happening; a law in every state requires certain professionals, usually teachers, child care providers, doctors, and so on, to report suspected child abuse

media exploitation—exploiting children through their use in the media

medical neglect—not providing adequate mental health, medical, and dental care for a child

mesosystem—used to explain the relationships between people and things in the child's microsystem or other systems and their effects on the child

microculture—a social group that shares distinctive traits, values, and behaviors that set it apart from the larger culture; refers to groups of people within a larger society who are set apart by certain common characteristics, practices, artifacts, values, and ideas

microsystems—those things that directly affect the child

mongolian spots—a congenital mark that looks like bruising and is often seen on young children, especially young children of color

motivation—encourages one to repeat the observed behavior on a continuing basis

multicultural—race, culture, language, life experiences, and power that shapes understanding and represents several different groups of people

Munchausen by proxy syndrome—a rare form of child abuse that occurs when a parent purposely makes a child ill or falsifies tests and child histories so that the child is subjected to hospitalizations and testing that are either unnecessary or brought on by the parent's behaviors

N

natural consequence—one that will occur automatically as a result of behavior; if a child forgets to take his coat, he will be cold

neglect—failure to provide for a child's basic needs

nonfamilial foster homes—those in which families not related to the child are identified for child placement

nonfamily abuse—abuse by perpetrators who are not family members, for example, an unmarried partner, a friend, or a neighbor

O

online victimization—harassment of a child by one or more children online in chat rooms, instant messages, e-mail, and on websites; threats, lies, or confidential details of a child's life are shared virtually, which often leads to humiliation, loss of friendships, and in some cases suicide

orphan train—children were placed with families chosen by local ministers or by town committees to learn the virtues of hard work and a Christian life; these children often became a cheap labor source for farm families, and many were treated harshly

outcry—a child's asking for help

outing—sharing the victims' secrets or personal information for the purpose of embarrassment or harm

P

pandemic—a term referring to the widespread existence of child maltreatment in large segments of the population

parent knowledge—knowing how children grow and develop and what to expect at different ages and stages; this helps parents and adult caregivers cope with stressful situations with children

partnerships—based on mutual respect and the understanding that professionals, parents, families, and children all have rights and responsibilities

pedophiles—people who are sexually aroused by children, usually men, but can also be women

permanent custody—full legal custody of the child is given to a person or the state, and the rights of the parents are severed; requires a court system

permissive parenting—parenting style in which the child is allowed to do what she wants as long as safety is not a factor

perpetrators—those who abuse children; many factors influence their behavior

petition—a complaint or allegation of child abuse or neglect

physical abuse—any type of injury to a child that is physically inflicted or causes physical harm

physical neglect—anything that results in a child's physical needs being unmet

policy—a definite course of action

post–traumatic stress disorder (PTSD)—a cluster of emotional, physiological, and psychological symptoms following an extremely stressful event

prejudice—having an opinion, attitude, or feeling formed beforehand without reason, thought, or knowledge of a person, place, or group

prevention—methods used to keep child maltreatment from happening or from being repeated

primary prevention—local in nature; such programs may be developed from a national pilot or model program, but they are administered locally with the aim of preventing abuse and neglect by providing direct services to families

prosocial skills—positive ways that children learn how to be autonomous with one another

psychodynamic theory—Sigmund Freud addressed abuse and neglect by using this theory

psychosocial development—Erik Erikson, a developmental psychologist, identified eight stages a child and adult go through and tasks they need to accomplish in order to function well socially

psychosocial short stature (PSS)—a disorder of short stature, or growth failure, and/or delayed puberty of infancy, childhood, and adolescence, which is observed in association with emotional deprivation and/or a pathological or psychosocial environment

R

race—the identification of a group based on perceived physical characteristics, which may or may not be accurate

rape—sexual intercourse that usually involves violence toward the child

ratios—providing enough adults for the number of children in a classroom; critical to healthy functioning in a classroom

recidivism—repeating abuse and/or neglect of a child

reciprocity—seeking to balance power between people in conversation, and recognizing that everyone has something of value to contribute

relative care—the placement of a child with a relative other than the custodial parent or relative; provides a child with a known caregiver who already has a relationship with the child

religion—a set of beliefs concerning the cause, nature, and purpose of the universe, especially when involving creation by a superhuman agency

reprimanding—verbal or nonverbal behaviors toward a child that are hostile or negative and critical

reproduce—behavior that is acted out because of what is seen and heard repeatedly

resiliency—the ability of a child to endure adversity, threat, or risk and to adapt positively in areas of functioning, even in the face of difficult circumstances

respect—the ability to make oneself vulnerable to another while recognizing different boundaries

responsiveness—an openness in allowing other individuals to be who they are without trying to reshape them into who you want them to be

retention—the ability to remember and/or imagine what has been seen or what has occurred

role model—a person whose behavior is copied or imitated by others

routines—regular courses of action; everyday activities that are done at the same time intervals during the day

rules—principles or regulations that tell people how they should conduct themselves and act

S

schedules—a plan of procedure written for a proposed sequence of and time allotted for each item; a series of things to be done or of events to occur at once during a particular time or period

secondary prevention—a strategy providing resources and support to all families, with child abuse prevention as a secondary goal; programs that benefit families in more general ways

self-directed parent education—occurs when parents read materials or watch audiovisual information on their own in an effort to improve their parenting

self-discipline—the ultimate goal of guidance and discipline should be for children to internalize values and appropriate behavior

severity—the nature and intensity of maltreatment

sexual abuse—any involvement of a child in sexually related activities

sexual solicitation and approaching—the child is brought into online sexual activities or sex talk

shaken baby syndrome (SBS)—severe trauma caused by violent shaking of a child

sibling abuse—when a child becomes psychologically, physically, or sexually aggressive toward a sibling in a way that can cause consistent or permanent harm

situational factors—factors that put a person at risk for child maltreatment

skilled dialogue—positive conversations, understanding, and interactions with parents that can improve relationships within families; approaching the challenge posed by cultural diversity when interacting with families is important

social learning theory—adapts behavioral theory to take into account the effects of relationships with other people and with the world on behavior

social support—strong families have many resources

Society for the Prevention of Cruelty to Children—an organization formed as a result of the Mary Ellen case in New York, which helped pass new laws and legislation for the protection of children

socioeconomic status—the combination or interaction of social and economic factors; groups distinguished by the amount of money they have, for example, those living in poverty, middle class, and wealthy

spanking—using the hand to hit a child on the buttocks, hand, or leg with the purpose of correcting behavior

stages of psychosocial development—a series of eight stages developed by Erik Erikson through which a person must progress in order to be emotionally healthy and fully developed

stress—physical, mental, or emotional strain or tension that interferes with or disturbs the normal physiological development of an individual

substantiated case—a case that is opened and on which action is taken

sudden infant death syndrome (SIDS)—the most common cause of death between the ages of 1 and 6 months; involves the sudden death of an infant during sleep without any obvious explanation, even after autopsy has been performed

superego—the conscience according to Freud

supervisory neglect—leaving children alone or with someone unable to adequately supervise them

T

teacher behavior—the ability of a teacher to influence a child or classroom through attitude, actions, and communication

temperament—the innate traits of a person that form a basis for behavior and personality

temporary custody—often given to protective services so that they can have the legal right to make decisions and placements for children

Trafficking Victims Protection Act—passed in 2000, this law monitors and sanctions countries that allow trafficking, and provides penalties to traffickers and protection services for adults and children who are victims

trickery—tricking someone into sharing personal information and then sharing it with others electronically

truancy—when a child has an unexcused absence from school, often without parental knowledge

type—the form of maltreatment

U

unsubstantiated case—where there is not enough evidence to indicate abuse and the incident is closed

V

voyeurism—watching children perform sexual acts they are forced to participate in, or having children watch as sexual acts are performed

W

wet nurses—women who had given birth during the previous year and still had breast milk

References

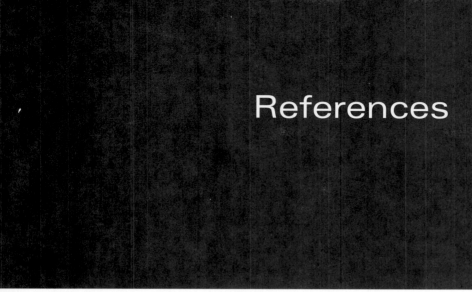

Abel, E. (2004). Paternal contribution to fetal alcohol syndrome. *Addiction Biology, 9*, 127–133.

Action for Child Protection, Inc. (2007, October). *The absence of basic resources as a threat to a child's safety.* Retrieved 3-28-08 from http://www .actionchildprotection.org.

Adventists Beliefs. (2007). Retrieved September 16, 2007, from Seventh Day Adventist Church: http://www .adventist.org/beliefs/statements/main_stat2.html.

Ainsworth, M., Blehar, M., Waters, E., & Wall, S. (1978). *Patterns of attachment: A psychological study of the strange situation.* Hillsdale, NJ: Erlbaum.

Aldridge, J., & Goldman, R. (2002). *Current issues and trends in education.* Boston: Allyn and Bacon.

Aluedse, O. (2006). Bullying in schools: A form of child abuse in schools. *Educational Research Quarterly, 30*(1), 37–49.

American Academy of Pediatrics (AAP). (2003). Policy statement: Family-centered care and the pediatrician's role. *Pediatrics, 112*(3), 691–696.

American Academy of Pediatrics (AAP). (1998). Guidance for effective discipline. *Pediatrics, 101*(4), 723–728.

American Association of University Women Educational Foundation (AAUW). (2001). *Hostile hallways: Bullying, teasing, and sexual harassment in school.* Retrieved May 28, 2008, from http://www.aauw .org/research/hostile.cfm.

American Humane Society. (2007). *The real story of Mary Ellen Wilson.* Retrieved April 27, 2007, from http:// www.americanhumane.org/.

American Professional Society on the Abuse of Children. (1995). *Guidelines for the psychosocial evaluation of suspected psychological maltreatment in children and adolescents.* Chicago: Author.

Anderson, M., Kaufman, J., Simon, T., Barios, L., Paulizzi, L., Ryan, G., et al. (2006). School-associated violent deaths in the United States, 1994–1999. *Journal of American Medical Association, 286*(1), 2695–2702.

Aries, P. (1970). *Centuries of childhood* (R. Baldick, Trans.). New York: Knopf. (Original work published 1962.)

Ashby, P. (2002). Child combatants: A soldier's perspective. *Lancet, 360*, 11–12.

Ashton, R. (Ed.). (1851). *The works of John Robinson. Vol. I.* (pp. 246–247). Retrieved May 6, 2007, from: http:// www.swarthmore.edu/Humanities/kjohnso1/brad-street.html.

Baker, C. (2002). *Female survivors of sexual abuse: An integrated guide to treatment.* Hove: Brunner-Routledge.

Bandura, A. (2002). Social cognitive theory in cultural context. *Applied Psychology: An International Review, 51*(2), 269–290.

Barnett, O., Miller-Perin, C., & Perin, R. (2005). *Family violence across the lifespan.* Thousand Oaks, CA: Sage.

Barr, R., Trent, R., & Cross, J. (2006). Age-related incidence curve of hospitalized shaken baby syndrome cases: Convergent evidence for crying as a trigger to shaking. *Child Abuse and Neglect, 30*, 7–16.

Barrera, I., Coso, R., & Macpherson, D. (2003). *Skilled dialogue: Strategies for responding to cultural diversity in early childhood.* Baltimore: Brookes.

Bass, S., Shields, M., & Behrman, R. (2004). Children, famillies, and foster care: Analysis and recommendations. *Future of Children, 14*(1), 5–31.

Baumrind, D. (1971). Correct patterns of parental authority. *Developmental Psychology Monographs, 4*, 1–103.

Baumrind, D., Larzelere, R. E., & Cowan, P. A. (2002). Ordinary physical punishment: Is it harmful? Comment on Gershoff. *Psychological Bulletin, 128*, 4, 580–589.

Beale, A. (2001). Bullybusters: Using drama to empower students to take a stand against bullying behavior. *Professional School Counseling, 4*, 300–306.

Beamen, R. (2000). Teachers' use of approval and disapproval in the classroom. *Educational Psychology, 20*(4), 16–32.

Beers, S., & De Bellis, M. (2002). Neuropsychological function in children with maltreatment related posttraumatic stress disorder. *American Journal of Psychiatry, 159*, 483–486.

Benbenishty, R., Zeira, A., Astor, R. A., & Khoury-Kassabri, M. (2002). Maltreatment of primary school students by educational staff in Israel. *Child Abuse and Neglect, 26*, 1291–1309.

Berger, L. (2005). Income, family characteristics, and physical violence toward children. *Child Abuse and Neglect, 29*, 107–133.

Besaw, A., Akalt, J., Lee, A., Sethi, J., Wilson, J., & Zemler, M. (2004). The context and meaning of family strengthening in Indian America. A report to the Annie E. Casey Foundation by The Harvard Project on American Indian Economic Development: Harvard University. Retrieved January 27, 2008, from http://www.ksg.harvard.edu/hpaied.

Beyer, C. (2004). Global child trafficking. *Lancet, 364*, 16–17.

Bifulco, A., Moran, P., Ball, C., Jacobs, C., Baines, R., & Cavagin, J. (2002). Childhood adversity, parental vulnerability and disorder: Examining intergenerational transmission of risk. *Journal of Child Psychology and Psychiatry, 43*(8), 1075–1086.

Bioethics, C. O. (1997). Religious objections to medical care. *Pediatrics, 99*, 279–281.

Block, R., & Krebs, N. (2005). Failure to thrive as a manifestation of child neglect. *Pediatrics, 116*(7), 1234–1237.

Bolger, K., & Patterson, C. (2001). Developmental pathways from child maltreatment to peer rejection. *Child Development, 72*(2), 549–568.

Boss, P. (2003). *Family stress: Classic and contemporary readings.* Thousand Oaks, CA: Sage.

Bostrom, M. (2003). *Discipline and development: A meta-analysis of public perceptions of parents, parenting, child development and child abuse.* Accessed February 2008, Frameworks Institute: http://www.frameworksinstitute.org/products/pca_americaameta.pdf.

Boswell, J. (1990). The kindness of strangers. New York: Vintage Books.

Botha, P. (2002). Young bodies and religion: Exploring the role of religion in child abuse. *Religion and Theology, 9*(1), 42–62.

Bowlby, J. (1988). *A secure base: Parent-child attachment and healthy human development.* New York: Basic Books.

Boynton, M., & Boynton, C. (2005). *The educator's guide to preventing and solving discipline problems.* Alexandria, VA: ASCD.

Breiner, S. J. (1990). Slaughter of the innocents: Child abuse through the ages and today. New York: Plenum Press.

Briscoe-Smith, A. M., & Hinshaw, S. P. (2006). Linkages between child abuse and attention-deficit/hyperactivity disorder in girls: Behavioral and social correlates. *Child Abuse and Neglect, 30*, 1239–1255.

Brok, P., Brekelmans, M., & Wubbels, T. (2004). Interpersonal teacher behavior and student outcomes. *School effectiveness and school improvement, 15*(3/4), 407–442.

Bronfenbrenner, U. (1979). *The ecology of human development: Experiments by nature and design.* Cambridge, MA: Harvard University Press.

Bronfenbrenner, U. (1977). The fracturing of the American family. *Washington University Daily*, October 5, p. 5 (summary of a lecture).

Brown, J., Ye, H., Bronson, R., Dikkes, P., & Greenberg, M. (1996). A defect in nurturing in mice lacking the immediate early gene fosB. *Cell, 86*, 297–309.

Burden, P. R. (1990). Teacher development. In W. R. Houston (Ed.), *Handbook of research on teacher education* (pp. 311–328). New York: Macmillan.

Burnett, P. C. (2002). Teacher praise and feedback and students' perception of the classroom environment. *Educational Psychology, 22*(1), 5–16.

Burrows-Horton, C., & Cruise, T. (2001). *Child abuse and neglect: The school's response*. New York: Guilford.

Cadogan, W. (1749). An essay upon nursing and the management of children, from their birth to three years of age. *Neonatology on the web*, Retrieved October 25, 2007, from http://www.neonatology.org/classics/cadogan.html.

Carpenter, A., & Donahue, B. (2006). Parental satisfaction in child abuse and neglect: A review of standardized measures. *Aggression and Violent Behavior, 11*, 577–586.

Center for the Study of Social Policy. (2003). *Protective factors literature review: Early care and education programs and the prevention of child abuse and neglect* [strengthening families through early care and education]. Available from: http://www.cssp.org/uploadFiles/horton.pdf.

Chalk, R., Gibbons, A., & Scarupa, H. (2002). *The multiple dimensions of child abuse and neglect: New insights into an old problem*. Washington, DC: Child Trends. Retrieved October 10, 2007, from http://www.childtrends.org.

Chaney, S. (2000). Child abuse: Clinical findings and management. *Journal of the American Academy of Nurse Practitioners, 12*(11), 467–471.

Chang, J., Rhee, S., & Weaver, D. (2006). Characteristics of child abuse in immigrant Korean families and correlates of placement decisions. *Child Abuse and Neglect, 30*(8), 881–891.

Chase, R., & Moser Nelson, S. (2002). *Home visiting program to prevent child abuse*. Minnesota Department of Health: Wilder Research Center.

Child Labor Coalition. (n.d.). *An overview of federal child labor laws*. Retrieved July 20, 2007, from http://www.stopchildlabor.org/.

Children's Aid Society. (2007). *History*. Retrieved May 8, 2007, from http://www.childrensaidsociety.org/.

Children's Defense Fund (CDF). (2005). *Child abuse and neglect fact sheet*. Retrieved September 15, 2007, from http://www.childrensdefense.org/site/DocServer/factsheet0805.pdf?docID=397.

Children's Trust Funds (CTF). (2005). *History*. Retrieved October 25, 2007, from National Alliance of Children's Trust and Prevention Funds: http://www.ctfalliance.org.

Child victims of human trafficking. (2007). Retrieved July 18, 2007, from Administration for Children and Families Campaign to Rescue and Restore Victims of Human Trafficking website: http://www.afterschool.ed.gov/?trafficking.

Child Welfare Information Gateway. (2007a). *Definitions of child abuse and neglect*. Retrieved September 26, 2007, from http://www.childwelfare.gov.

Child Welfare Information Gateway. (2007b, December 7). *Definitions in federal law*. Retrieved May 17, 2008, from http://www.childwelfare.gov/can/defining/federal.cfm.

Child Welfare Information Gateway. (2006). *Child abuse and neglect fatalities: Statistics and interventions*. Washington, DC: U.S. Department of Health and Human Services.

Child Welfare Information Gateway. (1990). Parenting the sexually abused child. In *Fact sheet for families*. Washington, DC: Author.

Christian, L. (2006). Understanding families: Applying family systems theory to early childhood practice. *Young Children, 61*(1), 12–20.

Church of Jesus Christ of Latter-Day Saints (LDS). (n.d.). FAQ. Retrieved September 15, 2007, from *LDS:* http://www.lds.org.

Cicchetti, D., & Blender, J. (2004). A multiple-levels-of-analysis approach to the study of developmental processes in maltreated children. *Proceedings of the National Academy of Sciences of the United States of America, 101*(50), 17325–17326.

Cicero. (450 B.C.). *Ancient history sourcebook, Law of the twelve tables*. Retrieved April 27, 2007, from http://www.fordham.edu/halsall/ancient/12tables.html.

Cloitre, M. (1998). Sexual revictimization: Risk factors and prevention. In V. M. Follette, J. I. Ruzed, & F. R. Abueg (Eds.), *Cognitive-behavioral therapies for trauma* (pp. 278–304). New York: Guilford.

Coffin, A. (1878). *Dr. Coffin's treatise on midwifery and the diseases of women and children, with remedies*. London. Retrieved April 25, 2007, from http://www.neonatology.org/classics/coffin.html.

Committee on Early Childhood, Adoption, and Dependent Care (CECADC). (2005). Quality early education and child care from birth to kindergarten. *Pediatrics, 115*, 187–191.

Cooke, B. (2006). Competencies of a parent educator: What does a parent educator need to know and do? *Child Welfare, 85*(5), 785–802.

Corby, B. (2006). *Child abuse: Towards a knowledge base.* New York: McGraw-Hill.

Court Appointed Special Advocates for Children (CASA). (2006). *The importance of family dinners III.* New York: Columbia University.

Covey, S. (1997). The 7 habits of highly effective families. New York: Golden Books.

Cowan, A. (2004). New strategies to promote the adoption of older children out of foster care. *Children and Youth Services Review, 26*, 1007–1020.

Crosson, T. (2005). *Understanding child abuse and neglect.* Boston: Pearson.

Crosson-Tower, C. (2003). *The role of educators in preventing and responding to child abuse and neglect.* In Child abuse and neglect user manual series. Washington, DC: U.S. Department of Health and Human Services; Administration for Children and Families; Administration on Children, Youth and Families; Children's Bureau; Office on Child Abuse and Neglect.

Crosson-Tower, C. (2002). *When children are abused: An educator's guide to intervention.* Boston: Allyn and Bacon.

Cushner, K., McClelland, A., & Safford, P. (2006). *Human diversity in education.* New York: McGraw-Hill.

Dale, K. A., & Alpert, J. (2007). Hiding behind the cloth: Child sexual abuse and the catholic church. *Journal of Child Sexual Abuse, 16*(3), 59–74.

Davidson, H. (n.d.) *Summary of some key changes to the federal child abuse prevention and treatment act (CAPTA).* Retrieved July 2, 2007, from http://www.abanet.org/child/capta.shtml.

DeBord, K., & Matta, M. (2002). Designing professional development systems for parenting educators. *Journal of Extension, 40*(2). Retrieved August 3, 2008, from http://joe.org/joe/2002april/a2.html.

Degh, L. (1979). Grimm's "household tales" and its place in the household: The social relevance of a controversial classic. *Western Folklore, 38*(2), 83–103.

deMause, L. (1998). The history of child abuse. *Journal of Psychohistory, 25*(3). Retrieved April 25, 2007, from http://www.psychohistory.com/htm/05_history.html.

DePanfilis, D. (2006). *Child neglect: A guide for prevention, assessment, and intervention.* In Child abuse and neglect user manual series. Washington, DC: U.S. Department of Health and Human Services; Administration for Children and Families; Administration on Children, Youth and Families; Children's Bureau; Office of Child Abuse and Neglect.

DePanfilis, D., & Salus, M. (2003). *Children protective services: A guide for caseworkers.* Washington: USDHHS.

Derluyn, E., Broekaert, G., Schuyten, G., & Temmerman, E. (2004). Post-traumatic stress in former Ugandan child soldiers. *Lancet, 363*(9412), 861–863.

Division for Early Childhood of the Council for Exceptional Children (DEC). (2007). Promoting positive outcomes for children with disabilities: Recommendations for curriculum, assessment, and program evaluation. Missoula, MT: Author.

Division for Early Childhood Research Committee Executive Work Group. (2006). *Research priorities for early intervention and early childhood special education.* Missoula, MT: Division for Early Childhood.

Dixon, L., Browne, K., & Hamilton-Giachritis, C. (2005). Risk factors of parents abused as children: A mediational analyis of the intergenerational continuity of maltreatment (Part I). *Journal of Child Psychology and Psychiatry, 46*(1), 47–57.

Dixon, L., Hamilton-Giachritsis, C., & Browne, K. (2005). Attributions and behaviors of parents abused as children: A mediational analysis of the intergenerational continuity of child maltreatment (Part II). *Journal of Child Psychology and Psychiatry, 46*(1), 58–68.

Dobner, J. (2007, September 26). Utah polygamist convicted of sex charges. *Seattle Times.*

Dombrowski, S., & Gischlar, K. (2006). Supporting school professionals through the establishment of a school district policy on child maltreatment. *Education, 127*(2), 234–243.

Drapeau, S., Saint-Jacques, M., Lepine, R., Begin, G., & Bernard, M. (2007). Processes that contribute to resilience among youth in foster care. *Journal of Adolescence, 30*(6), 977–1000.

Dreikurs, R. (1991). *Children the challenge: The classic work on improving parent-child relations—Intelligent, humane, and eminently practical.* New York: Plume.

Dube, S., Felitti, V., Dong, M., Chapman, D., Giles, W., & Anda, R. (2003). Childhood abuse, neglect, and household dysfunction and the risk of illicit drug use: The adverse childhood experiences study. *Pediatrics, 111*(3), 564–572.

Dubowitz, H. (2005). Maltreatment's wake: The relationship of maltreatment dimensions to child outcomes. *Child Abuse and Neglect, 29*(5), 597–619.

Dubowitz, H. (1999). *Neglected children*. Thousand Oaks, CA: Sage.

Dubowitz, H., & Bennett, S. (2007). Physical abuse and neglect of children. *Lancet, 369*, 1891–1899.

Dyslin, C. W., & Thomsen, C. J. (2005). Religiosity and risk of perpetrating child physical abuse: An empirical investigation. *Journal of Psychology and Theology, 33*(4), 291–298.

Eisenberg, N. (1992). *The caring child*. Cambridge, MA: Harvard University Press.

Elliot, G. (2003). *School mobbing and emotional abuse*. New York: Brunner-Routledge.

El Paso Intelligence Center (EPIC) National Clandestine Laboratory Seizure System. (2003). *Statistics*. Available at http://www.usdoj.gov/dea.

End Child Prostitution, Child Pornography and Trafficking of Children for Sexual Purposes (ECPAT-USA). (2003). *Child prostitution in the USA*. Retrieved October 1, 2007, from ECPAT: http://www.ecpatusa.org/child_prosti_us.asp.

English, D., Upadhyaya, M., Litrownik, A., Marshall, J., Runyan, D., Graham, J., Derluyn, I., Broekaert, E., Schuyten, G., & Temmerman, E. (2005). Post-traumatic stress in former ugandan child soldiers. *Lancet, 363*, 861–863.

Entenman, J., Murnen, T., & Hendricks, C. (2006). Victims, bullies, and bystanders in K–3 literature. *Reading Teacher, 59*(4), 352–364.

Erikson, E. H. (1963). *Childhood and society* (2nd ed.). New York: Norton.

Espelage, D., & Swearer, S. (2003). Research on school bullying and victimization: What have we learned and where do we go from here? *School Psychology Review, 32*(3), 365–383.

Estevan, F., & Baland, J. (2007). Mortality risks, education and child labor. *Journal of Development Economics, 84*, 118–137.

Etheridge, Susan. (2007, April 21). Personal interview.

Feeney, S., & Freeman, N. (1999). *Ethics and the early childhood educator. Using the NAEYC code.* Washington, DC: National Association for the Education of Young Children.

Feeney, S., Freeman, N., & Moravcik, E. (2000). *Teaching the NAEYC code of ethical conduct*. Washington, DC: National Association for the Education of Young Children.

Feixas, M. (2001). *What changes as new university teachers develop? Models and issues*. Paper presented to the 9th Conference of the European Association for Research on Learning and Instruction (EARLI): Bridging Learning to Instruction, Fribourg, Switzerland.

Fekkes, M., Pijpers, F., Fredriks, A., Vogels, T., & Verloove-Vanhorick, S. (2006). Do bullied children get ill, or do ill children get bullied? A prospective cohort study on the relationship between bullying and health-related symptoms. *Pediatrics, 117*, 1568–1574.

Feldman, D. H. (2004). Piaget's stages: The unfinished symphony of cognitive development. *New Ideas in Psychology, 22*, 175–231.

Fields, M., & Boesser, C. (2002). *Constructive guidance and discipline* (3rd ed.). Upper Saddle River, NJ: Merrill Prentice Hall.

Finn, J., Gerber, S., & Boyd-Zaharias, J. (2005). Small classes in the early grades, academic achievement and graduating from high school. *Journal of Educational Psychology, 97*(2), 214–223.

Flaherty, E. (2006). Analysis of caretaker histories in abuse: Comparing initial histories with subsequent confessions. *Child Abuse and Neglect, 30*, 789–798.

Fomby, P., & Cherlin, A. (2007). Family instability and child well-being. *American Sociological Review, 72*, 181–204.

Fontes, L. (2002). Child discipline and physical abuse in immigrant Latino families: Reducing violence and misunderstandings. *Journal of Counseling and Development, 80*, 31–40.

Freeman, K. A., & Morris, T. L. (2001). A review of conceptual models explaining the effects of child sexual abuse. *Aggression and Violent Behavior, 6*(4), 357–373.

Friesen, B. (2007). Recovery and resilience in children's mental health: Views from the field. *Psychiatric Rehabilitation Journal, 31*(1), 38–48.

Fuchs, R. (1982). Crimes against children in nineteenth-century France. *Child Abuse, Law and Human Behavior, 6*(3/4), 237–259.

Gahagan, S. (2006). Failure to thrive: A consequence of undernutrition. *Pediatrics, 27*(1), 1–11.

Gallagher, B. (2000). The extent and nature of known cases of institutional child sexual abuse. *British Journal of Social Work, 30*, 795–817.

Gallagher, S. (2005). Caring for the child who is obese: Mobility, caregiver safety, environmental accommodation and legal concerns. *Pediatric Nursing, 31*(1), 17–20.

Gardner, H. (1991). *The unschooled mind.* New York: Basic Books.

Garrett, A. (2001). *Keeping American schools safe.* Jefferson, NC: McFarland.

Geenen, S., & Powers, L. (2007). "Tomorrow is another problem": The experiences of youth in foster care during their transition into adulthood. *Children and Youth Services Review, 29*, 1085–1101.

Gershater-Molko, R., Lutzker, J., & Wesch, D. (2003). Project safecare: Improving health, safety and parenting skills in families reported for, and at-risk for child maltreatment. *Journal of Family Violence, 18*(6), 377–386.

Gershoff, E. (2002). Corporal punishment by parents and associated child behaviors and experiences: A meta-analytic and theoretical review. *Psychological Bulletin, 128*(4), 539–579.

Gilliam, W. (2005). *Prekindergartners left behind: Expulsion rates in state prekindergarten systems.* New Haven, CT: Yale University Child Study Center.

Ginsberg, K. (2007). The importance of play in promoting healthy child development and maintaining strong parent-child bonds. *Pediatrics, 119*(1), 182–191.

Glaser, D. (2002). Emotional abuse and neglect (psychological maltreatment): A concpetual framework. *Child Abuse and Neglect, 26*, 697–714.

Glaser, D. (2000). Child abuse and neglect and the brain—A review. *Journal of Child Psychology and Psychiatry, 41*(1), 97–116.

Glaser, S. (2001). Cultivating a healthy classroom. *Teaching PreK, 32*(1), 136–138.

Gold, S. (2000). *Not trauma alone.* Philadelphia: Taylor and Francis.

Goldman, J., & Salus, M. (2003). *A coordinated response to child abuse and neglect: The foundation for practice.* Washington, DC: U.S. Department of Health and Human Services.

Goldman, R. (2005). Educating teachers about child abuse. *Focus on Teacher Education, 5*(3), 1–4.

Goldstein, S. (2007). Understanding and managing children's classroom behavior (2nd ed.). New York: Wiley.

Gordon, A., & Browne, K. (1996). *Guiding young children in a diverse society.* Boston: Allyn and Bacon.

Graham, L., Rogers, P., & Davies, M. (2007). Attributions in a hypothetical child sexual abuse case: Roles of abuse type, family response and respondent gender. *Journal of Family Violence, 22*, 733–745.

Green, B., Furrer, C., & McAllister, C. (2007). How do relationships support parenting? Effects of attachment style and social support on parenting behavior in an at-risk population. *American Journal of Community Psychology, 40*, 96–108.

Greenberg, M. (2002). Attachment and psychopathology in childhood. In Cassidy & Shaver (Eds.), *Handbook of attachment: Theory, research, and clinical applications* (pp. 469–496). New York: Guilford.

Gregorc, A. F. (1973). Developing plans for professional growth. *NASSP Bulletin, 57*, 108.

Grogan-Kaylor, A., & Otis, M. (2007). The predictors of parental use of corporal punishment. *Family Relations, 56*(1), 80–91.

Gullotta, T., & Blau, G. (2008). *Family influences on childhood behavior and development: Evidence-based prevention and treatment approaches.* Boca Raton: CRC Press.

Hagen, C. (1999). Decision making factors in child caregiver reporting of child abuse and neglect. (Doctoral Dissertation, University of North Texas, 1999). *Dissertation Abstracts International, 63*(09), 3104.

Hall, R., & Hall, R. (2007). A profile of pedophilia: Definition, characteristics of offenders, recidivism, treatment outcomes and forensic issues. *Mayo Clinic Proceedings, 82*(4), 457–471.

Hamman, J. (2000). The rod of discipline; Masochism, sadism, and the Judeo-Christian religion. *Journal of Religion and Health, 39*(4), 319–327.

Hanson, E. (2008). *Overview of forensic interviews.* PowerPoint presentation at Collin College, April 8, 2008.

Hazzard, A. (2004). *Child sexual abuse prevention: Teacher training workshop.* Retrieved on March 5, 2006, from http://www.promising practices.net /program.asp.

Helfer, M., Kempe, R., & Krugman, R. (1999). *The battered child* (5th ed.). Chicago: University of Chicago Press.

Henry, B., Reiko, U., Shinjo, M., & Yoshikawa, C. (2003). Health education for nurses in Japan to combat child abuse. *Nursing and Health Sciences, 5*, 199–206.

Herman, K. C., Tucker, C. M., Ferdinand, L. A., Mirsu-Paun, A., Hasan, N. T., & Beato, Ch. (2007). Culturally sensitive health care and counseling psychology: An overview. *Counseling Psychologist, 35*, 633–649.

Herrenkohl, R. (2005). The definition of child maltreatment: From case study to construct. *Child Abuse and Neglect, 29*(5), 413–424.

Herrenkohl, T., & Herrenkohl, R. (2007). Examining the overlap and prediction of multiple forms of child maltreatment, stressors, and socioeconomic status: A longitudinal analysis of youth outcomes. *Journal of Family Violence, 22*, 553–562.

Hershkowitz, I., Fisher, S., & Lamb, M. H. (2007). Improving credibility assessment in child sexual abuse allegations: The role of the NICHD investigative interview protocol. *Child Abuse and Neglect, 31*, 99–110.

Hetzel-Riggin, M., Brausch, A., & Montgomery, B. (2007). A meta-analytic investigation of therapy modality outcomes for sexually abused children and adolescents: An exploratory study. *Child Abuse and Neglect, 31*(2), 125–141.

Hibbard, R., & Desch, L. (2007). Maltreatment of children with disabilities. *Pediatrics, 119*(5), 1018–1025.

Hines, D. A., & Morrison, K. (2005). *Family violence in the United States.* Thousand Oaks, CA: Sage.

Hirschy, S. (2001). What is parent education? In *Public policy facts on families* (http://www.cpe.unt.edu/). Denton: University of North Texas Center for Parent Education.

Hirschy, S., & Jacobson, A. (2001). Identifying the attitudes, knowledge and skills of parent education. *Enhancing Consumer and Business Independence Annual of Refereed Papers, 83*, USDA.

Horton, C. B., & Cruise, T. K. (2001). *Child abuse and neglect: The school's response.* New York: Guilford Press.

Hughes, P. (2005). New responsibilities for adapted physical educators: Watchdogs for abuse and neglect. *Palaestra, 21*(2), 20–25.

Hummell, L. (2007, Spring). Cyber-bullying: What it is and how to prevent it. *Delta Kappa Gamma Bulletin*, 26–29.

Humphrey, K., Turnbull, A., & Turnbull, H. (2006). Impact of the Adoption and Safe Families Act on youth and their families: Perspectives of foster care providers, youth with emotional disorders, service providers, and judges. *Child and Youth Services Review, 28*, 113–132.

Hymel, K. (2006a). Distinguishing sudden infant death syndrome from child abuse fatalities. *Pediatrics, 118*(1), 421–447.

Hymel, K. (2006b). When is lack of supervision neglect? *Pediatrics, 118*(3), 1296–1298.

Innocenti Research Center. (2005). *Trafficking in human beings, especially women and children, in Africa.* New York: United Nations Children's Fund (UNICEF).

Innocenti Research Center. (2002). *Child trafficking in West Africa.* New York: United Nations Children's Fund (UNICEF).

Institute for Family Centered Care. (2007). *What is patient and family centered care?* Available from http://www.familycenteredcare.org/.

Irvine, J. (2003). *Educating teachers for a diverse society: Seeing with the cultural eye.* New York: Teachers College Press.

Irvine, M., & Tanner, R. (2007, October 21). Sexual misconduct plagues U.S. schools. Retrieved October 21, 2007, from *Pocono Record:* http://blog.oregon live.com/oregonianextra/teacher_sex_abuse_ series/.

Iversen, V. (2002). Autonomy in child labor migrants. *World Development, 30*(5), 817–834.

Jenny, C. (2006). Evaluating infants and young children with mulitple fractures. *Pediatrics, 118*(3), 1299–1303.

Johnson, A. (2006). Using families as faculty in teaching medical students family-centered care: What are students learning? *Teaching and Learning in Medicine, 18*(3), 222–225.

Johnson, J., Cohen, P., Gould, M., Kasen, S., Brown, J., & Brook, J. (2002). Childhood adversities, interpersonal difficulties, and risk for suicide attempts during late adolescence and early adulthood. *Archives of General Psychiatry, 59*, 741–749.

Johnson, K. (2007, September 22). Case against Utah polygamist leader goes to the jury in Utah. *New York Times.* Retrieved September 20, 2008, from http://www.nytimes.com/2007/09/22/us/22jeffs .html.

Jones, B. J. (2007). The Indian Child Welfare Act: The need for a separate law. Downloaded January 20, 2008, from American Bar Association website: http://www.abanet.org/.

Jones, W. (2006). Working with the courts in child protection. Washington, DC: U.S. Department of Health and Human Services, Administration for Children and Families, Office on Child Abuse and Neglect.

Journey Back in Time (JBIT). (2004). School rules 1860. Retrieved May 20, 2008, from http://www.jbit.org/guide/index.htm#rules.

Juby, C., & Rycraft, J. (2004). Family preservation strategies for families in poverty. *Families in Society, 85*(4), 581–587.

Kairys, S., Johnson, C., and the Committee on Child Abuse and Neglect. (2002). The American Academy of Pediatrics: The psychological maltreatment of children—Technical report. *Pediatrics, 109*(4), 1–3.

Kaiser, B., & Rasminsky, J. (2003). *Challenging behavior in young children: Understanding, preventing, and responding effectively.* Boston: Pearson.

Katz, L. (1972). Developmental stages of preschool teachers. *Elementary School Journal, 73*(1), 50–54.

Katzman, G. (2005). A bioethical analysis of a form of psychologic abuse: Teaching hatred to children. *Clinical Pediatrics, 44*(2), 143–150.

Kaufman, P., Rudy, S. A., Chen, X., Choy, S. P., Miller, A. K., Fleury, J. K., Chandler, K. A., Rand, M. R., Klaus, P., & Planty, M. G. (2000). *Indicators of school crime and safety, 2000* (NCJ 184176/NCES, 2001-017). Washington, DC: U.S. Department of Justice, Bureau of Justice Statistics; U.S. Department of Education, Office of Educational Research and Improvement. [Also available on the World Wide Web: http://www.ojp.usdoj.gov/bjs/abstract/iscs00.asp.]

Kellogg, N. (2007). Evaluation of suspected child physical abuse. *Pediatrics, 119*(6), 1232–1241.

Kellogg, N., & Committee on Child Abuse and Neglect. (2005). Oral and dental aspects of child abuse and neglect. *Pediatrics, 116*(6), 1565–1567.

Kempe, C., Silverman, F., Steele, B., Droegemueller, W., & Silver, H. (1985). The battered-child syndrome. *Child Abuse and Neglect, 9*(2), 143–154.

Kempe, C., Silverman, F., Steele, B., Droegemueller, W., & Silver, H. (1962). The battered-child syndrome.

Journal of the American Medical Association, 251, 3288–3300.

Kendall-Tackett, K. (2000). Physiological correlates of childhood abuse: Chronic hyperarousal in PTSD, depression, and irritable bowel syndrome. *Child Abuse and Neglect, 24*(6), 799–810.

Kendall-Tackett, K., Lyon, T., Taliaferro, G., & Little, L. (2005). Why child maltreatment researchers should include children's disability status in their maltreatment studies. *Child Abuse and Neglect, 29,* 147–151.

Kenny, M. (2001). Child abuse reporting: Teacher's perceived deterrents. *Child Abuse and Neglect, 25,* 81–92.

Keogh, Barbara K. (2003). *Temperament in the classroom: Understanding individual differences.* Baltimore: Brookes.

KERA/North Texas Public Broadcasting. (2007). *Temperament traits quiz.* Retrieved May 26, 2008, from KERA website: http://www.readyforlife.org/temperament/quiz/.

Kessler, D., & Dawson, P. (1999). *Failure to thrive and pediatric undernutrition: A transdisciplinary approach.* Baltimore: Brookes.

Kim-Cohen, J., Moffitt, T., Caspi, A., & Taylor, A. (2004). Genetic and environmental processes in young children's resilience and vulnerability to socioeconomic deprivation. *Child Development, 75*(3), 651–668.

Kiselica, M., & Morrill-Richards, M. (2007). Sibling maltreatment: The forgotten abuse. *Journal of Counseling and Development, 85,* 148–160.

Kitsantonis, N., & Brunwasser, M. (2006, December 18). Baby trafficking is thriving in Greece. *International Herald Tribune.* Retrieved September 14, 2008, from http://www.iht.com/articles/2006/12/18/news/babies.php.

Knight, B. (1985). The history of child abuse. *Forensic Science International, 30,* 135–141.

Koenig, A. L., Cicchetti, D., & Rogosch, F. A. (2004). Moral development: The association between maltreatment and young children's prosocial behaviors and moral transgressions. *Social Development, 13*(1), 87–106.

Kosmin, B., Mayer, E., & Keysar, A. (2001). *American religious identification survey.* City University of New York, Graduate School and University Center. Retrieved on February 12, 2008, from http://www.trincoll.edu/NR/rdonlyres/AFCEF53A-8DAB-

4CD9-A892-5453E336D35D/0/
NEWARISrevised121901b.pdf.

Krugman, R. (1998). Keynote address: It's time to broaden the agenda. *Child Abuse and Neglect, 22*(6), 475–479.

Krugman, S., & Dubowitz, H. (2003). Failure to thrive. *American Family Physician, 68*(5), 886–887.

Labbe, J. (2005). Tardieu: The man and his work on child maltreatment a century before Kempe. *Child Abuse and Neglect, 29,* 311–324.

Lalor, K. (2004a). Child sexual abuse in sub-saharan Africa: A literature review. *Child Abuse and Neglect, 28,* 439–460.

Lalor, K. (2004b). Child sexual abuse in Tanzania and Kenya. *Child Abuse and Neglect, 28,* 833–844.

Larrivee, B. (2005). *Authentic classroom management: Creating a learning community and building reflective practice* (2nd ed.). Boston: Allyn and Bacon.

Lascarides, V. C., & Hinitz, B. F. (2000). *History of early childhood education*. New York: Palmer Press.

Lau, A., Takeuchi, D., & Alegria, M. (2006). Parent-to child aggression among Asian American parents: Culture, context, and vulnerability. *Journal of Marriage and Family, 68,* 1261–1275.

Leishman, J. (2005, March). *Cyber-bullying*. Retrieved October 7, 2007, from CBC News Online: http://www.cbc.ca/news/background/bullying/cyber_bullying.html.

Leventhal, J. (2003). The field of child maltreatment enters its fifth decade. *Child Abuse and Neglect, 27*(1), 1–4.

Lohman, J. (2004, August 4). OLR research report. Retrieved October 15, 2007, from Connecticut General Assembly Office of Legislative Research, http://www.cga.ct.gov/2004/rpt/2004-R-0615.htm.

Loseke, D., Gelles, R., & Cavanaugh, M. (2005). *Current controversies on family violence*. Thousand Oaks, CA: Sage.

Lundahl, B., Nimer, J., & Parsons, B. (2006). Preventing child abuse: A meta-analysis of parent training programs. *Research on Social Work Practice, 16*(3), 251–262.

Lundahl, B., Risser, H., & Lovejoy, M. (2006). A meta-analysis of parent training: Moderators and follow-up effects. *Clinical Pyschology Review, 26,* 86–104.

Luthar, S., Cicchetti, D., & Becker, B. (2000). The construct of resilience: A critical evaluation and guide-lines for future work. *Child Development, 71*(3), 543–562.

Maccoby, E. E., & Martin, J. A. (1983). Socialization in the context of the family: Parent–child interaction. In P. H. Mussen (Ed.) & E. M. Hetherington (Vol. Ed.), *Handbook of child psychology: Vol. 4. Socialization, personality, and social development* (4th ed., pp. 1–101). New York: Wiley.

MacLaggan, C. (2007, June 18). Day care owners balk at costly new background checks for employees. Retrieved October 17, 2007, from *American Statesman,* http://www.statesman.com/news/content/region/legislature/stories/06/18/18daycare.html.

MacLeod, J., & Nelson, G. (2000). Programs for the promotion of family wellness and the prevention of child maltreatment: A meta-analytic review. *Child Abuse and Neglect, 24,* 1127–1149.

Maestripieri, D., Higley, D., Lindell, S., Newman, T., McCormack, K., & Sanchez, M. (2006). Early maternal rejection affects the development of monoaminergic systems and adult abusive parenting in rhesus macaques. *Behavioral Neuroscience, 120,* 1017–1024.

Maguire, S., Mann, M., Siber, J., & Kemp, A. (2005). Are there patterns of bruising in childhood which are diagnostic or suggestive of abuse? A systematic review. *Archives of Disease in Childhood, 90,* 182–186. Retrieved July 10, 2007, from http://adc.bmj.com.

Manheimer, A. (Ed.). (2006). *Child labor and sweatshops*. Detroit: Thompson Gale.

Mannes, M. (1995). Factors and events leading to passage of the Indian Child Welfare Act. *Child Welfare, 74*(1), 264–282.

Marsh, J., Ryan, J., Choi, S., & Testa, M. (2005). Integrated services for families with multiple problems: Obstacles to family reunification. *Child and Youth Services Review, 28,* 1074–1087.

Martinez, C., & Forgatch, M. (2002). Adjusting to change: Linking family structure transitions with parenting and boys' adjustment. *Journal of Family Psychology, 16,* 107–117.

May-Chahal, C. (2006). Gender and child maltreatment: The evidence base. *Social Work and Society, 4*(1), 53–64.

McCurdy, K., & Daro, D. (2001). Parent involvement in family support programs: An integrated theory. *Family Relations, 50*(2), 113–121.

McEachern, A., Aluede, O., & Kenny, M. (2008). Emotional abuse in the classroom: Implications and interventions for counselors. *Journal of Counseling and Development, 86*(1), 3–10.

McNichol, T., & Tash, C. (2001). Parental substance abuse and the development of children in family foster care. *Child Welfare, 80,* 239–255.

McSherry, D. (2007). Understanding and addressing the "neglect of neglect": Why are we making a mole-hill out of a mountain? *Child Abuse and Neglect, 31,* 607–614.

Melton, G., & Flood, M. (1994). Research policy and child maltreatment: Developing the scientific foundation for the effective protection of children. *Child Abuse and Neglect: International Journal, 18*(1), 1–28.

Mennen, F. (2004). PTSD symptoms in abused Latino children. *Child and Adolescent Social Work Journal, 21*(5), 477–493.

Mertensmeyer, C., & Fine, M. (2000). ParentLink: A model of integration and support for parents. *Family Relations, 49*(3), 257–265.

Messina, N., Marinelli-Casey, P., West, K., & Rawson, R. (2007). Children exposed to methamphetamine use and manufacture. *Child Abuse and Neglect,* 1–10. Available online March 23, 2007, from Elsevier.

Miller-Perrin, C., & Perrin, R. (2007). *Child maltreatment.* Thousand Oaks, CA: Sage.

Moore, K., Chalk, R., Scarpa, J., & Vandivere, S. (2002). Family strengths: Often overlooked, but real *[Child trends research brief].* Available from http://www.childtrends.org/Files/FamilyStrengths.pdf.

Morton, N., & Browne, K. (1998). Theory and observation of attachment and its relation to child maltreatment: A review. *Child Abuse and Neglect, 22*(11), 1093–1104.

Moulden, H., Firestone, P., & Wexler, A. (2007). Child care providers who commit sexual offenses. *International Journal of Offender Therapy and Comparative Criminology, 51*(4), 384–406.

Mulinge, M. (2002). Implementing the 1989 United Nations' convention on the rights of the child in sub-saharan Africa: The overlooked socioeconomic and political dilemmas. *Child Abuse and Neglect, 26,* 1117–1130.

Mullings, J., Marquart, J., & Hartley, D. (2003). *The victimization of children: Emerging issues.* New York: Haworth Maltreatment and Trauma Press.

Muris, P. (2006). Freud was right . . . About the origins of abnormal behavior. *Journal of Child and Family Studies, 15*(1), 1–12.

Myers-Walls, J. (2003). Children as victims of war and terrorism. *Journal of Aggression, Maltreatment, and Trauma, 8*(1/2), 41–62.

Nanse, T., Overpeck, M., Pilla, R., Ruan, W., Simons-Morton, B., & Scheidt, P. (2001). Bullying behaviors among U.S. youth: Prevalence and association with psychosocial adjustment. *Journal of American Medical Association, 285*(6), 2094–2100.

National Association of Child Care Resource and Referral Agencies (NACCRRA). (2007, September 17). *Child care provider background checks: Policy e-conference.* Retrieved October 15, 2007, from the NACCRRA website: http://www.naccrra.org/policy/background_issues/.

National Association for the Education of Young Children (NAEYC). (2008). Building circles, breaking cycles. Preventing child abuse and neglect: The early childhood educator's role. Washington, DC: Author. Retrieved October 10, 2008, from http://www.naeyc.org/ece/pdf/Duke.pdf.

National Association for the Education of Young Children (NAEYC). (2006). *Guidance matters: Try these techniques with children you find challenging.* Washington, DC: Author. Retrieved March 2, 2006, from http://www.journal.naeyc.org.

National Association for the Education of Young Children (NAEYC). (2005). *Teacher-child ratios within group size.* Washington, DC: Author. Retrieved November 4, 2007, from http://www.naeyc.org/academy/criteria/teacher_child_ratios.html.

National Association for the Education of Young Children (NAEYC). (2004). *Where we stand on child abuse prevention.* Washington, DC: Author. Retrieved November 2, 2007, from http://www.naeyc.org/about/positions/pdf/ChildAbuseStand.pdf.

National Association for the Education of Young Children (NAEYC). (2003). *Early childhood educators and child abuse prevention: NAEYC's perspective, research findings, and future actions.* Washington, DC: Author. Retrieved February 8, 2008, from http://www.naeyc.org.

National Association for the Education of Young Children (NAEYC). (1996). *Prevention of child abuse in early childhood programs: A position statement of the National Association for the Education of Young*

Children. Washington, DC: Author. Retrieved November 2, 2007, from http://www.naeyc.org/about/positions/pdf/pschab98.pdf.

National Child Care Information Center. (2007). *Promoting family centered care*. Fairfax, VA: U.S. Department of Health and Human Services; Administration for Children and Families; Administration on Children, Youth, and Families; Child Care Bureau.

National Clearinghouse on Child Abuse and Neglect. (2000). *Fact sheets: What is child maltreatment?* Retrieved May 19, 2007, from http://www.calib.com/dvcps/facts/harmway.doc.

National Council on Family Relations. (NCFR). (2007). *Family life education*. Available from http://www.ncfr.org.

National Education Association. (NEA). (2006). *Class size: Issues in education*. Retrieved November 3, 2007, from the NEA website: http://www.nea.org/classsize/index.html.

National Institute on Disability and Rehabilitation Research. (2003). *Long-range plan 1999– 2003*. Washington, DC: U.S. Department of Education.

Native Americans and child maltreatment: The past, present, and the future. Washington, DC: National Center on Child Abuse and Neglect.

Naylor, P., Cowie, H., Cossin, F., Bettencourt, R., & Lemme, F. (2006). Teachers' and pupils' definitions of bullying. *British Journal of Educational Psychology*, *76*, 553–576.

Neill, S. (1991). *Classroom nonverbal communication*. London: Routledge.

Nesbit, W. C., & Philpot, D. F. (2002). Confronting subtle emotional abuse in classrooms. *Guidance and Counseling*, *17*(2), 32–38.

Newberger, E., Newberger, C., & Hampton, R. (1983). Child abuse: The current theory base and future research needs. *American Academy of Child Psychiatry*, *22*(3), 262–268.

Newton, C. (2001). Child abuse: An overview. *Mental Health Journal*. Retrieved June 15, 2007, from http://www.FindCounseling.com.

Nixon, L. (2003). *Best practices for ethnic, cultural, and language diversity in intervention settings*. Retrieved 3-28-08 from http://www.infantva.org/documents/conf-CulturalDiversity.

Noble, K. G., Tottenham, N., & Casey, B. J. (2005). Neuroscience perspectives on disparities in school readiness and cognitive achievement. *Future of Children*, *15*(1), 71–89.

Northam, E. (2004). Neuropsychological and psychosocial correlates of endocrine and metabolic disorders: A review. *Journal of Pediatric Endocrinological Metabolism*, *17*(1), 5–15.

Official Report of the Nineteenth Annual Conference of Charities and Correction. (1892). Reprinted in Richard H. Pratt, *The advantages of mingling Indians with whites. A way out. Remarks on Indian education*. In F. P. Prucha (Ed.), *Americanizing the American Indians: Writings by the "Friends of the Indian," 1880–1900* (Cambridge, MA: Harvard University Press, 1973), pp. 260–271. Retrieved January 2, 2008, from http://socrates.bmcc.cuny.edu/bfriedheim/pratt.htm.

Onyskiw, J. E., & Hayduk, L. A. (2001). Processes underlying children's adjustment in families characterized by physical aggression. *Family Relations*, *50*(4), 376–385.

Ooserman, M., Schuengel, C., Slot, N., Bullens, R., & Doreleijers, T. (2007). Disruptions in foster care: A review and meta-analysis. *Children and Youth Services Review*, *29*, 53–76.

Oren, M. (2006). Child temperament, gender, teacher-child relationship, and teacher-child interactions. Dissertation submitted to Florida State University.

Orpinas, P., & Horne, A. (2006). *Bullying prevention: Creating a positive school climate and developing social competence*. Washington, DC: American Psychological Association.

Osei-Hwedie, K., & Hobona, A. K. (2001). Secondary school teachers and the emotional abuse of children: A study of three secondary teachers in Gaborone, Botswana. *Journal of Social Development in Africa*, *16*, 139–163.

Paolucci, E. & Violato, C. (2004). A meta-analysis of the published research on the affective, cognitive, and behavioral effects of corporal punishment. *Journal of Psychology*, *138*(3), 197–221.

Parault, S., Davis, H., & Pellegrini, A. (2007). The social contexts of bullying and victimization. *Journal of Early Adolescence*, *27*(2), 145–174.

Parent Teacher Association (PTA). (2007). *About PTA*. Retrieved October 22, 2007, from http://www.pta.org/.

Paulsen, D. (2003). No safe place: Assessing spatial patterns of child maltreatment victimization.

Journal of Aggression, Maltreatment and Trauma, 8(1), 63–85.

Pears, K. C., & Capaldi, D. M. (2001). Intergenerational transmission of abuse: A two-generational prospective study of an at-risk sample. *Child Abuse and Neglect, 25*, 1439–1461.

Pederson, W., & Hegna, K. (2003). Children and adolescents who sell sex: A community study. *Social Science and Medicine, 56*, 135–147.

Perez-Albeniz, A., & de Paul, J. (2004). Gender differences in empathy in parents at high and low risk of child physical abuse. *Child Abuse and Neglect, 38*, 289–300.

Perkins, D. F., & Jones, K. R. (2004). Risk behaviors and resiliency within physically abused adolescents. *Child Abuse and Neglect, 28*, 547–563.

Perry, B. D. (2002). Childhood experience and the expression of genetic potential: What childhood neglect tells us about nature and nurture. *Brain and Mind, 3*(1), 79–100.

Perry, B. D. (2001). Bonding and attachment in maltreated children. ChildTrauma Academy, *Parent and caregiver education series, 3*, pp. 1–18. Accessed November 9, 2007, at http://www.childtrauma.org/ctamaterials/AttCar4_03_v2.pdf.

Perry, B. D. (2000). Brain structure and function 1: Basics of organization. ChildTrauma Academy, *Parent and caregiver education series, 2*(3). Retrieved July 18, 2007, from http://www.childtrauma.org/CTAMA-TERIALS/brain_i.asp.

Perry, B., Runyan, D., & Sturges, C. (1998). Bonding and attachment in maltreated children: How abuse and neglect in childhood impact social and emotional development. ChildTrauma Academy, *Parent and caregiver education series, 1*(5). Retrieved July 18, 2007, from http://www.childtrauma.org.

Perry, B., & Szalavitz, M.. (2006). *The boy who was raised as a dog.* New York: Basic Books.

Pew Charitable Trust. (1996). *See how we grow: The status of parenting education in the U.S.* Philadelphia: Pew Charitable Trust.

Piaget, J. (1965). *The moral judgment of the child.* New York: Free Press.

Pollock, L. (1984). *Forgotten children: Parent-child relations from 1500 to 1900.* New York: Cambridge University Press.

Prater, M., Johnston, M., Dyches, T., & Johnstun, M. (2006). Using books as bibliotherapy for at-risk students: A guide for teachers. *Preventing School Failure, 50*(4), 5–13.

Pratt, R. H. (1892). The advantages of mingling Indians with whites. A way out. Remarks on Indian education. In F. P. Prucha (Ed.), *Americanizing the American Indians: Writings by the "Friends of the Indian," 1880–1900* (Cambridge, MA: Harvard University, 1973), pp. 260–271. Retrieved October 28, 2008, from http://socrates.bmcc.cuny.edu/bfriedheim/pratt.htm.

Price, J. L., Hilsenroth, M. J., Petretic-Jackson, P. A., & Bonge, D. (2001). A review of individual psychotherapy outcomes for adult survivors of childhood sexual abuse. *Clinical Psychology Review, 21*(7), 1095–1121.

Prosser, L. A, & Corso, P. S. (2007). Measuring health-related quality of life for child maltreatment: A systematic literature review. *Health and Quality of Life Outcomes, 5*(42), 1–10.

Reijneveld, S., van der Wal, M., Brugman, E., Sing, R., & Verloove, V. S. (2004). Infant crying and abuse. *Lancet, 364*, 1340–1342.

Reynolds, L., & Birkimer, J. (2002). Perceptions of child sexual abuse: Victim and perpetrator characteristics, treatment efficacy, and lay vs. legal opinions of abuse. *Journal of Child Sexual Abuse, 11*(1), 53–73.

Roditti, M. (2005). Understanding communities of neglectful parents: Child caregiving networks and child neglect. *Child Welfare, 84*(2), 277–284.

Rogers, P., & Davies, M. (2007). Perceptions of credibility and attributions of blame towards victim in a childhood sexual abuse case: Gender and age factors. *Journal of Interpersonal Violence, 22*(5), 566–584.

Rose, L. C., & Gallup, A. M. (2006). 38th annual Phi Delta Kappa/Gallup poll of the public's attitudes toward the public schools. Online: http://www.pdkintl.org/kappan/k0609pol.htm [accessed April 2008].

Rossman, B., & Rea, J. (2005). The relation of parenting styles and inconsistencies to adaptive functioning for children in conflictual and violent families. *Journal of Family Violence, 20*(5), 261–277.

Rousseau, J. (2005). *Emile* (G. Gutek, Trans.). New York: Barnes and Noble. (Original work published in 1762.)

Ryan, R., Salenblatt, J., Schiappacasse, J., & Maly, B. (2001). Physician unwitting participation in abuse and neglect of persons with developmental disabilities. *Community Mental Health Journal, 37*(6), 499–509.

Salehi-Had, H., Brandt, J., Rosas, A., & Rogers, K. (2006). Findings in older children with abusive head injury: Does shaken-baby syndrome exist? *Pediatrics, 117*(5), 1039–1044.

Sand, K. (2002). *Child performers working in the entertainment industry around the world: An analysis of the problems faced.* Geneva: International Labor Office.

Saunders, B. E., Berliner, L., & Hanson, R. F. (2004, April 26). *Child physical and sexual abuse: Guidelines for treatment* (revised report, pp. 61–68). Charleston, SC: National Crime Victims Research and Treatment Center.

Schaeffer, C. M., Alexander, P., Bethke, K., & Kretz, L. (2005). Predictors of child abuse potential among military parents: Comparing mothers and fathers. *Journal of Family Violence, 20*(2), 123–129.

Scher, C. D., Forde, D. R., McQuaid, J. R., & Stein, M. B. (2004). Prevalence and demographic correlates of childhood maltreatment in an adult community sample. *Child Abuse and Neglect, 28*(2), 167–180.

Schmidt, S. (2005). *Liberian refugees: Cultural considerations for social service providers.* Retrieved February 20, 2008, from Bridging Refugee Children and Youth Services: http://www.brycs.org/documents/Liberian_Cultural_Considerations.pdf.

Schneider, M., Ross, A., Graham, C., & Zielinksi, A. (2005). Do allegations of emotional maltreatment predict developmental outcomes beyond that of other forms of maltreatment? *Child Abuse and Neglect, 29*, 513–532.

Sheehan, R. (2006). Emotional harm and neglect: The legal response. *Child Abuse Review, 15*, 38–54.

Sheppard, M. (2001). The design and development of an instrument for assessing the quality of partnership between mother and social worker in child and family care. *Child and Family Social Work, 6*, 31–46.

Sher, J. (2007). *Caught in the web.* New York: Carol and Graf.

Shields, A., & Cichetti, D. (2001). Parental maltreatment and emotional dysregulation as risk factors for bullying and victimization in childhood. *Journal of Clinical Psychology, 30*(3), 349–363.

Shumba, A. (2002). The nature, extent and effects of emotional abuse on primary school pupils by teachers in Zimbabwe. *Child Abuse and Neglect, 26*, 783–791.

Simeon, D. (2006). Emotional maltreatment of children: Relationshp to psychopathology. *Psychiatric Times, 23*(7), 29–30.

Simpson, A. (1997). *The role of mass media in parent education.* Boston: Center for Health Communication, Harvard University.

Singer, P. (2005). *Children at war.* New York: Pantheon.

Singh, R., & Clarke, G. (2006). Power and parenting assessments: The intersecting levels of culture, race, class and gender. *Clinical Child Psychology and Psychiatry*, 9–25.

Sirotnak, A. P. (2001). Child abuse and neglect: Psychosocial dwarfism. *eMedicine Journal, 2*(2), 2–11.

Skinner, B. (1953). *Science and human behavior.* Basingstoke: Collier Macmillan.

Skinner, J. (2001). Teachers who abuse: The impact on school communities. *Educational Research, 43*(2), 161–174.

Slaby, R. (1997). Psychological mediators of violence in urban youth. In J. McCord (Ed.), *Violence and childhood in the inner city* (pp. 171–206). New York: Cambridge University Press.

Smith, B., & Test, M. (2002). The risk of subsequent maltreatment allegations in families with substance-exposed infants. *Child Abuse and Neglect, 26*, 97–114.

Smokowski, P., & Kopasz, K. (2005). Bullying in schools: An overview of types, effects, family characteristics, and intervention strategies. *Children and Schools, 27* (1), 101–110.

Snyder, H. (2000). *Sexual assault of young children as reported to law enforcement: Victim, incident and offender characteristics.* Washington, DC: Bureau of Justice Statistics, U.S. Department of Justice, National Center for Juvenile Justice.

Sobsey, D. (2002). Exceptionality, education, and maltreatment. *Exceptionality, 10*(1), 29–46.

Spertus, I., Yehuda, R., Wong, C., Halligan, S., & Seremetis, S. (2003). Childhood emotional abuse and neglect as predictors of psychological and physical symptoms in women presenting to a primary care practice. *Child Abuse and Neglect, 27*, 1247–1258.

Statistics, F. I. (2007). *America's children: Key national indicators of well-being, 2007.* Retrieved September 12, 2007, from http://www.childstats.gov/americaschildren/famsoc7.asp.

Steffy, B. E., & Wolfe, M. P. (2001). A life cycle model for career teachers. *Kappa Delta Pi Record, 38*(1), 16–19.

Stein, N., Gaberman, E., & Sjostrom, L. (1996). *Bullyproof: A teacher's guide on teasing and bullying for use with fourth and fifth grade students.* Wellesley, MA: Wellesley College Center for Research on Women.

Sternber, K., Lamb, M., Guterman, E., & Abbot, C. (2006). Effects of early and later family violence on children's behavior problems and depression: A longitudinal, multi-informant perspective. *Child Abuse and Neglect, 30,* 283–306.

Stinnett, N., & DeFrain, J. (1985). *Secrets of strong families.* Boston: Little, Brown.

Stirling, J. (2007). Beyond Munchausen syndrome by proxy: Identification and treatment of child abuse in a medical setting. *Pediatrics, 119*(5), 1026–1030.

Straus, M. (2005). Children should never, ever be spanked no matter the circumstances. In D. Loseke & R. C. Gelles (Eds.), *Current controversies on family violence* (pp. 137–158). Thousand Oaks, CA: Sage.

Sullivan, J. (2002). Professional perpetrators. *Child Abuse Review, 11,* 153–167.

Sullivan, J., & Beech, A. (2004). A comparative study of demographic data relating to intra- and extra-familial child sexual abusers and professional perpetrators. *Journal of Sexual Aggression, 10*(1), 39–50.

Teasly, M. (2004). Absenteeism and truancy: Risk, protection, and best practice implications for school social workers. *Children and Schools, 26*(2), 117–128.

Thomas, A., & Chess, S. (1977). *Temperament and development.* New York: Brunner/Mazel.

Thompson, M., Kingree, J. B., & Desai, S. (2004). Gender differences in long-term health consequences of physical abuse of children: Data from a nationally representative survey. *American Journal of Public Health, 94*(4), 599–604.

Timmer, S., Urquiza, A., Zebell, N., & McGrath, J. (2005). Parent-child interaction therapy: Application to maltreating parent-child dyads. *Child Abuse and Neglect, 29*(7), 825–842.

Tittle, G. (2002). Caseload size in best practice literature review. Unpublished doctoral dissertation, University of Illinois, Urbana-Champaign.

Tomison, A., & Wise, S. (1999). *Community-based approaches in preventing child maltreatment. Issues in child abuse prevention.* Retrieved April 2008 from http://www.aifs.gov.au/nch/issues11.html.

Tschannen-Moran, M., Woolfolk Hoy, A., & Hoy, W. K. (1998). Teacher efficacy: Its meaning and measures. *Review of Educational Research, 68,* 202–248.

Turney, D., & Tanner, K. (2001). Working with neglected children and their families. *Journal of Social Work Practice, 15*(2), 193–204.

Ung, L. (2001). *First they killed my father.* New York: Harper Perennial. Retrieved September 20, 2007, from The Campaign to Rescue and Restore Victims of Human Trafficking: http://www.acf.hhs.gov/trafficking.

U.S. Advisory Board on Child Abuse and Neglect. (1991). *Creating caring communities: Blueprint for an effective federal policy on child abuse and neglect.* Washington, DC: U.S. Government Printing Office.

U.S. Children's Bureau. (2007). *Trends in foster care and adoption—FY2000–FY2005.* Retrieved November 1, 2007, from Administration for Children and Families: http://www.acf.hhs.gov/programs/cb/stats_research/afcars/trends2000-2005.pdf.

U.S. Department of Health and Human Services (USDHHS). (2008). *Child maltreatment, 2006.* Washington, DC: U.S. Government Printing Office. Administration on Children, Youth and Families. Retrieved August 4, 2007, from http://www.acf.hhs.gov/programs.

U.S. Department of Health and Human Services (USDHHS). (2007a). *Child maltreatment, 2005.* Washington, DC: U.S. Government Printing Office. Administration on Children, Youth and Families. Retrieved June 15, 2007, from http://www.acf.hhs.gov/programs.

U.S. Department of Health and Human Services (USDHHS). (2007b). *News release: U.S. surgeon general releases advisory on alcohol use in pregnancy.* Retrieved October 2, 2007, from Office of the Surgeon General at http://www.surgeongeneral.gov/pressreleases/sg02222005.html.

U.S. Department of Health and Human Services (USDHHS). (2007c). *Promoting healthy families in your community.* In 2007 Resource Packet. Washington, DC.

U.S. Department of Health and Human Services (USDHHS). (2006a). *The AFCARS report.* Retrieved November 1, 2007, from Administration for Children and Families: http://www.acf.hhs.gov/programs/cb/stats_research/afcars/tar/report13.pdf.

U.S. Department of Health and Human Services (USDHHS). (2006b). *Child maltreatment.* Washington, DC: U.S. Government Printing Office. Administration on Children, Youth and Families. Retrieved August 2, 2007, from http://www.acf.hhs.gov/programs.

U.S. Department of Health and Human Services (USDHHS). (2005). *Mandatory reporters of child abuse and neglect: Summary of state laws*. Administration on Children, Youth and Families. Retrieved July 19, 2007, from http://www.childwelfare.gov/systemwide/laws_policies/statutes/mandaall.pdf.

U.S. Department of Health and Human Services (USDHHS). (2004, September). *Fact sheet: Child victims of human trafficking*. Administration on Children, Youth and Families. Retrieved June 12, 2007, from http://www.acf.hhs.gov/trafficking/about/factsheets.html.

U.S. Department of Health and Human Services (USDHHS). (2003). *Child maltreatment, 2001*. Washington, DC: U.S. Government Printing Office. Administration on Children, Youth and Families. Retrieved June 15, 2007, from http://www.acf.hhs.gov/programs.

Van Hook, L. (1920). The exposure of infants at Athens. *Transactions and proceedings of the American Philological Association, 51*, 134–145.

Venkateswarlu, D., Kasper, J. M., Reis, C., Lacaopoino, V., & Wise, P. (2003). Child labour in India: A health and human rights perspective. *Lancet, 362*, 32–33.

Virginia Department of Social Services. (2006). Sexual abuse by educators and school staff. *Virginia Child Protection Newsletter, 76*, 1–16.

Walsh, W. (2002). Spankers and nonspankers: Where they get information on spanking. *Family Relations, 51*(1), 81–88.

Ward, C., Martin, E., Theron, C., & Distiller, G. (2007). Factors affecting resilience in children exposed to violence. *South African Journal of Psychology, 37*(1), 165–187.

Wark, M., Kruczek, T., & Boley, A. (2003). Emotional neglect and family structure: Impact on student functioning. *Child Abuse and Neglect, 27*, 1033–1043.

Wattendorf, D., & Muenke, M. (2005). Fetal alcohol spectrum disorders. *American Family Physician, 72*, 279–282.

Way, I., Chung, S., Jonson-Reid, M., & Drake, B. (2001). Maltreatment perpetrators: A 54-month analysis of recidivism. *Child Abuse and Neglect, 25*, 1093–1108.

Weissman, A., Jogerst, G., & Dawson, J. (2003). Community characteristics associated with child abuse in Iowa. *Child Abuse and Neglect, 27*, 1145–1159.

Wekerle, C., Wall, A., Leung, E., & Trocme, N. (2007). Cumulative stress and substantiated maltreatment: The importance of caregiver vulnerability and adult partner violence. *Child Abuse and Neglect, 31*, 427–443.

Willard, N. (2007, April). *Educator's guide to cyberbullying and cyberthreats*. Retrieved October 7, 2007, from Cyberbully.org: http://www.cyberbully.org/cyberbully/docs/cbcteducator.pdf.

Windham, A., Rosenberg, L., Fuddy, L., McFarlane, E., Sia, C., & Duggan, A. (2004). Risk of mother-reported child abuse in the first 3 years of life. *Child Abuse and Neglect, 28*, 645–667.

Winterfeld, A., & Sakagawa, T. (2003). *Investigation models for child abuse and neglect—Collaboration with law enforcement*. Retrieved September 18, 2008, from http://www.americanhumane.org/site/DocServer/PC_EMC_Report_6_03.pdf?docID=1141.

Wolak, J., Mitchell, K., & Finkelhor, D. (2006). *Online victimization of youth: Five years later*. Retrieved February 12, 2008, from National Center for Missing and Exploited Children: http://www.missing-kids.com/en_US/publications/NC167.pdf.

Wolfe, D. (1999). *Child abuse: Implications for child development and psychopathology* (2nd ed.). Thousand Oaks, CA: Sage.

Wolfe, D. A., Jaffe, P. G., & Jette, J. (2003). The impact of child abuse in community instititions and organizations: Advancing professional and scientific understanding. *Clinical Psychology: Science and Practice, 10*(2), 179–191.

Wolk, R. (2002). Tragic flaws. *Teacher Magazine, 13*(5), 3.

World Health Organization (WHO). (1999). *World report on violence and health*. Retrieved July 10, 2007, from http://www.who.int/violence_injury_prevention/violence/global_campaign/en/chap3.pdf.

Xu, X. T. (2000). Cultural, human, and social capital as determinants of corporal punishment: Toward an integrated theoretical model. *Journal of Interpersonal Violence, 15*, 603–630.

Younes, L. (1986). *Protection of Native American children from abuse and neglect*. In Child abuse and neglect user manual series. Washington, DC: U.S. Department of Health and Human Services; Administration for Children and Families; Administration on Children, Youth and Families; Children's Bureau; Office on Child Abuse and Neglect.

Index

A

A to Z, 219
Abandoned Infants Assistance Act, 16
abdominal injuries, 30
abrasions, 31, 33
absenteeism, 45
abuse. *See* child abuse
Active Parenting, 175
Adam Walsh Child Protection and Safety Act, 16
  adjudication by, 76
adjudication, 76, 77, 78
Adler, Alfred, 175
adoption, 82, 83
Adoption Assistance and Child Welfare Act, 16
Adoption and Safe Families Act, 16, 82
adult self-abusive factors, 102
affection, in families, 148, 150
age of onset, 2
aggressive behavior, following abuse, 110
alcohol, 31, 102, 111, 133
Alert Program, 219
Amber Alert, 16
American Academy of Pediatrics, 79, 126, 168, 171
  Conference on Child Abuse of, 13
  Council on Exceptional Children of, 25
American Association of University Women, 197
anger
  of children, 170
  of teachers, 194
Annie E. Casey Foundation, 179

appreciation, in families, 148, 149
art, as resource, 218
assessment, 63–65
  informal, 63
  sample questioning techniques for, 64
attachment, 108
  problems of, 215
  theory of, 23, 24
attention, need for, 170
attention deficit disorder (ADD), 110
attention deficit/hyperactivity disorder (ADHD), 109
AVANCE, 174

B

baby trafficking, 51
Bandura, Albert, 17
battered child syndrome, 2, 10, 12, 30
behavior, ways of changing, 171
behavioral issues, working with, 218
behavioral theories, 15–17, 18, 24
beliefs, in families, 148, 150
Bergh, Henry, 8
bibliotherapies, 222
bio-ecological systems theory, 19, 20, 24
  relationship of neglect and poverty in, 42
biological theories, 20–22, 24
bites, 31, 33
body language, 193
Bowen, Murray, 17
Bowlby, John, 23